W9-AYB-504

MABEL

BETTY HARPER FUSSELL

TICKNOR & FIELDS

NEW HAVEN AND NEW YORK

1982

Library of Congress Cataloging in Publication Data

Fussell, Betty Harper.
Mabel.
1. Normand, Mabel, 1894 – 1930. 2. Moving-picture
actors and actresses — United States — Biography.
I. Title.
PN2287.N57F87   791.43'028'0924 [B]   81 – 23286
ISBN 0 – 89919 – 090 – 1   AACR2

Designed by Sally Harris / Summer Hill Books

Printed in the United States of America

V 10 9 8 7 6 5 4 3 2 1

To Charles Sumner Harper, Carrie Hadassah Erskine,
Josias Meryl Harper, & Ruby Hazel Kennedy

The way folk talk about us too,
For the smallest thing we do —
'Nuff to make a girl feel blue.
          Ain't it awful, Mabel?

          — J. E. Hazzard, 1908.

CONTENTS

Illustrations follow pages 18, 82, 146, and 210.

ACKNOWLEDGMENTS

I want to thank all those who searched their memories — actors, directors, writers, producers, stuntmen, cameramen, publicity men, newspaper men — and all those who helped me search — historians, archivists, friends: Scott Bailey, Rowland Barber, Bea Benjamen, Bebe Bergsten, Billy and Arline Bletcher, David Bradley, Kevin Brownlow, David Butler, James Crenshaw, J. J. Cohn, J. F. Conneally, Viola Dana, Sampson De Brier, Digby Diehl, Lucinda Ballard Dietz, Lonnie D'Orsa, Donald Driver, William Dufty, Allan Dwan, I. V. Edmonds, William K. Everson, Al Fariello, Georgine Hall Freedman, Paul Fussell, Tay Garnett, Jetta Goudal, Albert Hackett, John and Dorothy Hampton, Tom Hanlon, Bernard Harris, George James Hopkins, William Hornbeck, Jake Jacoby, Leatrice Joy, Kathy Karr, Barrett Kiesling, Paul Killiam, Henry King, Albert Kopec, Edward Leveque, Anita Loos, Bessie Love, Arthur Mayer, Mary MacLaren, Elsie Hanneman McEvoy, Mio Mennes, Mary Miles Minter, Colleen Moore, Molly Moynahan, Jack Mulhall, Kemp Niver, Liam O'Leary, Harriet Parsons, Ruby Predmore, Glenna Putt, Eddie Quillan, Robert Remer, Glen Rinquist, Hal Roach, Bobby Rose, Mabel Rycowitch, Adela Rogers St. Johns, Philip Scheurer, Don Schneider, Mrs. Lee Shumway, Barnett Shepherd, Eric Sherman, Patricia Sides, Anthony Slide, Ethel Smallwood, Valerie Sorelle, Maynard T. Smith, Victoria Smith, Leonard Spigelgas, Andrew Stone, Blanche Sweet, Violet Unholtz, Rudy Villaseñor, King Vidor, Raoul Walsh, Marc Wanamaker, Sparky Wetherington, Bart Williams.

Special thanks to the staffs of the Margaret Herrick Library of the Academy of Motion Picture Arts and Sciences; Performing Arts Library of the New York Public Library at Lincoln Center;

Film Study Center, Library and Stills Archive of the Museum of Modern Art; Motion Picture Section of the Library of Congress; Library and National Film Archives of the British Film Institute; Special Collections of the General Research Library of the University of California at Los Angeles; Theater Collection of the Firestone Library of Princeton University; American Film Institute; Walter Hampden-Edwin Booth Theatre Collection and Library of the Players Club; Staten Island Historical Society, Museum, and Institute of Arts and Sciences; Snug Harbor Cultural Center; Cork County Library, Ireland.

Last and best thanks to the memorialists: Julia Benson, Lee Westerlund, Stephen Normand. I could not tell the story of Mabel without telling their story — in their own words. But for the sake of brevity I have made composites of Julia's letters to Stephen, so that the letters as they appear here are not historical documents but fictional ones. In this way I too have turned fact into fiction.

Picture Credits

Photographs in this book appear by permission of: Witzel Studio; Electric Theater Movie Museum of Hollywood; Albert J. Kopec; Billy Rose Theatre Collection, the New York Public Library at Lincoln Center; Lindstedt; American Slide Co.; British National Film Archive/Stills Library; Museum of Modern Art/Film Stills Archive; Stagg; Mishkin; Moody; Melbourne Spurr; International; Ernest Bihler; Henry Waxman.

CAST OF CHARACTERS

Time: the Twenties
(Ages at Mabel's death in 1930)

MABEL NORMAND: (38) queen of silent comedy, first bathing beauty, first personality star, Mack's girl.

MACK SENNETT: (50) king of slapstick, creator of Keystone, Mabel's sparring partner.

SAMUEL GOLDWYN: (46) producer, starmaker, Mabel's suitor.

WILLIAM DESMOND TAYLOR: (died 1922, at 49) director, English gentleman, murder victim, Mabel's lover.

LEW CODY: (43) actor, bon vivant, drunk, Mabel's husband.

CHARLES CHAPLIN: (41) the Keystone Tramp, Mabel's cockney romancer.

ROSCOE "FATTY" ARBUCKLE: (43) the Keystone Fat Boy, slander victim, Mabel's Fatty.

COURTLAND DINES: (36) millionaire playboy, boozer, shooting victim, Mabel's drinking pal.

50 Years Later
(Ages in 1982)

STEPHEN NORMAND: (34) Mabel's grandnephew.

JULIA BREW BENSON: (94) Mabel's nurse-companion.

LEE WESTERLUND: (82) Mabel's handyman-masseur-cook, Julia's companion.

MINTA DURFEE ARBUCKLE: (died 1975, at 86) comedienne, Fatty's wife, Mabel's pal.

MARY MILES MINTER: (80) juvenile star, in love with Taylor.

ADELA ROGERS ST. JOHNS: (88) Hearst reporter, Mabel's pal.

WHO WAS MABEL?

OCTOBER 26, 1973, LOS ANGELES

Dear Steve —

Was it a dream or was it for real? Just hung up from talking at least an hour to you in New York, Steve, the living flesh and blood of Mabel Normand!!!!

Precious friend, where will I begin? That was like a voice of heaven when I got your letter. . . . Steve are you married?

With love,
Julia Benson

AUGUST 2, 1976, HOLLYWOOD

Mabel? Everybody knew who Mabel was. But what happened to her? That was the question. And how the hell did I get into this? Here I was on the third floor of the Lincoln Heights Jail in Hollywood, staring at Mabel's trunk. How did a movie star's trunk, fifty years after the girl had died, end up behind bars in a Hollywood jail?

I had to see it to believe it. I followed directions exactly because it's easy to get lost in the tangle of seedy streets east of the Hollywood Freeway and south of Elysian Park. I turned left on Avenue Nineteen under the railroad tracks and parked in the back lot of the old jail. I entered a small unmarked door at the rear of the building, climbed three flights of empty cell blocks to find an open cell filled by a big florid man with his feet on a desk smoking a cigar. He looked like a sheriff in a Western, but he wasn't. He was an ex-stuntman, collector of King Tut-iana, founding member of the Gothic Horror Club and curator of the official Hollywood Museum of the City of Los Angeles.

1

I came to Hollywood that summer looking for clues to the mystery of Mabel Normand. The official Hollywood Museum seemed a good place to start, even if the museum was almost never open.

"Call the museum after 10:00 A.M. on Monday morning," the curator, who called himself the "Senior Preparitor," told me on the phone. "If I answer the museum's open, and if I don't, it's closed."

That August Monday the museum was open. A year later it was closed for good. Spilling cigar ash on a metallic cobra radiator cap that had once belonged to Valentino, on cowboy boots once worn by Gary Cooper, on early peep-show machines gathering dust, on albums of publicity stills nibbled by silverfish, the Senior Preparitor led me at last to a small Louis Vuitton wardrobe trunk. He gestured to "the final remains of Mabel Normand."

I opened the cracked leather top as Mabel's grandnephew had done two years earlier. He was Stephen Normand, Mabel's living flesh and blood and, like him, I felt as if I were opening the tomb of Tutankhamen. I brushed aside the cobwebs to touch Mabel's pink powder puff, an onyx cigarette holder engraved with her initials, a pack of Mogul Egyptian cigarettes and eight loose Lucky Strikes, a pair of jodhpurs and a riding crop, a moulting ostrich-plume fan, a couple pair of darned white silk stockings, and a paper-covered book labeled by hand, "THESAURUS." The same hand had inscribed

> To my Darling Mabel,
>   the most Scintallating Mind I know — also one of
> the Loveliest of Women,
>
> > Lovingly,
> > Minta
> > 1922

I knew who Minta was. She was Araminta Durfee Arbuckle, an early comedienne who married Roscoe "Fatty" Arbuckle before he became famous as the Keystone Fat Boy and then infamous for rape and murder. She was also one of Mabel's best pals. In 1922, Mabel had needed both a pal and a thesaurus for the poetry she was writing. In 1922, poetry was a special comfort to Mabel when Arbuckle was on trial and when Mabel herself was suspected of murder. Mabel was suspected of murdering her friend and lover William Desmond Taylor in one of Hollywood's most sensational murder mysteries.

Stephen Normand was lucky enough to meet Minta the year before she died in the fall of 1975. She was then eighty-six, her hair still flaming red and her heels six inches high. Stephen also met that year the one living person who had known Mabel even better than Minta. This was Mabel's nurse and companion for the last decade of her life. Her name was Julia Brew Benson, and Stephen was certain that she held the answers to what happened to Mabel before Mabel died in 1930. When she died, Mabel was thirty-eight years old, but she denied it. Officially, she was thirty-six.

Julia survived them all. Julia survives now at ninety-four, but she was a mere eighty-seven when Stephen met her, tiny and frail as a bird, he said, but with a will and memory of iron. Julia warmed to Stephen's person but was cool to his inquiries. By the time I got to Hollywood, after Stephen had gone back home to Staten Island, the trail was cold and Julia froze me out. She talked to me once on the phone, but the next time I called, a man's voice answered and said, "Don't call again."

The man was her companion of forty years, a man who had been handyman, cook, and masseur to Mabel and to her husband before they died. His name was Lee Westerlund, or Cowboy Lee as he became to me, and he had just moved Julia from their Ingraham Street bungalow in Los Angeles to a house he built in Pacoima, in one of the flattest and bleakest pockets of the San Fernando Valley. Lee put up a six-foot link fence first off, with a sign saying "Beware the Dog." He named the dog "Cody" after Lew Cody, the bon-vivant actor Mabel married at a drunken party in 1926.

"They used to put the drunks in this cell," the Senior Preparitor told me while I was inventorying Mabel's trunk. If I counted the eight loose Lucky Strikes as one, Mabel's final remains numbered less than three dozen. I could see from her peach silk kimono how tiny she was, from a pair of silk pumps how long and narrow her feet, from a pair of French doeskin gloves how small her hands, but the cigarettes told me most. Mabel died slowly and painfully of tuberculosis, but she was not about to stop smoking. Or drinking. "She was a little Queen," Julia had said. Had the little Queen known her regalia would end in the drunks' cell of the Lincoln Heights Jail, she would have laughed herself into a coughing fit.

The Preparitor clanged the bars shut behind me and locked them as I made my way down the stairs, past a movie crew shooting a prison film in the cell block below. In the old days, Mabel would have dashed into the middle of them and "done her stuff" while Mack Sennett's cameras ground out another 500 feet of instant slapstick. Mack founded his Keystone company on just such petty larceny. But in the old days, Mack and Mabel would have turned real cops and criminals into Keystone comics. Art poached on life, life on art. Nobody worried then about what was real and what was fake.

But I did — now. I felt defrauded when I learned that Mabel's trunk was not, in fact, Mabel's. The contents, donated by Julia, were real enough, but the trunk itself was a fake. When I mentioned Mabel's trunk to one of Hollywood's most colorful film historians, a man named Kemp Niver, another ex-stuntman, bodyguard, cowboy, and cameraman turned archivist, Niver exploded. "When that museum guy says 'We've got a trunk owned by Mabel Normand,' I want to hit the sonuvabitch right in the mouth," Niver said. "Prop-room-wise, we don't know whose goddamn trunk it is."

Prop-room-wise, the trunk of Mabel Normand was typical of my three-year search for Mabel in the Hollywood smog of fake and real. Every time I said "Gotcha," she vanished. I should have listened to historian Niver when he told me at the beginning, flat out, "Listen young lady, in Hollywood, if you don't know the answers before you start, forget it." Many times I wished I could. I wished I had.

MAY 12, 1976, STATEN ISLAND
Dear Mrs. Fussell:
I regret that I am unable at this time to give you

any information about my great-aunt, Mabel Normand.

Sincerely yours,
Stephen Normand

MAY 15, 1976, PRINCETON, NEW JERSEY

For a moment, when I saw the return address of Drumgoole Road, Staten Island on the brown envelope, I was hopeful. I had written to a "Mr. Stephen Normand" a couple of weeks before because I was playing a hunch. So much for hunches.

I had seen Mabel for the first time a month or so earlier, and I couldn't get her out of my mind. I had seen her image flicker into life on a roll-up screen, where she jerked at the rate of eighteen frames a second on an 8-mm print of an early Keystone comedy called *A Muddy Romance.* She was a revelation in black and white. Here was a dark-haired round-chinned beauty with eyes like headlights. She was dressed in Gibson-Girl velvet and taffeta, cinched like an egg-timer, but when she stepped from the porch into the sunlight, she was the girl next door stepping out to meet her beau. When she stepped into a rowboat for a quick row around Echo Lake, she was flirty and adorable. When the water crazily drained away and Mabel emerged from the lake bottom like a creature from the black lagoon, a mud-dripping monster, she was irresistible. I liked the story. I loved the girl. "The story," Stephen said when I finally met him, "is the story of Mabel's life."

Stephen set out for Hollywood in 1974 to straighten out the story of Mabel's life. He was determined to clear the Normand name from the scandals of drugs, booze, sex, and murder that shook Hollywood in the early twenties and ended Mabel's career. He had a soft-focused image in his head of a haloed Mabel whom the screen and press had muddied.

I began the other way round. Where Stephen was looking for tragedy, I was looking for comedy, and at the beginning each of us found only what we sought. Mabel had stuck in my mind because she stirred memories. She stirred memories of a childhood lost in the dark of the Fox Movietone Theater in Riverside, California, in the thirties. But the dark was crowded with faces, unreal faces larger than life, livelier than life, funnier than life. The faces that inhabited my memory were all sexy clowns — Jean Harlow, Carole Lombard, Mae West, Jean Arthur, Ginger Rogers, Katharine Hepburn, Rosalind Russell, Judy Holliday, Lucille Ball. I loved them because they were so American. They were wisecrackers, tomboys, and rebels who kidded sex while seducing every man in sight. They had the best of all possible worlds. They were collectively the Comedian Girl I wanted to be, lost in the dark of the Fox Movietone Theater, where I escaped the sorrows of Riverside.

Later, when I found I was being "liberated" from my sexist past and I needed to define the American girl and my own tomboy rebellion, I looked for other Comedian Girls. To my surprise, I found a full-blooded theatrical tradition that ran unbroken from Eva Tanguay and Fanny Brice in vaudeville and burlesque at the turn of the century to Goldie Hawn and Gilda Radner in movies and television today. America bred funny girls, and among them Mabel was unique. She was the first funny girl to be created by the screen and for the screen. She was a movie pioneer, a revolutionary, an original whom every one of her peers called "the premiere comedienne of silent film." Her peers were Chaplin, Sennett, Pickford, Goldwyn, Zukor. Where had she been all my life?

She had been disintegrating on nitrate film that oxidizes rapidly and dangerously. Between 1909 and 1926, Mabel had made at least 167 comic shorts and probably more, but of them all only 66 survive today. She had made 23 full-length features, but of these only four survive. The rest are now lost, junked, or have already combusted spontaneously. Unlike Mary Pickford, who hoarded and preserved her films in a temperature-controlled vault, Mabel was as careless of her future as of her past. She was called the I-Don't-Care Girl with reason. Today, whoever wants to find Mabel on film has to search her out in museums and film archives, except for the handful of silent comedies like *Tillie's Punctured Romance* that are revived fitfully on television.

If Mabel has nearly vanished on film, I soon discovered that she was scarcely ever present in print. Many of her peers tried to write about her, or intended to and thought they had, but Mabel was a shapechanger who reflected back what others wanted to see. Every man Mabel met fell in love with her. Just like that. She tripped over men's lives and tangled herself up in them, so that when they tried to write about her they often told lies, sometimes about her and sometimes about themselves, sometimes to preserve her image and more often to preserve their own. Most often they told lies without knowing it, because they were all involved in the business of making and projecting graven images.

Sam Goldwyn was the first to project an image of Mabel in his 1923 memoir *Behind the Screen,* but he screened out the central fact that in creating Mabel the star Goldwyn had tried and failed to win Mabel the girl. Chaplin, in *My Autobiography,* confessed readily enough that he had tried and failed to woo the girl, but he distorted his relation to Mabel the professional because he could not stand the idea of a woman director. Mack Sennett, Mabel's partner in love and comedy, told the biggest lies of all. Through his biographer Gene Fowler in *Father Goose* and his ghost-writer in *King of Comedy,* Mack worried his aborted romance with Mabel like the Ancient Mariner his albatross. Long after Mabel's death, Mack still threw up smoke screens to cover the entangled story of love and money that lay behind the screen.

I found that the only writers on Mabel I could trust were a pair of studio publicists, ordinarily the slenderest of reeds but better than starmakers. Sidney Sutherland was one, a twenties publicist who told the story of "Madcap Mabel Normand: The True Story of a Great Comedienne" in six issues of *Liberty* magazine just after Mabel died. The other was Norbert Lusk, a Goldwyn publicist who told her story in his 1940 unpublished memoir *I Love Actresses.* But both men were in love with her, and while Sutherland veiled her in gentility, Lusk wrapped her in cellophane.

Everyone who wrote about Mabel wrapped her in something because she needed all the protection she could get. She was not only the first comedy girl of the movies; she was the first "personality" girl of the movies, and she became as famous for her wildness off the screen as on. She was "reckless, spectacular, unorthodox," Lusk wrote, and he was the one who best caught her gutsy and quirky idiom as she jazzed herself into oblivion.

In Hollywood's first decade, Mabel and the movies went wild together among the faked rainbows, the instant chateaux and supermobiles, the real gin bottles and diamonds and guns. Mabel got fame and money by spending her personality and her talent as recklessly as the $1000 bills she lavished on shop girls and other waifs. The starmakers played up her spending until Mabel spent herself so liberally that she was played out by the mid-twenties and wasted the last of the twenties dying. In that, too, Mabel was first. She was the first of the bad-luck girls. Before Clara Bow or Judy Garland or Marilyn Monroe, or any other of those funky angels of fun and sex, there was Mabel.

MAY 30, 1976, STATEN ISLAND
Dear Mrs. Fussell:
At this time, it is now possible for me to discuss my great-aunt, Mabel Normand, with you.
Sincerely yours,
Stephen Normand

JUNE 3, 1976, PRINCETON
A month after the first, a second brown envelope turned up in the mail with a message as brief as before. Only this time, the front of the envelope had been stamped in black ink with the words

MABEL LIVES

Within the week, a station wagon pulled up to my house, and a tall young man got out. He had the same large brown heavy-lidded eyes, curling lashes, white skin, and curved mouth that Mabel had on the screen. From the tailgate he unloaded stacks of photo albums, scrapbooks, Mabel's silver tea set, books from her library, silver-backed brushes from her dressing table, get-well notes from Mary Pickford, an invitation to Valentino's funeral, telegram forms with Mabel's penciled scrawl, an inch-long eyelash taped to a Holy Communion card, a couple of dozen reels of 8-mm film, and an ancient roll-up screen that had belonged to Stephen's grandfather. Stephen brought with him everything of Mabel's left him by his grandmother, who had married Mabel's brother. Everything, that is, that she had not burned the day she found her husband hanging from a rope in the basement of the house Mabel had bought for her parents on St. Marks Place in Staten Island. Stephen had grown up there, "under the doom of Mabel Normand," as his grandmother had said. Stephen introduced himself to me not as the living flesh and blood but as "the caretaker of the memory of Mabel Normand."

"All I want is to set the facts straight," Stephen said as he laid out the memorabilia. "About Mabel's genius," he added.

When Stephen went to Hollywood to set the facts straight, he ran into a cement-brick wall. Before he got there, he questioned Julia a number of times by phone and taped the conversations.

> *Stephen: Do you think Mabel took dope?*
> *Julia: No!!! Steve, they made up such awful lies that*
> *it just burns me up and makes me sick all over. The*
> *only thing she ever took anyone could buy over the*
> *counter, phenobarbitol. But if you took a thimbleful*
> *of liquor, they said you were a booze hound. The*
> *bigger the star, the harder they made you fall.*

I knew nothing about Mabel and dope until I read the piece Stephen wrote for *Films in Review* (August – September, 1974) to prove that Mabel's rumored drug addiction was false. Julia told him so. But such testimony was very like Mabel's trunk where, prop-wise, you couldn't tell fact from fiction.

"Oh I could write a book about Mabel Normand," Julia told him, "and there wouldn't be anything in it but what was beautiful."

The more Stephen tried to write what Julia saw, the more the caretaker of Mabel's memory became possessed by his charge. "I just want you to understand that when you're talking to me you're talking to Mabel because Mabel is in me," Stephen said to me once in anger. "I'm Stephen Normand, but I'm also Mabel Normand, and I think you ought to take that into account."

To the Normand family, "Bad Luck Mabel," as she called herself, cast a blight on all of them after her death. Brother and sister and husband and wife quarrelled over the spoils of her

9

fortune. Stephen's mother, named for Mabel, did not speak to her brother for years because each claimed some possession of Mabel's that the other one had. Stephen, born Rycowitch, changed his surname to Normand to make his role of memorialist official. No one else in his family would even mention her name.

Stephen wanted to discover the facts of Mabel's past as long as they squared with his fictions. I wanted to discover the fictions that had made the facts of my California past bearable. We were an unlikely pair of sleuths, Stephen and I, the Staten Island boy and the middle-aged exile from Riverside, but Mabel seemed to offer some sort of clue to both our identities. I wanted to exorcise something unresolved in my memory of the past. Stephen wanted an exorcist for the doom of the Normand name.

FEBRUARY 4, 1922, LOS ANGELES
Question: Please state your name?
Answer: Mabel Normand.
Question: What is your occupation?
Answer: Motion Pictures.

JULY 15, 1976, HOLLYWOOD
The first document that I got my hands on when I flew out to Hollywood to look for the facts was a seventeen-page Coroner's Report of the inquest held at Ivy H. Overholtzer's Undertakers, Tenth and Hill streets on February 4, 1922. The coroner's questions were as simple and direct as Mabel's answers. Too simple. I knew that what had happened to Mabel involved murder and that the mystery of Mabel Normand hinged on a Hollywood murder mystery which had never been solved. I decided to solve it. I was deaf to historian Niver's warning, "If you don't know the answers before you begin, forget it." I was blind to the fact that Mabel's answer to the second question, "What is your occupation?" undid her answer to the first, "Please state your name?" I was dumb.

I got to Hollywood as soon as I could. Time, after all, was against me. I wanted to track down everyone who had known Mabel and who had known the murder victim, William Desmond Taylor. Of the hundred or so people I talked to, a third would be dead by the time I knew enough to write her story. Sometimes I felt as if I were playing out *The Mummy's Curse.*

I stayed at the Montecito Hotel, just two blocks north of Hollywood Boulevard, at the corner of Franklin and Whiteley avenues, because it called itself "Hotel of the Stars." It was an Art Deco memorial to thirties optimism.

"Not the Montecito," warned an elderly actress friend whose hair was orange and whose weight was a good two hundred pounds. "You'll be mugged or raped."

Itinerant and aging actors filled the Montecito because it was cheap and it was handy. True enough, the parking lot was risky, the pool was rimmed with sludge, and the switchboard was permanently out to lunch, but the view from my ninth-floor window was like a peak in Darien.

Before me lay the Hollywood Wax Museum, the pagodas of Grauman's Chinese Theater, the Pussycat Theater, Larry Edmond's Bookshop, the Admiral and Commodore motels, the Church of the Blessed Sacrament behind the Scientology Center, and Max Factor in a tube of smoked glass. By night, I watched the neon wax and wane on Gordon's Gin, next to the red neon heart of Love's Barbecue, while helicopter searchlights fingered the streets. By day, I watched child prostitutes and ageless druggies ply the Avenue of the Stars.

On the Avenue of the Stars I found Mabel's star laid in cement just in front of the Dollar-Rent-A-Car. Mabel's star was unattended by the Japanese tourists who crowded Grauman's Chinese. A block to the west, I found the moldering grandeur of the Garden Court Apartments. Its palms were dusty and its fountain dry where Mack Sennett had once killed off the goldfish by spitting tobacco from his balcony. The Garden Court put up a brave if peeling front, just as Sennett had done until they laid him in front of the altar at the Church of the Blessed Sacrament. Every hour, its mission bells tolled the time, time past and present, numbering my childhood memories of cockroaches and the hot Santa Ana wind that drove folks mad in August.

For July and August I rented a Ford Cortina from the Dollar-Rent-A-Car, cheapest rates, no air-conditioning, and I spent my money buying Mitock maps of the Greater and Greater

Los Angeles Freeway System. I also bought *Michael's Memory Map: A Guide to the Memorials and Final Resting Places of the Stars.* Nobody died in Hollywood. They rested, between takes. Good. Bodies were facts. I would begin with the resting places of Mabel and the men in her life.

Mabel's resting place was Crypt No. D7, Block 303, in the thirties wing of Calvary Mausoleum. Calvary Cemetery was not on *Michael's Memory Map* at all. Perhaps the stars there were too immemorial to be remembered. To get to Calvary from the Montecito, I headed south on the Hollywood Freeway to the Santa Ana Freeway and turned east on Whittier Boulevard at Boyle Heights. When Mabel died, the mausoleum was a spanking new Hollywood-Mission showcase of terra-cotta angels on top of Corinthian pillars at the end of a grand *allée* of palms. Today, the cemetery is an island encircled by wave after wave of Mexican-pink bungalows.

In 1930, Mabel's marble slab, equipped like a bureau drawer with a pair of brass knobs, cost $1125. For this sum, Mabel was granted exclusive right of interment by the Roman Catholic Bishop of Los Angeles and San Diego, "a corporation sole." Mabel rests in good company in her marble wall next to the Pre-Raphaelite Chapel donated by one of the architects of the Teapot Dome scandal. The Barrymores rest on her left — Ethel, Lionel, and John. John Hodiak rests on her right. Her mother, Mary Drury Normand, 1869 – 1932, rests above her and her husband, Lew Cody, 1887 – 1934, below. Mabel's slab is inscribed with the birthdate of her choice:

MABEL NORMAND CODY

1895 – 1930

"Rest in Peace"

Julia did not think Mabel was resting in peace. "Why Mabel Normand would turn over in her grave if she knew that Cody name was on her tomb," Julia told Stephen. Julia hated Cody, but Cody outlived Mabel by only four years. It was Lee who found Cody dead in his bed the morning after a Memorial Day beach party of unusual vigor. Cody died as he had lived, dead drunk.

I went on to other resting places. To get to Sennett's place,

I took the Santa Monica Freeway west and turned south on the San Diego Freeway until Slauson Avenue. Holy Cross Cemetery is just south of Culver City, and Holy Cross *is* on *Michael's Memory Map* because of Gary Cooper, Rosalind Russell, Bing Crosby, and Sharon Tate ("Left of Grotto"). Mack is not on the map, however, and I would never have found him had not a comedian named Billy Bletcher, once the voice of Disney's Big Bad Wolf, "rounded up the boys" to collect a tombstone for Sennett's unmarked grave. "I couldn't get over it," Billy told me the year before Billy himself died, "Poor Mack didn't even have a headstone." Now his headstone read

MACK SENNETT

1880 – 1960

When Sennett died, he willed his estate to the Los Angeles Orphan Asylum and the Jewish Orphans Home, not knowing he had nothing left to will.

To reach Sam Goldwyn's place, I took the San Diego Freeway north, turned east on the Santa Monica Freeway, then north on the Harbor Freeway to the Golden State Freeway and exited at Glendale Boulevard in order to reach Forest Lawn Memorial Park, Glendale branch. Forest Lawn was on *Michael's Map* because Humphrey Bogart, among others, was in the Garden of Memory, and Jean Harlow, among others, was in the Great Mausoleum past the Last Supper Window on the left. But Goldwyn's place was not marked, and after I'd circled the Court of Freedom three times, I gave up. I knew his tomb would read 1884 – 1974. When Goldwyn died, he knew he had plenty left to will.

My final stop was Hollywood Memorial Park Cemetery. I wanted to find William Desmond Taylor. From Forest Lawn, I took Glendale Boulevard west and turned south on Hyperion Avenue, then west on Santa Monica Boulevard to Van Ness. Hollywood Cemetery is conveniently adjacent to Paramount Studios on the south. Many of Mabel's friends rest in Hollywood Memorial Park — Marion Davies, Douglas Fairbanks, Rudolph Valentino, Norma Talmadge (in the Shrine of Eternal Love). The girl Fatty Arbuckle was supposed to have killed by raping rests there too. Just five months after her death, William Desmond Taylor was laid to rest, on February 7, 1922, after the biggest funeral Hollywood had ever had. That year set a kind of record for resting.

Taylor's funeral set a precedent for funerals that rivaled premiers. Mabel's limousine led Taylor's funeral cortege, behind a band of Scotch bagpipers, from St. Paul's Cathedral in Pershing Square through the mobs massed along Vine to the grave site in the Park. There the Canadian Honor Squad fired three volleys, and a British bugler from a visiting warship played "Taps." Mabel had two favorite songs, Julia said. One was "The Indian Love Call" and the other was "Taps."

Taylor's grave was inscribed with the dates 1872 – 1922 and with the name he assumed after he disappeared from New York in 1908, abandoning wife, child, occupation, and name — William Cunningham Deane Tanner. His new occupation? Motion Pictures. Taylor's grave was the opposite of Mabel's trunk. The grave was certain, but what about the contents?

FEBRUARY 12, 1974, STATEN ISLAND
[From a telephone conversation written down by Stephen]
Stephen: Do you think Mabel had anything to do with the murder of Taylor?
Julia: On her deathbed she said to me, "Julia, do you think God is going to let me die and not tell me who killed Bill Taylor?"
. . . Steve, the town car sat out at the curb, and the driver said that Bill Taylor put Mabel in the car and walked back into the house. She wasn't there when the man was killed. My god, the woman was as innocent as you or me.

AUGUST 12, 1977, LOS ANGELES
I looked up one of the veteran police reporters for the *Los Angeles Times* in the press room of the Central Police Building at 150 North Los Angeles Street. Jake Jacoby's first assignment in 1938 had been a startling "new" development in the Taylor

case. Before the state grand jury, a woman had just accused her mother of killing Taylor, but there was no evidence and no indictment. God had let Mabel die without telling her or anyone else who killed Bill Taylor, but not everyone believed that Mabel was as innocent as you or me. Reporter Jake, eating peanuts like a reformed chainsmoker, told me that a reporter who covered the original case in 1922 told him — off the record — that Taylor was shot by a woman jealous of another actress. The woman's name was Mabel Normand.

In the Taylor mystery, Hollywood had answers before there were questions. "Start from scratch," Jake advised me. "Go to the old newspaper files, try the police, try the coroner." In 1922, there had been seven daily papers in Los Angeles. I decided to begin with the files of Hearst's *Los Angeles Examiner,* but the original files had been shredded after the *Herald-Examiner* merger in 1958. "When they killed the old *Examiner,* they killed the files," a retired police reporter told me. "We gnashed our teeth over that."

I moved on to library archives and in UCLA's General Research Library in Westwood found the *Examiner* for February, 1922 on microfilm. I threaded the machine and idled through the news of February 1 and 2, anticipating by delay the first morning paper headlines of the murder on February 3. I noted that the jury of the second Arbuckle trial had not yet reached a verdict. Sweden had announced a new invention called "talking film." A pair of Prohibition agents had been arrested in a blackmail scam. Police seizure of Chinese girls in an opium den threatened a new tong war. I pushed the forward button on the machine and held my breath. The tape flipped from the reel. The end of the tape was jagged. It had been torn off, and the rest of the reel was missing.

There were other newspaper archives, of course, and there were the police. I contacted first the Records and Publications Division of the Los Angeles Police Department and was told that there was no file on anyone named William Desmond Taylor or Tanner. The file must be misplaced or missing. A call to the Public Affairs Division brought a different answer. "We do have records on the case," said a division member. "I know because

I've seen them." I tried the Homicide Division and cited California Public Records Act #6250. A lieutenant, in return, cited Act #6254 F, which exempts certain records from public access. When I suggested that after fifty-five years even an unsolved homicide belonged to history, the lieutenant countered my ploy by saying time has no limit on homicide and cited Agatha Christie's *Murder in Retrospect*. I was up against it. I said I was representing the Normand family who wished to clear the Normand name. "Wouldn't it be simpler if I just said there were no records?" he asked.

I had no better luck at the district attorney's office. Since there were dozens of suspects but never an indictment, there were no grand jury records. An archivist in the district attorney's office sent me to the Bureau of Investigation for house records. There, an officer told me that the internal house file had been purged five years ago. "Personally I regret this," he said. "I have some interest in history myself."

Only in the coroner's office did my luck change. After three weeks' wait and $11.50 for xeroxing, I received my single hard document in a mystery that had teased Hollywood for fifty-five years and that had bred more fictions than America had bred funny girls. The facts in the coroner's report merely confirmed what I had already pieced together from the newspapers. Only the style differed, since presumably the coroner was not being paid by the word. Mabel was summoned to the inquest because she was the last person to see Taylor alive on the night of February 1, 1922. The story she told to the coroner's jury she had told endlessly to reporters.

She had dropped by Taylor's apartment around 7:00 P.M. to exchange a bag of peanuts for a pair of books. One was by Friedrich W. Nietzsche, and the other was by Ethel M. Dell. Taylor was improving Mabel's mind. Mabel joked, drank a gin and orange, and Taylor walked her out to her car where her chauffeur was waiting. Taylor promised to call her at 9:00 P.M. to see how she liked the books. But he did not call as he had promised. Taylor could not call because he was lying face up on his living-room floor, his head in a pool of blood, his body neatly straightened by the person who shot him in the back within minutes after Mabel had waved goodbye.

It was a long goodbye. A single .38 caliber soft-nosed bullet changed Mabel's life almost as definitively as Taylor's. Until that moment, Taylor had been Hollywood's symbol of class. He was "Exhibit A," producer Jesse Lasky said, when Hollywood wanted to impress Pasadena society with "Hollywood's culture and refinement." Taylor was impressive. He was a first-rate director who, as president of the Motion Picture Directors Association, became a moral spokesman for the industry. Publicists called him "a crusader in quest of an ideal." Privately, he was a crusader who rescued fallen angels like Mabel. He also fell in love with Mabel, until the bullet ended his quest and exposed the faked identity of the crusader. Hollywood went into shock and so did Mabel.

For months, Mabel's name appeared in bold black letters on pink front pages. Everybody knew her name, all right, but what about her occupation? Prop-wise, Taylor's murder opened a Pandora's box. Apparently as many people had real cause to kill Taylor as Hollywood had cause to cover it up. An embarrassment of confessions, witnesses, motives, and suspects was matched by an embarrassment of suppressed and stolen evidence, of bribery and conspiracy between industry officials and the law. Taylor's faked identity uncovered the fakery native to motion pictures and to their performers. Motion picture actors were worse than other kinds because they would not stand still. Mabel and the movies were already suspect after the Arbuckle scandal in September had unmasked the Fat Boy as a rapist. Now the Taylor murder unmasked Fatty's Mabel as a druggie. Now everybody in Hollywood had a stake in keeping the Taylor mystery a mystery. His corpse was real enough but everything else that could be faked was.

FEBRUARY 1, 1979, CLAREMONT, CALIFORNIA
Dear Mrs. Funnell [sic]:
I have begun to think you are a professional
scandal writer . . . trying for money to open a murder
mystery which is more than fifty years old and should
be forgotten. . . .
This brings our contacts to a close.
Barrett C. Kiesling

In Hollywood, mysteries are trickier than elsewhere because fakery, or "hokum" as they once said, is its business. When people in Hollywood say "I know — I was *there,*" they say it with the rehearsed authenticity of performers. I found many who knew because they were *there,* but often I wondered where exactly "there" was. Among the cacti and jacuzzis of Desert Hot Springs, I found former Hearst reporter Adela Rogers St. Johns writing *The Missing Years of Jesus,* when Jesus went to England to learn from the Druids. Adela had been in New York at the time of the murder, but she was so much a part of the Hollywood scene that she wrote as if she had been *there.* "Everybody *there* knew who shot William Desmond Taylor," she told me. "There was never any question about it." She named straight out the mother of actress Mary Miles Minter.

In her decaying house on the rim of Santa Monica canyon, I found Mary Miles Minter, now a diabetic invalid named Mrs. O'Hildebrandt. The scandal of Taylor's killing killed young Mary's career, and she had certainly been *there.* But she called Adela "a sob sister, a lying wretch." Amid French antiques and Hollywood Oscars for set design in his Normanesque chateau, I found Taylor's art director, George James Hopkins, who also had been *there* and who knew "too much" about cleaning out the police files. But that information was going into a book of his own. Amid the retirement groves of Claremont, I found Taylor's publicity director, Barrett C. Kiesling, who at 92 had been *there* so long he had known them all, known them all, but had had enough of Hollywood questions.

"Why do you go back so far to someone like Mabel Normand?" more than one nonagenarian asked me in my search. In the Motion Picture Country Home in Woodland Hills, I found many who shared Mabel's and Taylor's past, actors and actresses who hugged their memories to them like afghans while Johnny Weissmuller, invalided in the hospital wing, let loose a Tarzan cry. In the neighboring valleys, I found survivors like Hollywood's publicity czar Howard Strickling, who reigned for three-quarters of a century, but for whom the past was only pain. "It gets me all upset," he said. "I just can't talk about it."

In Hollywood, I found the truth of an American novelist's

Top   Mabel Normand in 1912, when she was Mack's girl and Lew's pal. Mack Sennett to her left, Lew Cody to her right.

Bottom   Mabel's final resting place between her mother Mary and her husband Lew at Calvary Mausoleum in Boyle Heights. Her dates should have read 1892 to 1930.

Top left   Mabel's French grandmother, Adrienne Marie Beraud.
Middle left   "Baby," about age ten, at Staten Island.
Bottom left   Mabel's French father, Claude G. Normand.
Bottom right   Claude and Mabel, at eight, a melancholy "Baby."
Middle right   Mabel's Irish mother, Mary Drury.

Top left   Mabel's brother Claude in 1928, his wife Winifred and daughter named for Mabel.
Middle left   Mabel's nurse Julia Benson, left, with Mabel, right, in 1925 in front of Mabel's new house in Beverly Hills.
Bottom left   Mabel's niece Mabel Normand Rycowitch as a model in the 1940s.
Bottom right   Mabel's grandnephew Stephen Normand.
Middle right   (*l. to r.*) Lee Westerlund, Stephen Normand, Minta Durfee Arbuckle, Julia Benson in 1974.

Top left Mabel the photographer's model in 1909.
Middle Mabel the Gibson Girl posing for illustrator Charles Dana Gibson.
Bottom left Mabel in 1910 posing for a postcard ad.

"BETTY BECOMES A MAID"

Top   Mabel's first funny-girl role in a 1911 Vitagraph film with
James Morrison and Lou Delaney.
Bottom   Bad-Girl Mabel with Edwin August and Blanche Sweet in
D. W. Griffith's *The Eternal Mother*, 1912, Biograph.

Top Mabel the Diving Girl in the first Keystone comedy, *The Water Nymph*, in August 1912.
Bottom Mabel as Wild Flower, with a real Indian, Dark Cloud, in D. W. Griffith's *The Squaw's Love*, in August 1911.

Top   Keystone Mabel projected on a colored glass slide of 1913 to advertise next week's split-reel comedy.
Bottom   Mabel, "The Sugar on the Keystone Grapefruit," in her first cheesecake shots for Keystone in 1914.

Mabel Normand

Top Mabel mugging in *Zuzu the Band Leader*, December 1913, when the Keystone band infiltrated a real crowd.

Middle Mabel with trombone and Ford Sterling in *Prof. Bean's Removal*, July 1913.
Bottom Mabel giving Minta Durfee (?) a piece of her pie in *A Misplaced Foot*, January 1914.

remark, "Anything processed by memory is fiction." How fool-hardy to think I could solve any mystery at all in a place that denied its past by eternally processing the present. If truth was the daughter of time, time was what Hollywood killed. "I lugged the whole world onto a twenty-foot screen," the director D. W. Griffith said of his *Birth of a Nation.* "I condensed history into three hours and made them live it." The camera changed the way we saw and lived and remembered. It changed history into cinerama and memory into dream and people into performers.

Wherever I turned, I was stuck with real props in a fake trunk. I was stuck with images projected in the interior studios of memory. Mabel herself was no help. In her real-unreal occupation, the person named Mabel Normand colluded with Hollywood in inventing images of herself. She invented a dozen Mabels to fit the fragments of herself she saw distorted on a screen that seemed to reverse fake and real. Mary Pickford gradually surrendered to the image she invented and, at the end of the twenties, immured herself alive in the mausoleum called Pickfair. But Mabel was too naive, too honest and too spontaneous for that. She was also too combustible. She exploded with contradictions that made her a mystery to herself. She knew her name and occupation, but who was she? She never stopped searching for an identity that eluded her. In the end, Mabel told publicist Lusk to call her simply "a very dissatisfied seeker of what life really means."

In the end, the camera that made her undid her. "She was enchanting, she was funny, she was gay," art director Hopkins remembered, "until she was drunk, and she was drunk a lot of the time." The camera that gave Mabel form as an image dispossessed her of herself and turned substance into shadow. But I didn't know that when I began. I was a mystery-solver; just give me the facts. I didn't know that searching for Mabel was like searching for Velma in Raymond Chandler's *Farewell, My Lovely.* I didn't know that I was in a placeless place searching for a missing person with a faked identity.

GIBSON GIRL

Dear Steve,

I sometimes believe Mabel's spirit is near us, is with us. Is there something MN is trying to tell us? Somehow she seems to be telling me to avoid all that pertains to murder, dope. . . .

As God is my judge a few years ago on Mabel's birthday I dreamed she was in my bed, seemed to be awake and I could actually feel MN's presence.

We must deny lies and other made-up stories.

God bless, Love,
Julia.

OCTOBER 15, 1976, STATEN ISLAND

Stephen and I stood in front of the Music Hall at Sailors' Snug Harbor that Mabel's father had helped build in the early 1890s. Claude G. Normand, a carpenter, was proud of his French ancestry and was proud to be part of a Frenchman's design to tame island wildness with a Beaux Arts facade. Claude was proudest of all of the Music Hall. The theater, he felt, was in his blood. His mother, Adrienne Marie Beraud, had been an actress in Toulon before she gave up the theater for a Parisian cabinetmaker and a new start in Quebec.

Born in Providence, Rhode Island, Claude grew up in its local theaters, playing the piano in the pit and working backstage until he was snapped up by a square-jawed Irish girl named Mary Drury. Mary was the daughter of a Kerry blacksmith who had brought his village bride to Providence in the 1860s. He was a sensible man, and when his daughter squared her jaw for Claude, the blacksmith said "No!" So Mary and Claude eloped. Claude did odd jobs while she produced three children, all of whom died of tuberculosis. Claude and Mary moved south to better work and weather in Staten Island.

On both sides Mabel was a Celt. From her Irish mother Mabel inherited black hair, inch-long eyelashes, determination, energy, and not a grain of common sense. From her French father Mabel inherited a love of music, art, romance, and strong drink, along with recklessness and melancholy. As the youngest of the family, Mabel was both spoiled and neglected, but her father knew that the theater ran in her blood.

Claude was at work on the Music Hall when Mabel was born prematurely, November 9, 1892. She weighed only five pounds, and her head was covered with a caul. Her parents took that as a sign of luck and sold it for "a handsome sum." At her birth her sister Gladys was three and her brother Claude was two, but the new baby was special. They christened her Mabel Ethelreid Normand, but her name was always "Baby."

As Baby grew up, she stayed small. She was half the size of the rest of her family, who were either short and stout or tall and thin. Mabel was closest in size to her later rival, Mary Pickford. Fully grown, Mabel was 5'1" to Mary's 5'; both weighed just under 100 pounds; and both had large heads in proportion to their bodies. Mabel's body, however, developed curves where Mary's did not. Mary kept her little girl look because her legs were extremely short for her torso. Mabel developed the full bosom, tiny waist and rounded hips of a vaudeville queen. But her body also developed the eccentricities of a clown. Her feet were long and thin and turned in, pigeon-toed, while the little fingers of each hand turned out, at an angle of 30°.

Mabel was lucky in the place of her birth. Claude had built a narrow frame house at 91 Tysen Street, at the corner of Fillmore, just opposite the east gate of Snug Harbor. Stephen showed me the house that still stands in a row of similar upright houses built by the Irish, Polish, and German immigrants who poured into Staten Island in the eighties and nineties. Today the houses are shaded by plane trees planted as saplings when Mabel was born. Mabel was lucky because she had the hundred acres of Snug

Harbor for a playground and the mouth of the Hudson for a swimming hole. To learn to swim, Mabel merely toddled to the end of Tysen Street and jumped into the waters of the Kill Van Kull. She was a born athlete and took to water like a minnow.

She also took to the Music Hall where Thursday night entertainments were provided for the thousand or so "aged, decrepit and worn-out" sailors for whom Snug Harbor was built. Baby played backstage while her father, a Gilbert and Sullivan fan, built the sets and props for *H.M.S. Pinafore and The Mikado.* By the time she was eight, she had sampled a full variety of vaudeville acts, from a Dancing and Whistling Artiste with her Trio of Equilibrists to the Louisiana Troubadours singing "Take a Trip to Coon Town Tonight." By the time she was twelve, she had seen with her own eyes the "Latest Scientific Wonder of the Age: Edison's Marvellous Kinetograph, Most Wonderful of Moving Pictures."

If Hollywood kills time, Staten Island marks it. To visit the island with Stephen was to step into Mabel's Victorian childhood. All her houses were intact. The house the Normands moved to from New Brighton on the north of St. George to Stapleton on the south still stands at 71 Sands Street, bordered by Wave. It stands in a congested black neighborhood now that was then dominated by prosperous German breweries. The house Mabel proudly bought her parents at 125 St. Marks Place in St. George still stands, still asserting its dignity against the odds of a bulging bay front and a gnome roof. This was the house the Normands fought over and fought in after Baby's good luck turned bad.

Here Mabel's brother Claude married an Irish girl who worked as a maid for a prominent island family and who thought Hollywood the work of the devil. Mabel got jobs for Claude in Hollywood a couple of times, but when the Great War came he joined the infantry and was sent to France. He returned shell-shocked, Stephen said, and when he took to drugs, his wife blamed Mabel. Twenty years later, a construction accident left him an invalid with crushed legs. This was the house where in 1945 he hung himself from a basement pipe, and this was the house that his wife tried to purge of Mabel by throwing all her clothes, costumes, furniture, and letters onto a bonfire in the backyard.

Mabel invented herself as she went along. Unlike Mack Sennett (born Michael Sinnott) or Mary Pickford (born Gladys Smith) Mabel's name was real, but her places and dates were fake. Mabel usually chose Boston to be born in, or a Southern plantation in Atlanta. When invention flagged, she named Providence. Sennett was so certain that Mabel had been born in Providence that he was baffled when his researchers found no trace of her baptismal records. Mabel told her biographer Sutherland that she "thought" she'd been born on Staten Island and she "thought" the date was November 10, 1895, but "thought" neither fact very important. Mabel lied. If the place wasn't important to her, the date was. She was wholly consistent about a year which kept her two years younger than Pickford.

Where Mabel went to school was another unimportant fact. There were no records of her in any of the likely parish or public schools. Mabel liked to say that she never went to school at all. Sometimes she said that her mother taught her to read, her father taught her to play the piano, and she taught herself to swim. Sometimes she chose to be educated at an art school in Boston where she studied to be a painter, sometimes at a private school like the Westerleigh Collegiate Institute in Staten Island where she studied to be a lady, and sometimes at St. Mary's Convent in Northwestport, Massachusetts, where she studied to be a nun.

Mabel liked to make up stories for herself and others. In her memoir *The Honeycomb*, Adela Rogers St. Johns described Mabel's struggles as an orphan, slaving in the hell-holes of the garment factories of New York, attacked by consumption before she was eight — "No mother, father, sister, uncles, aunts or cousins." In 1976, Stephen the grandnephew wrote Adela an angry letter "to set the facts straight." Adela's reply was forthright:

I am sure that Mabel would have thought it very bad for her "image," as we say now, if she came from a routine Staten Island respectable ordinary family. . . .

*Maybe she got the factory bit out of David
Copperfield, her favorite book. We all told a lot of
big stories, I guess.*

When Stephen showed me Adela's letter I thought of Jean Harlow's remark, "I love people to think I came up from the gutter. Wouldn't it be dull to know that my Grandpa's present to me on my *fifth* birthday was an ermine bedspread?"

While Mabel always romanticized the ordinary, she observed sharply. Her real education was the island itself, which was then a vast playground and theater of social extremes who could be remembered and mimed as comic types. At the turn of the century, Staten Island was both a fashionable resort for the rich and a port of entry for the immigrant poor. The rich — the Vanderbilts, Roosevelts, Sir Edward Cunard — built their mansions around Clove Lakes Park and played polo at Manor Farm. Rich ladies in boaters introduced a new game called lawn tennis to the Staten Island Cricket and Tennis Club. Rich yachtsmen like Kaiser Wilhelm christened their new yachts at the New York Yacht Club based at Clifton.

But there were plenty of country pleasures for the poor. There were oystering and iceskating and blackberrying in season, along with Coney Island razzmatazz. Showmen of cash and vision were fast developing bathing beaches and amusement parks along South Beach, and there the masses, as Sennett would say, could rub elbows with the swells. There Mabel could develop her swimming skills in the Olympic swimming pool built by showman Erastus Wiman between his casino and ten-thousand-seat amphitheater. There Mabel could thrill to Buffalo Bill and His Wild West Show and to mighty spectacles like *!!!The Fall of Babylon!!!* At nearby Prohibition Park, "a temperance resort" founded by the future president of the Women's Christian Temperance Union, Mabel could thrill to the pleasures of demon rum by hearing William Jennings Bryan damn them. At John Bechtel's brewery on Sunday afternoons, she could thrill to the new "motion picture common shows" that entertained the workers for free and that would soon attract folk into the casinos as a come-on to the gaming tables. "Free-and-easys," the casinos called them.

As a teenager, Mabel might have seen free-and-easys being made on Fred Scott's farm. Scott had bought up coaches and wagons from Buffalo Wild Bill Cody and rented them out to the first maker of Westerns, Edwin S. Porter, who shot *The Life of an American Cowboy* within spitting distance of Manhattan. Mabel learned to bust real bronchos when she got to California, but she may have picked up a few pointers by watching fake cowboys gallop down Fingerboard Road to shoot Indians behind papier-mâché rocks.

Its beaches and meadows and carnival mobility made the place an island paradise for a tomboy to run wild in. Mabel remembered riding bareback and stealing her brother's bike and doing things "like the boys used to do," as one of her school chums put it. Mabel was too young and too poor to have met one of the most amazing tomboy rebels of the island, the socially posh photographer Alice Austen. But Mabel might have seen Alice set up her camera in front of her mansion Clear Comfort to record her friends in bicycle bloomers and herself in knickers and cigar. By the time Mabel was rich, Alice was poor and had removed to a house almost next to the one Mabel bought at St. Mark's Place. Although they never met, they should have. Their daring and their talent placed them on that equal ground where extremes so often meet.

From the beginning, Mabel was split between poor and rich, between tomboy and lady. While Mabel outswam all the boys her age and, the family bragged, swam the Hudson regularly to Bayonne and back, she looked yearningly at the ladies in white gloves who paraded along the fashionable avenues of New Brighton. What Mabel remembered most about her childhood was not how much fun she'd had but how lonely she had been. "While she knew all the neighbor children and divined what they were thinking about," her biographer Sutherland wrote, "they never really knew her." Did anyone ever really know her? In my pilgrim's tour with Stephen, I felt Mabel's spirit was near us, was with us, as Julia would say, in only two places. One was a snapshot Stephen showed me of Mabel when she was about eight. It shows a sad-faced little girl sitting on a park bench, eyes cast down, unsmiling, a big bow in her hair, her feet bare. She looks lonely.

The other was the Music Hall, too far gone to be restored under landmark grants. In front of its Greek Revival portico, a Neptune in a dried-up fountain stares at the oil tankers passing through the narrow Kill Van Kull. Within the theater, mold has rotted the walls and seats. Without, a sign chained across two fluted pillars warns, "Danger — Falling Objects."

MARCH 1, 1974, LOS ANGELES

Dear Steve:

Something keeps telling me you are going about the story in the wrong way. Your Aunt Mabel would not want the horrid past all hashed up again. Yesterday I was never going to write you again, but changed my mind.

Love,
"Judy" (Mabel christened me "Judy.")

MARCH 1, 1974, P.O. BOX 326, BEVERLY HILLS

Greetings Steve:

Julia was dined and wined and offered fabulous amounts by reporters to tell the true story of Mabel, but she wouldn't tell any of the shady side of Mabel's life. So — no story.

Most babies are born in bed and most stars are born on a sofa — which is the most familiar place for them (the stars).

And the more famous they become the more sofas — So Julia isn't telling anyone, not even you Steve, and it is making a nervous wreck out of her to be reminded of the past — much of which isn't too good.

Sincerely,
Lee Westerlund

APRIL 24, 1909, MANHATTAN

It was a cold wet day, and Mabel was glad for the warmth of Mr. Gibson's studio in Carnegie Hall. Mabel idolized Charles

Dana Gibson, for whom she had posed for nearly a year now. She was disappointed when he told her that he would have to cancel the day's sitting to attend the funeral of his publisher.

To Mabel, Mr. Gibson was kind and fatherly and "truly a master." When she looked around the studio, she saw drawings of hundreds of girls just like her, Gibson Girls with round chins, wide liquid eyes, clear brows, cupid mouths, and masses of dark hair swept under a boater or a velour heaped with silk roses. She hated to see the drawings go when an editor's messenger came for them, but the painter had told her, "Mabel, if we don't sell them you don't get paid for posing and I don't eat."

Mabel was being paid ten times as much for posing as that first day she boarded the Staten Island ferry for Manhattan with fifty cents and the address of the Butterick Company at Spring and MacDougal streets in her pocket. Her mother had told her to apply for a job in the pattern-mailing room, but the clerk took a close look and sent her on to the art department. The department head told her he would pay her fifty cents an hour, hours 9:00 to 12:00 and 1:00 to 4:00, to model patterns for *Delineator* magazine.

Sometimes Mabel liked to say that she had set off for Manhattan from Boston, after inheriting a legacy from a seafaring uncle "enriched by Oriental trade." Other times she liked to say that her mother sent her out when she was only thirteen "to bear her share of earning for the needy household." The facts were that Mabel was sixteen when she set out in 1908 in a routine respectable ordinary way to seek her fortune. Like Mary Pickford, she "wanted nice things," and she wanted to earn them respectably. At sixteen, Mabel was working-class respectable but far too pretty to be ordinary.

Her modeling introduced her to the fast-growing world of commercial advertising. At photography studios like Eddowes on Broadway, she posed for "hats, cold cream, hairbrushes, shoes, stockings, combs, hair tonics, veils, gloves, satchels, lingerie, umbrellas, necklaces, frocks, evening wraps, furs, bracelets." For one dollar she posed for a set of real luggage next to a fake Pekingese. For five dollars she posed for a set of a dozen hats.

Mabel and her friends freelanced at photographers' studios

while "the real artists" were out to lunch. Photography was suspect. There was something cheap and fake about it. Like the
lantern-slides for which Mabel posed, at five dollars a set, that
vaudeville houses projected on a screen while some aspiring tenor
like Fatty Arbuckle sang the latest popular ballad. A photographer
would prop Mabel under a fake peach tree, she remembered, and
tell her to gaze at an imaginary youth departing for the city to
make a lot of money so he could marry her.

Mabel had in fact departed for the city to make a lot of
money for herself, but money and jobs were scarce. She had to
compete with one million immigrants each year who left farm and
country for the city of New York and who thought themselves
lucky to find jobs as maids, rag pickers, shoeshine boys, garment
workers, chimney sweeps.

Mabel would make her modeling rounds on foot to save
carfare, walking from the ferry dock at the Battery to Carnegie
Hall and back. Most of the "real" artists had studios midtown,
illustrators like Hamilton King, the Leyendecker Brothers, James
Montgomery Flagg, and her favorite Mr. Gibson. The real artists
put her on the covers of the Saturday Evening Post and Life as
"The Sand Witch" or "The Girl at the Spinning Wheel" or they
posed her for a new soft drink, Coca Cola. Real artists treated
models with respect, and Mabel, as late as 1927, wanted her
biographer to understand that "the better artists never had the
time or inclination to misbehave." In 1909, Mabel was too naive
to know that some of the better artists had other commitments.
The lover of J.C. Leyendecker, for example, was his model
Charles Beck, the same Arrow Collar Man who received 17,000
fan letters a month from adoring women until he died of drugs
in 1924.

What Mabel remembered most about 1909 was the shame
of being poor. She remembered her embarrassment when she
took the wrong umbrella from Flagg's studio, a silk one for her
cheap cotton. She remembered her humiliation when Mr. Gibson
caught her trying to snitch a silver rosebud from the ball gown
she was modeling to put it on a cheap felt hat her mother had
made her. Mr. Gibson had smiled, while Mabel cried, and told
her to take all the silver rosebuds she wanted.

Mabel also remembered that on the day Mr. Gibson cancelled her sitting for a funeral she ran into a modeling friend who had just landed a job with a motion picture company called Kalem, and she urged Mabel to apply. A male model, much in demand as a "calendar Indian," had been telling Mabel for weeks about the good pay at Biograph, a motion picture company down on 14th Street. To top it off, one of the "real" artists had long urged Mabel to give pictures a go because she was funny as well as pretty, and why not get paid for being both?

Mabel hesitated. She was afraid of two things, she told her biographer. She was afraid of her mother, and she was afraid she might fail. Her mother disapproved of pictures for the same reasons that united "all Christian denominations and the Society for the Prevention of Crime" in their efforts to get the licenses of the city's 550 nickelodeons revoked. Picture shows, they said, tended "to degrade the morals of the community," and respectable girls didn't even look. Mabel had been "a movie fan all my life," she confessed, and she had looked plenty but had never acted. Stage actresses like Mary Pickford, a veteran since the age of five, contemned pictures as they would street walking. "Oh no, not that, Mama!" Little Mary had cried. Models like Mabel were terrified of not knowing how to act.

Rather than lose a day's pay, however, Mabel took a trolley down to Union Square and looked for a four-story brownstone on East Fourteenth Street, not far from Tony Pastor's Theater and Luchow's Restaurant. She finally located number eleven next to a Singer Sewing Machine sign. Today, she wouldn't have found number eleven at all. She would have found instead a fifteen-story apartment building at number seven preempting the entire block east of Fifth Avenue. What was once number eleven is today an Off-Track Betting parlor, a shake of the dice that Mack and Mabel would have liked.

When Mabel found the right number, she climbed the stairs, entered a long dark hallway, and asked the first man she met for a job. The man was D. W. Griffith's assistant, Wilfred Lucas, for whom Arbuckle would name his famous dog Luke. Lucas sent Mabel to the basement where the wardrobe mistress dressed her in a pair of silk tights and velvet bloomers. Hustled upstairs in her page's costume, Mabel found the large ballroom where, under banks of blue Cooper-Hewitt lights, Lucas was yelling at actors in capes and crowns. Lucas yelled at Mabel to pick up a crowned lady's train and follow her out the door of the painted set.

Mabel did as she was told but was embarrassed by her tights and by the grin of "a stocky, red-faced Irishman." Then someone blew a whistle for lunch and turned off the lights. She was handed a sandwich which she was too excited to eat. After lunch, Lucas put her in another costume for another picture which he shot until 11:00 that night. For her work as an extra girl, she was paid five dollars plus five dollars overtime. When she got home long past midnight with her ten-dollar bill, she knew what she wanted to do. She wanted to be in the movies. Her mother, waiting in the parlor, said, "Not on your tintype."

Mabel dutifully returned to modeling until some three weeks later when she ran into the Irishman and a couple of other Biograph actors at Times Square. The Irishman scolded her for not returning "to kill the scene." When they wanted to film the noblewoman entering the next room, where was the little page carrying the train? Mabel later said that she returned to kill the scene and to make a few others. The Irishman, she said, was Mack Sennett.

What happened next is obscured by the process of Mack's and Mabel's memories. Mack had joined Biograph a couple of years before, when he found the pay was better than vaudeville and the employment steadier. Mack was desperate to direct comedies as well as to act in them, but Griffith already had a director for his comic line, and Mack had to bide his time. While Mack took to Mabel, Griffith did not, and he left her behind when the Biograph Company made their first trip to California in December of 1909.

Mabel had been no more than an extra girl, but she was unhappy at being left behind. Griffith told her to try the Vitagraph Studios in Flatbush. Mack told her that when he returned he was going to start his own company and put her in it. That's what Mabel remembered. She didn't remember anything about falling in love with Mack. She had tried to purge him from her memory as from her life.

It was Mack who remembered discovering in that first trip to California two things in the Hotel Alexandria: the pleasures of a six-foot bathtub and the pains of being in love. It was Mack who remembered having courted Mabel "in a mild sort of way" before he left. Mack was the one who remembered taking Mabel to cheap shows in the fall of 1909, buying her a cheap ring "with a lot of *shine* to it," and giving it to her one night on the ferry back to Staten Island when he finally got up nerve to kiss her. Mack was the one who remembered composing a love letter, while meditating in the Hotel Alexandria bathtub, in which he plagiarized a chorus of "Brown Eyes" and got the reply he wanted, "Your girl, Mabel." Mack was the one who said, "She was exactly that from then on." On the subject of love, Mabel was silent.

Yet I trusted Mack's garrulity less than Mabel's silence. Mack wanted to "spin a romance, a made-up boy-and-girl story," he confessed in *King of Comedy,* but he also wanted to spin a romance of money, the story of a Canadian farm boy who rose from boilermaker to multimillionaire. His fictions were no more compatible than his facts. When they first met, Mack was twenty-eight, twelve years older than Mabel, almost an "old man," with little to show for it after a decade of clowning in vaudeville and burlesque and a couple of years in picture acting. Mack was courting Mabel, but — he confessed — he was courting a career even more, and they both knew it. When Mack processed his memories in 1954, he said, "My happiest and my saddest memory is Mabel Normand, the actress who ate ice cream for breakfast." When Mabel processed her memories in 1927, her happiest and saddest memory of Mack was that "I made a tremendous fortune for that Irishman."

VITAGRAPH BETTY

MARCH 3, 1974, LOS ANGELES
Dear Steve:

*I had a premonition you would telephone. "Mabel
lives" for sure in your own flesh and blood. All
during the "probe" of your story I have felt nervous
of you dear, forgive me, for trying to keep a
well-guarded secret. Remember MN is looking down
on us and what we say better be to her way of right
good thinking!!*

*Love,
Judy*

JUNE, 1911, FLATBUSH

Mabel and Norma Talmadge were falling over themselves
laughing. They spent most of their time at Vitagraph's large
outdoor studio falling over themselves laughing. Today they were
laughing over the funniest fat man of the movies, John Bunny,
who was snoring in a chair. They had painted one half of his face
black with burnt-cork and the other half red with the clay they
used for Indian makeup. Bunny snored on. The girls hadn't had
so much fun since the day they ruined a take in a Civil War movie
to protest being cast as slaves; they blackened only the front of
their necks and shoulders and turned their lily-white backs on the
camera. Or since the last day they provoked their favorite short-
tempered director into stamping his bowler hat flat. Or since the
last night they lied to their mothers and bought a case of iced beer
and got tight with other Vitagraph girls like Norma's sister Constance and Lillian "Dimples" Walker.

Vitagraph was much more fun than Biograph, although it

took Mabel twice as long to get to the Vitagraph Studio in Flatbush. But Flatbush then was country like Staten Island and Mabel was right at home in the tank on the studio grounds and in the water of nearby Sheepshead Bay. Bay and studio were so close that Dimples Walker remembers swimming out to a raft and being called back by a prop boy to shoot the next scene. The studio was on land so countrified that the lease included the clause, "Wilhelmina Lot reserves the right to drive her cows to pasture through the premises."

How and when Mabel came to Vitagraph are unclear. Vitagraph's founder claimed in his memoirs that he had found "the prettiest girl in New York" posing for *Delineator* and hired her on the spot for an ingenue. But his memories were as fictional as other people's, and Mabel may well have taken Griffith's advice and boarded a trolley for Flatbush to ask for a job. She must have impressed someone at Vitagraph more than she did Griffith because she landed a role with the company's major romantic stars, Maurice Costello and Florence Turner, in the romance of "a Double Love-Tale Sweetly Told." *Over the Garden Wall* got Mabel's name and picture as a featured player in Vitagraph's "Life Portrayal" ads in the trade magazines for June, 1910. But what had she been doing since December, when Mack and Biograph took off for Hollywood? Or before that, when the Biograph company, without Mabel, spent the summer on location in Cuddebackville in New York State?

I hoped to find that Mabel had appeared as an extra girl in a film Vitagraph made in the fall of 1909, *Miss Annette Kellerman*, when they hired a chorus of girls to swim and play diabolo with the world champion swimmer and diver. When Mabel became the Diving Girl of the screen, she owed much to Annette and the one-piece bathing suit known as "the Kellerman tights" that got Annette arrested in Boston. A Gibson Bathing Girl had shocked audiences with her stockings and bloomers in Ziegfeld's first Follies in 1907, but the Kellerman tights bared all and critics responded: "The dripping silk of the fleshings appears almost iridescent . . . with each sinuous move," they wrote of this Salomé of the Sea. Mabel was not allowed to wear Kellerman "fleshings" until her first Keystone comedy in 1912, *The Water Nymph*, but when she did, she was a knockout. From then on Mabel was Mack's and America's first Bathing Beauty.

But there was no visible trace of Mabel the extra girl in *Miss Annette Kellerman,* and the wish was a biographer's trap. Mabel's early career was nothing but traps, and I fell into most of them. What happened to Mabel after her first major picture in the spring of 1910, for example? She went right back to Biograph as an extra girl to make a single film in July after the company had returned from California. Why? The answer had to be Mack. Mack always called himself a slow-brained tongue-tied rube. In fact, he was a mighty persuader. He must have persuaded Mabel to quit her good job at Vitagraph to share a working vacation with him in Cuddebackville, in the Orange Mountains above Port Jervis. Griffith was going to film *Wilfull Peggy* there, in July, to star Mary Pickford. Since it was an eighteenth-century costume drama set in Ireland, he hired a bevy of extra colleens for this one film only. There is no sign of Mabel on the existing print, but we know she is there because her name appears on the hotel register of the Caudebec Inn, with other members of the company, for July 20, 1910. "Miss Norman" was assigned to Parlor 17 with two other girls.

There is also no sign that Mabel worked in movies again until seven months later. And when she did, she was back at Vitagraph. More puzzles. Maybe Mack believed he could persuade Griffith to keep her on. If so, he miscalculated. Mabel's sense of humor irritated Griffith, who had none. Sennett believed that Griffith missed out on Mabel because she was prankish and fooled around too much with the company clown, Mack. "Griffith never took her seriously," Mack said.

Somebody at Vitagraph took her seriously, however, as a comedienne. Vitagraph starred her in *Betty Becomes a Maid* and gave her a chance to create her own comic character. "Vitagraph Betty" was a girl who is pretty, funny, and shockingly "fast." Critics heralded the dawn of a new comedienne when she repeated "Vitagraph Betty" in *The Troublesome Secretaries* with her favorite John Bunny, but they worried about her morals. "Attractive Mabel Normand as Betty" is "extremely funny," the *Mirror* wrote, but wished that Betty had not been "so free in her hugging and kissing but had been more refined and dainty." Girls were dainty, boys were coarse. Mabel muddled the genres, and audiences were shocked as well as amused.

In her last comedy for Vitagraph, *The Subduing of Mrs. Nag*, Mabel got to play not only with Bunny but also with his comic partner, Flora Finch. Fat Bunny and scrawny Finch were the screen's funniest comic couple because they were equally ugly. Bunny was said to be so fat that only a beanpole like Finch could squeeze into the same camera frame with him. When Mabel squeezed her prettiness into the same frame, she unhinged the sexes. To avoid Nag's jealous wife, Mabel as "Miss Prue" disguises herself as a male secretary, only to arouse the lust of Mrs. Nag. Critics again praised the newcomer but thought the plot "coarse." "It will give offense to many observers," they warned. It was a warning that plagued Mabel throughout her career.

Had Mabel continued at Vitagraph, she would have made a comic trio with Bunny and Finch. But when Mack returned East with Biograph in May of 1911, after another Mabel-less winter in California, he had persuaded Griffith to hire Mabel as a leading player. Griffith could put her in melodramas, and Mack could put her in the comedies he was at last directing. To give offense, coarsely, was Mack's comic point. But even Mack was prudish when it came to girls and sometimes he got so genteel that Mabel had to call him "Aunt Prue."

In June, Mabel left Vitagraph after three more romance dramas as a lead ingenue: *Picciola, A Dead Man's Honor, The Changing of Silas Warner.* She left as a rising young comedienne with a future as bright as a penny. But when she "groped her strangely forgetful and disjointed way" through her memory trunk for biographer Sutherland, she remembered how quickly her early idols had fallen and how few of her friends were loyal when she herself fell. She remembered how Finch's career ended in 1915 when Bunny, "poor clown," died after a disastrous stage tour in England. She remembered how the career of the first matinee idol, Maurice Costello, was ruined in the 20's by a wife jealous of his fans. She remembered how the Vitagraph Girl, Florence Turner, was down and out when Buster Keaton gave her a bit part in *College*. In the precarious occupation of motion pictures, nothing lasted but friends.

And once down and out, you learned how short-lived those were. Except for a few like the Talmadges, who lasted. The Talmadge sisters — Norma, Connie, and Natalie — came to Vitagraph as a flying wedge from Erasmus Hall High School in Flatbush, propelled by their mother, Peg. Norma, the eldest, came first, to team with Mabel in leading her younger sisters astray. Of all Mabel's friends, Norma was the one who stood by Mabel during the Taylor blitz. And of all stage mothers, Peg was the one Mabel should have had and didn't to protect her in the California days and nights to come, when the air was so pure you could see a whole sky of falling stars.

DIVING GIRL

MARCH 25, 1974, LOS ANGELES
Dear Steve:

One subject, sacred and confidential about MN —
her big problem was the gin bottle. All her help,
especially Mamie, would cooperate with me in getting
rid of it by watering the bottle. We didn't want the
public to detect or see the least sign of liquor on
MN. We felt sure the gossip mongers would label it
dope.

Fans would mob Mabel wherever she went — had
to be rescued by plainclothesmen when she went to
Bloomingdale's one day. There was only one bad
incident, on stage in NYC, where someone yelled
out, 'Mabel when you left the sunshine in
Hollywood, why didn't you leave the moonshine too?'

Love,
Judy

SEPTEMBER 30, 1978, CUDDEBACKVILLE

I had driven north from Princeton through Port Jervis at the
Jersey border to Cuddebackville because I wanted to see for
myself the scene of Mabel's first big picture for Biograph that I
had already seen on a 16-mm print. I had seen Mabel the Indian
maid in *The Squaw's Love*, "An Indian Poem of Love in Pictures." I had seen Mabel thrown over a cliff by a rival squaw and
seen Mabel swim down river with a knife in her mouth to rip up
the enemy's canoes. With her dark hair and eyes and red clay
makeup they called "Bole Armenia," Mabel made a more authentic Indian than Pickford, I thought, because Mabel didn't require

37

a horsehair wig. Griffith used the services of a real Indian named Dark Cloud to make costumes and props authentic and Mabel was plausible enough as his daughter, Wild Flower.

For the first time, Griffith found a way in this romance-adventure film to exploit Mabel's athletic talent. But Sennett had already beat him to it, in July, in his first Mabel comedy, *The Diving Girl.* Mack put Mabel in a kerchief, knee-length bathing costume, black stockings, and slippers, and posed her at the end of a diving board at Coney Island, arms raised, ready to take the plunge. Like Venus from the foam, the Bathing Beauty was born from the coupling of sex and clowning that would make Sennett a fortune and Mabel a star. Sennett said no to Kellerman tights, but even Mabel's calves were enough to cause a sensation in the days "when knees were a treat and ankles were an orgy."

As a split-reel short, *The Diving Girl* was no more than a vaudeville skit brought out-of-doors. But a real seashore and a real girl made all the difference in the image. Mabel was not a burlesque queen. Mabel was the girl next door, or what America's pimply youth hoped the girl next door would be in a bathing costume. Mabel at a stroke had revolutionized the idea of the sexy by changing its image, by transplanting it from stage to screen to make it as innocent and as girlish as an ice cream cone.

Not to be outdone by the coarse Sennett, Griffith experimented by making the diving girl a heroine in a Western, and he made up a story around a girl who could dive and swim. "What Griffith saw in his mind we put on the screen," his cameraman used to say, and what Griffith saw in the little hills at Cuddebackville was the drama of the American wilderness. Griffith saw Wild Flower thrown off a cliff into the Neversink River, to be faked by Mabel in a real back dive. Movie legend claims that the dive was so risky Mabel refused to do it more than once. To make certain of his shot, Griffith set up three cameras to shoot simultaneously and so created movie history. But Mabel never refused anything risky. She only balked at the safe and dull. It was Griffith, I began to suspect, who worried about the risks.

When I got to Cuddebackville to look for the spot where Mabel had dived and to see what was left of the Caudebec Inn where Mabel had registered, I began to suspect everything. The Predmore family ran the inn when the Biograph company spent summers there, escaping the heat of Manhattan for the woods of pine and oak that line the Neversink. I found Ruby Predmore, the widow of the Predmore son who had loaded the actors into a hay wagon to take them to an eighteenth-century stone house, for "authenticity," where the owner would refresh the troupe after a day's shooting with pails of apple juice and ale poured over blocks of ice. Shandy gaff, they called it then. Mabel was supposed to have dived from a granite bluff near the house, but when Ruby and I tramped through the woods the twilight was so thick we couldn't even find the river.

We did find the one remaining structure of the old inn, an outbuilding captured now by mobile trailers above the pond they called "the Basin," formed by the Delaware and Hudson canals. Nothing else remains to confirm memories of the inn as "a comfy place three stories high, with one bathroom, a tiny parlor, rag-rugged, and a generously sized dining room whose cheerful windows looked upon apple orchards." Nobody was around to remember Mother Predmore's lemon meringue pies and her annual welcome to the troupe, "Glad to see you come." Nobody, except a wooden cigar-store Indian on the porch of the general store next door.

Somebody was around, however, in the white clapboard Reformed Church built two centuries ago on the far side of the Basin. Frank Cuddeback was somebody, and he was around, as his ancestors had been since the early 1600s, to give the place a name. Frank was in the Church kitchen, preparing a fish fry for the 300 inhabitants of Cuddebackville. Frank remembered the Griffith company well. He remembered the night Mary Pickford "tried to drown herself in the pond" by getting beamed by a log before a local lad jumped in and saved her. He remembered how he and the other boys would come running when they heard the cannon and guns go off. He did not remember seeing Mabel Normand take that dive. The Neversink had always been too shallow for diving, Frank maintained. "They faked those shots," he said, "You know how they do in the movies."

That summer of 1911 was a turning point for Mabel because her diving films, faked or real, identified her with the out-of-doors. Because she was an athlete, not a stage actress, the out-of-doors was her natural habitat. When the company returned in the fall to Manhattan, Mabel turned out a couple of more seaside comedies for Mack, but Griffith put her back indoors in vamp roles that were against her nature as much as straight melodrama was.

Griffith was colorblind. He saw the world in black and white, brunettes and blondes, bad girls and good. His moral vision made good epic but weak comedy, and with Mabel he couldn't see the girl for the type. To Griffith, Mabel was the "voluptuous type" in contrast to the "spirituelle." "The voluptuous type, blossoming into the full-blown one, cannot endure," Griffith said. "The years show their stamp too clearly. The other type . . . ah, that is different." If Mabel was his "voluptuous," Pickford, Blanche Sweet, Lillian Gish would become his "spirituelles."

For Griffith Mabel made five melodramas: *Her Awakening, The Unveiling, Saved from Himself, The Eternal Mother, The Mender of Nets.* Typical of the moral lesson Mabel incarnated for Griffith was her role in *The Eternal Mother,* where she played opposite Blanche Sweet. Biograph ads pointed the contrast in word and picture between "a restless, passionate, dark-haired girl with a red rose in her hair" and "a mere flaxen-haired girl as carefree as a May morning." The spirituelle transcended time because she was free of flesh and therefore eternally young. The voluptuous was time's victim and withered like a red red rose.

Mabel the voluptuous instructed the world for the last time in the only major film she made with her real-life opposite and counterpart, Mary Pickford. Swallowing her pride, Mary had applied to Biograph in April of 1909, the same month as Mabel. "Too little and too fat," Griffith told Mary and immediately cast her as a ten-year-old in *Her First Biscuits.* Mary looked young but was born old and in real life had never been the child she was forced to play for the rest of her career. When Griffith hired her at sixteen, she was a tough professional schooled by a decade of stage trouping and poverty that made Mabel seem like a child of the idle rich.

In *The Mender of Nets,* "a Seaside Romance," Mabel and Mary were a perfect Griffith pair. Cast as "The Weakness: His Old Infatuation," Mabel the voluptuous appeared with her dark hair cascading loose to her waist in contrast to spirituelle Mary, her blonde curls tucked chastely into a beret. In the story, Mary proves her spirituality by caring for Mabel's child after she dies, even though Mabel has seduced Mary's lover and wrecked her romance. The drama was the first film Mabel made in California, shot in January of 1912 on the beach at Santa Monica. But for Griffith, the sea was a stage backdrop, useless for voluptuous types who may take off their clothes but don't go near the water. It was Sennett, not Griffith, who put the diving girl into the sea to find her true element in the waters of the Pacific and to create a new genre of seaside comic sex.

Prowling Hollywood for Mabel clues, I came on a former diving girl named Elsie Hanneman McEvoy, secreted in a ferny dell off Fairfax Avenue. Elsie at eighty-seven was as spry as the day she retired in 1913 as the undefeated women's diving champion of the world. She followed Annette Kellerman into vaudeville with her own touring company, and she taught Mabel some dives for *Mr. Grouch at the Seaside,* shot at Gravesend Bay when the Biograph company returned East. She didn't do fancy work with Mabel, she recalled, "just front and back and front jack-knife and back jack-knife." She also recalled winning a dollar bet from friends who claimed Mabel's eyelashes had to be false. Elsie had worn the Kellerman tights in vaudeville, she said, to dive into the largest glass tank ever used on the stage. Under a glass pail she ate a banana, drank a bottle of grape juice and sang the verses of her special song,

> *There are lots of live lobsters at sea, oh yes,*
> *There are lots of live lobsters at sea.*

Sennett had wanted Elsie to join his new Keystone company and come to Hollywood with Mabel, but Elsie's father said "No!" "I thank the good God now because look how Mabel turned out," Elsie told me, as we looked through her albums of diving girl silhouettes. "She couldn't take it, definitely couldn't take it," Elsie went on, "and I would have been the same in movies. So I went into vaudeville and Mabel went into pictures and made a big name. But look what happened to Mabel."

MAY 1, 1974, LOS ANGELES
[Stephen wrote Julia that he would come to Hollywood in

41

June to take Julia and Lee to the opening of David Merrick's musical *Mack and Mabel* at the Aronson Music Center.]

Dear Steve:

What are you going to wear? I get a bit "up tight" and nervous, I am so thrilled at the thought of Mabel's own flesh and blood!! I'm sure your dear Aunt Mabel will find you a perfect media through which to express yourself.

You will never guess what caused me to fall head, line and sinker? On April 16 you wrote me a letter — one sentence of 11 words — the subject was 'love.' 'It is wonderful how the feeling of love can encompass one' — I applied it spiritually, you understand.

You make me so happy.

Love,
Judy

DECEMBER 28, 1912, ABOARD THE SANTA FE CALIFORNIA LIMITED

While the train was speeding West across Kansas and while Mack was drinking beer and playing poker in the observation car with his crony Henry "Pathé" Lehrman, Mabel was in her compartment teaching Blanche Sweet how to smoke. In 1977 I found Blanche in her Murray Hill apartment in New York, looking much as she did when she created a sensation as the spirituelle avenger for Griffith in 1913. Blanche laughed as she remembered Mabel's smoking lesson.

"Mabel taught me to take a puff of the cigarette and then a swallow of water and then puff the smoke out," Blanche said. "Of course I choked to death all the way across Kansas."

Mabel smoked because smoking was wicked and yet "she had this terrific innocence in her," Blanche recalled. Blanche had begun her acting career as "Baby Blanche" in the stage hit *Blue Jeans* before joining Biograph as a spirituelle. "We were all so young," she remembered. "We had to be." The camera exposed wrinkles that the stage could conceal, and youth was harder to fake. Mabel was not only young, Blanche remembered, but "so very beautiful, so wide-eyed, such a talented comedienne."

On December 27, Mabel had boarded the Black Diamond Express in Jersey City for Chicago, changing at LaSalle Street Station to catch the California Limited going West. Mabel was going West to see for herself the crystal sunshine, golden oranges, mackerel-crowded seas, and six-foot bathtubs that Mack had boasted of until she wanted to scream. Mabel was going West in luxury. She had three dollars a day to spend on food — and cigarettes. She would have fourteen dollars a week expense allowance when she checked in at the Hotel Alexandria. Escaping the hell-holes of her fictional past, Mabel was going West across Kansas, the Great Divide, the Mohave Desert, to reinvent herself in California.

When she stepped for the first time into the hot eucalyptic air of Los Angeles, Mabel knew that California was the kind of place she would have invented if asked to invent a place. California was made for comedy. "In the beginning," Mabel remembered, "we were golden lads and girls" who made money so fast "we didn't know what to do with it or ourselves and didn't care." "In the beginning," the native Californian Anita Loos remembered, "Hollywood was a gypsy camp and everything was fun." "In the beginning," Adela Rogers St. Johns remembered, "we were still so innocent, so young, with lots of money and no place to go." "In the beginning," Mack remembered, "we brought box lunches with us and picked oranges right off the trees . . . we had more fun then." "Remember, we were the beginning," Minta Arbuckle said, "and our comedies are classics now because they can *never* be made again."

They could never be made again because most of the split-reel comedies that Mack and Mabel made that first winter and spring were movies of Mack and Mabel having fun. In the films that survive we can still see them having fun in an orange grove, where Mack picks Mabel an orange. In a funicular up Mount Lowe, where Mabel hits Mack with a snowball. In a cactus grove, where Mabel with a dagger in her teeth threatens Mack in his sombrero. At the beach, where Mack beans Mabel with a beach ball. In the park, where Mabel snubs Mack to cuddle up with a live bear cub.

The titles were as extraneous as those old comic tags *As You*

Like It or *What You Will.* In a year's time, between August 1911 and August 1912, Mabel made twenty-five comedies for Biograph and Mack, most of which have survived today by means of paper prints: *The Diving Girl, The Baron, Through His Wife's Picture, A Victim of Circumstances, Why He Gave Up, The Fatal Choco-late, The Engagement Ring, A Spanish Dilemma, Hot Stuff, Oh Those Eyes!, Help! Help!, The Brave Hunter, The Fickle Spaniard, The Furs, Helen's Marriage, Tomboy Bessie, Neighbors, Katchem Kate, A Dash Through the Clouds, The Tourists, What the Doc-tor Ordered, The Tragedy of a Dress Suit, An Interrupted Elope-ment, Mr. Grouch at the Seaside, He Must Have a Wife.*

Without knowing it, Mack and Mabel were inventing a new style of Western comedy. Speed was the key. They took Griffith's interior scenes of sex and crime, put them out-of-doors, and speeded them up until everybody fell over laughing. Breakneck speed brought laughs and money. "We made pictures as fast as we could for money," Mack said. "We used to go into a park with a stepladder, a bucket of whitewash and Mabel Normand and make a picture," Chaplin said. For making comedy on the spot, Mabel was ideal. "Mabel was pure emotion," Mack said. If Mack said be a mother, she was a mother; be a girl, she was a girl. She could do, she dared do, anything. She dared to ride a bike, a horse, a burro, a balloon, a racing car, an airplane, anything that moved. Audiences had fun because Mabel had fun running wild in the West.

If Vitagraph Betty was sexually fast, Biograph Mabel was a speed demon. She dropped her long taffeta skirt for bicycle bloomers, bathing tights, riding dusters, and men's breeches. In *A Dash through the Clouds,* she took to the air in a display of Western speed and dash impossible to the inhibited East. "This is a farce comedy," Biograph advertised the film, "of a melo-dramatic type that has a thrill in every foot." It was a farce comedy in which Mack and Mabel discovered the formula of their Keystone comedies to come — farce, melodrama, and thrills. The catalyst was dashing Mabel. We can see her today, dancing with excitement when she sees a real two-seater twin-propelled Wright Brothers airplane piloted by a pro. She wants to go up. Her boyfriend objects. Mabel hops into the open seat side by side with the pilot, fastens one seat belt around her waist and another around her calves to keep her skirt down, before they take off. They take off over cows grazing in a meadow that would one day become the Los Angeles County airport. They take off leaving Mabel's boyfriend to get into a jam in Olvera Street when he peddles his "tutti-frutti" gum to the señoritas. Mabel rescues him from the air, pumping a pair of six-shooters like a Mexican revolutionary.

The American girl took note. Mabel's movies instructed girls in sexual liberation because "prop-wise" the girl, the place, the flying machines were real. In this movie, however, Mack faked the closeups of Mabel flying, by filming the plane while it was stationary on a hilltop. But the camera conspired with the airplane to make the fantasy of flight and of freedom real. Just as the camera conspired with California to make the fantasy of unlimited space and life and liberty real.

The California landscape was a surreal place to begin with, as surreal as Death Valley and the San Andreas Fault, or those surreal backdrops painted by the father of comic movies in France, George Méliès, that caused Mack to say, "I stole it all from the French." California was a ready-made geographic joke that bred joke cities like Hollywood and joke countries like Disneyland and jokers like Mack and Mabel. California's geographic excess violated decorum the way slapstick did. Its sunshine was too much, and its excess liberated cameras from the musty interiors and props of the East where, as Griffith's cameraman said, to indicate class they stuck in a potted palm and to indicate great class, two potted palms. Its space went too far, and its excess liberated actors and other gypsies from the mores and manners of the East.

Mack's cameras upset the stereotypes of real and fake the way Mabel's actions upset the stereotypes of boy and girl. When Mack and Mabel came back to California with their own company, their speed upset the stereotypes of East and West. They had no time to build plots or scenery or social types. "When we wanted to shoot a picture of a house," Mack said, "we had to shoot a picture of a house." When they wanted to shoot cops or firemen, they shot real cops and firemen. When they wanted action, they raced around real tracks at Santa Monica and raced from real lions at Colonel Selig's Zoo. Real was what you made up on the spot, fast. Speed was money, and the speed with which they made money was, like the landscape, surreal. They knew it and they captured its excess in the chase. The comic chase, by which Keystone would brand the West, exaggerated real Western mobility to make it funny. The rhythm of Keystone comedy would rev up the old Western rhythm of the brag to the speed of the new combustion engine.

KEYSTONE MABEL

MAY 23, 1974, LOS ANGELES

Dear Steve:

Petula Clark now singing "My Love" seems to be the right beat for my present thoughts of you! Dear, have you heard Capricorns never show their age? The new role I am asking to play fills me with love I have never experienced before. Your love will allow me to play the role of Nana — God rest.

I love you much,

God bless,

Judy

AUGUST 12, 1977, LOS ANGELES

I'd been told that the old Keystone lot was still on Allessandro Street, now Glendale Boulevard, and I went to look for it. From the Montecito, I drove east on Hollywood Boulevard until it drains into Sunset, then turned north at Echo Lake past the Angelus Temple to reach Glendale Boulevard just before it becomes the Glendale Freeway. On my right, set back from the street behind a vacant lot of rubble and tumbleweeds was a large warehouse with a sign, "Center Theatre Group, Scenic Shop." To the left of the warehouse, stage flats and props lined a fence that had once backed on the Hornbeck ranch, a combination boarding house, saloon, and poolroom. To the right of the warehouse, facing its entrance, a pair of cottages hid behind broken picket fences, battered cars, and a line of wash. The warehouse was built into a steep hill that ended in a ridge where Keystone cars had raced and crashed. Across the boulevard from the warehouse, some Mexican boys hosed down their cars where Greenberg's

Bakery had once furnished Mabel with pies. I was looking at the final remains of Keystone Studio in the place once called Edendale, halfway between Aimée Semple MacPherson's Four-Square Gospel Temple on the south and Forest Lawn Memorial Park on the north.

Before the movies arrived, Edendale was a valley of green pastures between Silver Lake Reservoir on the west and Elysian Park on the east. But not for long. I came on a 1905 photograph of the Hornbeck ranch that shows a line of horse-drawn wagons pulled up to the Edendale Grocery next to a billboard for McCan Mechanical Works. The mechanical works of cameras and cars would soon displace horse, wagon, and farm and empty the grocery for movie storeroom and stage. A traveling medicine man turned moviemaker, Colonel William Selig, was the first to discover that at Edendale the land was cheap and the transportation good. A trolley ran through it from Los Angeles to "Tropico," as Glendale was then. The New York Motion Picture Company moved in next and shot its first cowboys there under the mark of the buffalo nickel, for Bison Company. When Bison's director Tom Ince moved his cowboys over to "the prairie" at Santa Monica, Mack and Mabel moved in to make Keystone pratfalls give the lie to Eden without the fall.

Everything happened so fast. When Mack and Mabel came to Edendale, picture stars did not yet exist but what made them did — the chance to start over, to make a name, to become somebody. The people who had named Edendale, who had come with Bibles instead of cameras from Kansas, Ohio, Iowa, and Nebraska, had come seeking the same covenant as the picture people. It was the sermon of the West, from the gold rush to the present, preached still by Dr. Robert Schuller in his drive-in church in Garden Grove, executed by Philip Johnson as a star-shaped cathedral of glass: "YOU TOO CAN BE A STAR."

"The whole thing was a gamble," Mabel said, meaning lives as well as money. The success of those first picture gamblers in the teens was like the success of the Beatles in the sixties. All they asked was a chance. Because they were ordinary people, nameless and classless, Mack and Mabel embodied the hopes of the thirteen million immigrants each year who gambled everything on the chance of a new start in America. Mack and Mabel were projections of themselves, performing home movies on the screen and fulfilling in their lives immigrant dreams of money and fame. For all of them, the real lives of the actors were more fantastic than their photodramas. "One year we were nobodies, poor, untrained and uneducated," a Griffith actress remembered. "Overnight we were treated like royalty." Overnight Mack and Mabel became the king and queen of comedy, and almost overnight the screen became a social register for the proletariat.

After I had been to Edendale, I found a portrait of Mabel in *The Photoplayer's Weekly* of August 8, 1914, labeled "Mabel Normand, 'Queen of the Movies.'" One year a nobody. Overnight a queen. In the photo, Mabel is staring straight at the camera, unsmiling, and what struck me is that Mabel the Queen, at twenty-two, looks like the little girl in Staten Island who wore a hair bow and bare feet. She looks lonely.

In the beginning, I found, the story of Mack and Mabel was a comedy, a story of instant success, founded on the keystone of clowning and sex. When Biograph returned East in May of 1912, Mack split with Griffith to form his own company. As Mack tells it, he persuaded a pair of bookies to cancel a gambling debt and stake him to $2500 to make comedies only. The bookies were small Charles O. Baumann and big Adam Kessel, who had founded the New York Motion Picture Company in 1909 when a crusade against racetrack gambling threw them out of work. It was the crusading spirit that made the movies as it would make bootleg gin. As Mack tells it, he filched the logo of the Pennsylvania Railroad for his own heist, since comedy was the keystone of motion pictures and since *his* comedy was to outstrip all others in the race for gold.

But Mack's word is as reliable as other myths of origin, like "How the Elephant Got Its Trunk." Mabel remembered how the bookies took her to lunch at Luchow's and bid up her salary so fast that she was struck dumb. When they reached $125 a week, she recovered her wits and signed. The only trouble with Mabel's story is that Charlie Chaplin's is identical in *My Autobiography.* Whatever the facts, the point of the myth was not dates or sums but wonder. "My family wouldn't believe it," Mabel said, "until they saw the first week's pay."

Whenever Mabel talked about Keystone beginnings, she talked about somebody fiddling the funds. She remembered the "weird" financing that kept Keystone one step ahead of receivership. She remembered how the bookies exploited her name and her energy with five films at once in order to finance the first. "There'd be a Mabel Normand Amusement Co., Inc., and a Mabel Normand this and a Mabel Normand that," she told Sutherland. She never did understand how the system worked, and she never cared, she said. But when it was too late, she did care because she knew she'd been had. "I made more millionaires of men I never saw than anybody ever in pictures."

Mack liked to say that sex and crime, the subjects of serious drama, were the best source of his funny ideas, but he should have added money. From the beginning, sex, crime, and money were the source of Keystone comedy and the context of their lives. Mabel provided the sex, the male clowns provided the crime, and the combo brought in the money. Their first thousand feet of film, in fact, split a half-reel of sex, *The Water Nymph*, with a half-reel of crime, *Cohen Collects a Debt*. To get free locations, they shot one at Coney Island and the other at Central Park before taking off for California on July 4. Or so Mack and Mabel recalled. But July 4 was a ritual date with both of them, as I discovered when I tried to solve the mystery of their romance.

From the beginning, Mack and Mabel were a comically odd couple. They were hopelessly ill-matched, the dainty and the coarse. Mabel so pretty, Mack such a lout. The girls at Biograph had hated to work with him, Griffith's wife remembered, because he clowned so much and spent so little. He'd never buy a girl an ice cream soda until Mabel came along. When Mabel came along, he bought her a $75 diamond necklace and when they quarreled, he tried to sell it for $85. He was that kind of guy. "Very vulgar, uncouth," Blanche Sweet remembered, "but he didn't know it and wouldn't have cared if he did." He did care, I discovered; he cared a lot. He used vulgarity as the clown's defense against ridicule and years later remembered the snubs of the Biograph girls and legit actors who condescended to him.

Even Griffith condescended, Mack recalled, although "he was exactly my own age."

Mack saw himself as all elbows and arms and teeth. He always stuck his hands in his pockets, he said, to keep them from dangling to his knees. He always chewed tobacco, he didn't say, to keep from having to talk. Minta Arbuckle saw him as a "big handsome farm boy from Canada, with his ruddy complexion, great shock of black hair, big brown eyes, generous mouth, nice teeth but," she added, "terribly stained with tobacco." I saw him in photos as a man whose eyes contradicted his mouth. His eyes were so vulnerable. Stephen saw him as the man who ruined Mabel.

It was hard to tell how Mabel saw him because she seldom admitted to being his girl. Mabel understood Mack, Blanche felt, "For if she put up with him for so long his uncouthness must not have mattered to her." But I wondered if the opposite weren't true. His uncouthness was just what mattered. Vulgarity was their bond. They were shanty Irish together, and together they laughed at couthness, snobbishness, and pretense. When Mack forgot himself and put on airs, Mabel shot him down. "I used to call Mack Sennett Napoleon because it made him feel proud," Mabel told her biographer, "and changed it to 'Nappy' because it made him angry." The more she called him Nappy, the longer he sulked in the eight-foot marble bathtub he installed with Turkish masseur in the tower from which he ruled his Keystone kingdom.

But that was later. At the beginning, their teamwork was unique. Mack built his company around Mabel, and when she left him, he never could replace her. As a comic team, Mabel replaced a male partner at Biograph whom Griffith described as "tall, debonair, possessing the easy manner of the aristocrat." Mack, by contrast, was "a short, burly bearlike figure with long gorilla arms dropping from a pair of incredibly huge shoulders. . . . a wide good-natured grin on his face." For larks, when the pair entered a public place like a restaurant, Griffith added, the tall and debonair would lead Sennett by the hand and introduce him as "my idiot brother."

When Mack hired comics Fred Mace, Ford Sterling, and "Pathé" Lehrman for the original Keystone gang of four men and a girl, Mabel got not only top billing but equal billing with Mack. Their first ads announced "High Class Comedy and Dramatic Subjects acted by an All-Star Stock Co. including Max [sic] Sennett, Mabel Normand, and Others Heretofore with the Biograph Co., Directed by Mr. Sennett." By 1915 they were so well established as a team that the trades called them a double "Key to the Comedy in Keystone Comedies: Mack Sennett, Director, and Mabel Normand, Portrayer of Keystone Burlesque."

The combination offended some, like Chaplin. His first impression of the Keystone lot, Chaplin recalled, was "a strange and unique atmosphere of beauty and beast." Chaplin found the "he-man atmosphere" of the male comics — "ex-circus clowns and prize fighters" — intolerably vulgar. Their "crude melange of rough-and-tumble" was justified solely by "a pretty dark-eyed girl named Mabel Normand." It was the shock once again of coupling the dainty with the coarse, the same shock that jolted audiences into laughter. Anomaly was the basis of Keystone humor that they carried to vulgar excess. Mabel was an ideal human norm to set off Mack's menagerie of human idiots — the gorillas, fishfaces, walruses, and bears portrayed by Mack Sterling, Hank Mann, Harry McCoy, Edgar Kennedy, and Chester Conklin, among others, as the menagerie grew.

Mack knew that Beauty and the Beast was a miscegenation of sex and crime that would turn audience nickels into dimes. In Keystone's first ads Mack put Mabel in Kellerman tights to star as "the beautiful Diving Venus" in *The Water Nymph.* Beefy by today's standards, Mabel was a sylph for her time, and her image dazzled. Pioneer director King Vidor remembered that, as a boy in Galveston, Texas, he fell in love with the movies the day he fell in love with Mabel.

"I saw her in bathing tights on the screen and fell in love with her as a bathing beauty the way guys do," he said. "She was different from Annette Kellerman. Mabel was pretty and the movies were magic. I fell for the image of the girl on the high dive."

Mabel was different because she was natural, and movies were magic because Mack's camera loved Mabel. It couldn't get enough of her, it ate her up. And because Mack and Mabel were filming their lives, improvising in real locations like cinema verité, their cameras recorded a real romance. Real to their audiences because the audiences felt themselves to be as oafish, mismatched, ludicrous as their clowns. Since sex was both sacred and taboo, laughing at it was as liberating as showing it at all.

Crime, too, paid off. In *Cohen Collects a Debt* the clowns battled over money in a three-way con game that was an extension of their lives. When the Keystone gang reached Los Angeles around the end of August, they had to split for the Mexican border. One of the clowns, probably Sterling, had got a girl pregnant, and she threatened him with the Mann Act. The company producer sent them down to Tijuana until the "stinking mess" blew over. He remembered sending their weekly payroll down by chauffeur in a 1912 Losier touring car. Mack should have chosen for his logo the grill of the motorcar.

The stinking mess caused the producers to delay release of the first Keystone film until September 28, 1912, but from then on, the gang was committed to producing "two snappy subjects" every Monday. Time was the enemy, and their lives were a scramble to put anything down on film, from canning olives, Mabel said, to shooting the San Diego Exposition. When film was sold by the yard like gingham, Mack said, "anything on film made money." They literally stole scenes wherever they moved, like a pack of horse thieves. When they stepped off the train at the Santa Fe depot in Los Angeles, they stole the thunder of the Grand Army of the Republic as it paraded past the station. Or so Mack remembered. Mack handed Mabel a blanket and told her to find the father of "her baby" among the marchers while he cranked the camera. Sennett eternally confused pictures and dates, but the thieving was accurate. *Stolen Glory,* the title of an early Keystone, could have been the title for all. Mabel remembered stealing the glory of director Tom Ince by invading his cowboy and Indian territory at Santa Monica. "Mack, you damned thief! Get those infernal clowns off my set!" Ince would holler, after Mabel had dashed into the middle of a cavalry charge and done her stuff.

Mabel's stuff was the stuff of comedy because she was herself a comic anomaly. She could play a comic foil because she was pretty. She could play a buffoon because she was a natural mimic. She could play a daredevil because, as Adolph Zukor said, she was "a fine athlete [who] could swim, dive, run, jump, box and — the really important thing — take a fall wonderfully." This was why Chaplin called her "a good fellow." Her husband Lew Cody called her "two good fellows."

Unlike the male comics who brought with them the stock character types of stage Dutchman, Irishman, and Jew from vaudeville and burlesque, Mabel had only herself. To critics of early Keystone shorts, Mabel's naturalness made the grotesque caricatures of the clowns seem stagey and fake. A critic of *A Strong Revenge*, which has Mack and Sterling battling over Mabel with the weaponry of Limburger cheese, complained that the men's impersonations of Dutch and Irish characters were not credible. The Dutch and Irish, he affirmed, "do not make violent gestures with their *hands*, such as these actors would have us believe." Their stage gestures were too large for the camera. Thrusting Mabel into their midst produced some of the weirdness of Monty Python's mixture of real people and animated cartoons. We can see it in an early film, *When Dreams Come True*, which thrust Mabel and Sterling into a roomful of snakes. Snakes dangle from the chandelier, coil around Sterling's face, cling to his body as he goes into a St. Vitus fit. Mabel mugs cross-eyed into the camera, but in comparison to Sterling in his frenzy, Mabel is a model of restraint.

Mabel complained that she lacked stage experience, but she didn't know how lucky she was. "I had nobody to tell me what do do," she told biographer Sutherland. "I had to do something that nobody ever had done before." Mabel was the first comic at Keystone or elsewhere to have begun her performing career in front of a camera. Stage veterans like Pickford and Chaplin discovered that they had to unlearn stage technique in order to miniaturize their gestures for the camera's frame. Mabel's gestures were small, and often they were manic. Mabel had to learn to stand still, Mack said, but Mabel was never stagey in the way that Pickford often was in "indicating" comic moments. Mabel was right in sensing that she was an explorer. "No director ever taught me a thing," she boasted to Sutherland. "I created my own standard of fun."

Instead of making up comic characters like a Lily Tomlin, Mabel radiated personality like a Goldie Hawn. She became her own comic character, Keystone Mabel, to create a standard of fun matched only by her own standard of daredeviling. Mabel set up the girl adventure serials that followed, serials like *The Perils of Pauline,* by playing Superwoman: "She rides like a Centaur, swims like a Fish, with muscles as strong and springy as cold-rolled steel."

Because she could take a fall wonderfully, the male comics threw her over cliffs, ran over her with cars, drowned her in lakes, flattened her with sledge hammers, sent her up in balloons, and strapped her to railroad tracks. While burlesquing the weepy heroines of melodrama, Mabel was providing audiences with the thrill of seeing these feats done for real, at least in the beginning, in single takes, with few stand-ins or stage trickeries. In a burlesque like *The Battle of Who Run,* Mabel doesn't faint when she sees her lover's ghost, like the heroine of *The Battle of Bull Run.* She takes a fall head first down a flight of stairs. Laughs *and* thrills. She ridiculed the pretenses of spirituelle heroines — "Most emotional acting gave me a laugh," she said — by providing thrills of her own.

Mabel provided sex, laughs, and thrills in fifty-three pictures that first Keystone year, between August of 1912 and June of 1913. The number of films with Mabel titles shows how quickly she came into her own; as a full listing shows how much we have lost. Only seven (marked with asterisks) remain. *Cohen Collects a Debt, The Water Nymph*, The New Neighbor, Pedro's Dilemma, Stolen Glory, The Ambitious Butler, The Flirting Husband, At Coney Island, The Grocery Clerk's Romance, Mabel's Lovers, At It Again, The Deacon's Troubles, A Temperamental Husband, The Rivals, Mr. Fixit, A Desperate Lover, Brown's Seance, Pat's Day Off, A Family Mix-up, A Midnight Elopement, Mabel's Adventures, The Drummer's Vacation, The Duel, Mabel's Stratagem*, Saving Mabel's Dad, The Cure that Failed*, The Mistaken Masher, The Deacon Outwitted, Just Brown's Luck, The Battle of Who Run, Mabel's Heroes, Heinze's Resurrection,*

The Professor's Daughter, A Tangled Affair, A Red Hot Romance, A Doctored Affair, A Rural Third Degree, The Sleuths at the Floral Parade, A Strong Revenge*, Foiling Fickle Father, The Rube and the Baron, At Twelve O'Clock, Her New Beau, Hide and Seek*, Those Good Old Days, Father's Choice, The Bangville Police*, The Ragtime Band, A Little Hero, Mabel's Awful Mistake, Hubby's Job, The Foreman of the Jury, Barney Oldfield's Race for a Life*.

TOPSY

When I asked Hal Roach in Hollywood what had made Mabel funny, he told me, "Whatever she did the audience would roar with laughter and to this day I don't know why. She was sort of a pixie, I guess, but you knew that if a guy kicked her, she'd kick him back."

In the days of the Bionic Woman, a karate kick is expected. But in the days of the New Woman that Ibsen and Shaw put on the stage in *A Doll's House* and *Mrs. Warren's Profession,* a girl who kicked back was as scandalous as a girl who showed her ankles. In slapstick, Mabel did both and often showed her bloomers as well. "I wasn't satisfied with merely being kicked," Mabel said, and no more was Mary Pickford. They both rebelled personally against the Griffith type of child heroine who sniveled rather than kicked. Mabel was doing for slapstick what Pickford was doing for dramatic comedy, but both of them together were translating the New Woman of European playwrights onto the American screen — with the usual sea-change en route.

Ibsen's and Shaw's spokeswomen were largely middle-class ladies of family and dignity. Mabel and Mary were girls, usually foundlings, always spunky, always girls. Together they were recreating the image of the ideal American girl, as expressed by an American novelist in the mid-nineteenth century: "She am full of fun, an' I mout add as purty as a hen canary, an' I swear I don't believe the woman knows it." Naturalness was her birthright and her glory, as artifice was the glory of the European woman. Oscar Wilde caught the contrast exactly when one of his English aristocrats remarks on a visiting American, "She is painfully natural, is she not?"

My search for Mabel's uniqueness and for the mystery of her

craft took me back half a century before her time to the roots of that Yankee Girl I started with. I found Mabel, of all places, in *Uncle Tom's Cabin,* playing Topsy to Mary's Little Eva. Topsy was the first American funny girl to capture permanently the national imagination in the most popular and enduring play in American history. Topsy's power sprang from her slavery. As a pickaninny, she was absolved from the virtue and decorum of ladyhood and could be wicked with abandon. Little Eva could not exist without her. Little Eva needed Topsy to make her sainthood credible. Pickford sensed something of this paradox when she titled her 1954 autobiography, *Sunshine and Shadow,* after the title of an early Vitagraph film which told "A pretty and appealing story of child life in the South before the War — Sunshine is a little white girl and Shadow a little slave." They were linked like Siamese twins by innocence, an innocence which defused national guilt over sex as well as slavery. Topsy was never born. She "jus' grow'd." Topsy caught the American idiom of comic outrage, excess, and self-parody, and she made Eva a pale-faced foil for her comedy:

> *Eva: If you try, you will succeed.*
> *Topsy: I don't know nuffin' bout suckin' seed: I likes*
> *to suck eggs; but den I'se so drefful wicked!*

Topsy was beyond sex and was more often played by men and boys than by girls. If Pickford and a host of other spirituelles had played Little Eva on the stage, Spencer Tracy as a boy had played Topsy.

What I discovered about the Yankee Girl was that she came in pairs, like the musical-comedy Duncan sisters billed as "Burnt cork vyin' with blonde curls, the licorice and marshmallow pair." Or like the musical-comedy pairing of licorice Jane Russell with marshmallow Marilyn Monroe in *Gentlemen Prefer Blondes.* The good girls needed the baddies, as the careful needed the careless. Topsy was my first real clue to the doom of "Bad Luck Mabel" and her origin in the first of the "I-Don't-Care Girls," the girl who made vaudeville famous by putting Topsy in burlesque — the one and only Eva Tanguay. In 1900, Eva came shrieking from the wings like Bette Midler seventy-five years later. Eva shook and shimmied in outrageous parody to exploit a Topsy personality off the stage, as well as on, and to make vulgarity pay in the guise of "Topsy as Eva Tanguay." Eva's theme song became Mabel's tag:

I don't care! I don't care!
What they may think of me.
I'm happy-go-lucky,
Men say that I'm plucky,
So jolly and carefree.

Eva made $5000 a week by being jolly and carefree about sex and money and by making a vulgar display of both until, of course, she ran out of both by giving it all away. Eva was the reason a 1902 journalist enthused, "THE COMEDIAN GIRLS JUMP TO THE FRONT — the day of the comic actress has dawned." Mabel came up like thunder.

Good girls needed the baddies the way the elite needed the vulgar or high art needed pop. The story of Mack and Mabel was also the story of class warfare in the battle of the coarse against the refined. The same working-class rowdies who packed vaudeville houses at the turn of the century packed the nickelodeons in the early teens. As vaudeville took on airs and became respectable family entertainment, burlesque moved in to take its place. Sophie Tucker noted the change when she became the first of the Red Hot Mamas in the twenties. "And suppose burlesque was 'vulgar,' the way vaudeville said it was. Hell! folks were vulgar," she said. "Otherwise burlesque wouldn't be the good business it was, playing to full houses forty-five weeks of the year." When Keystone began in 1912, it played to full houses because it was vulgar the way folks were vulgar. As long as movies were cheap, like the ten, twent', thirt' seats of burlesque, it was vulgar slapstick, not the mellers, that packed them in. When ticket prices rose, along with the masses, vulgarity lost its good name and comedy its innocence.

To the Presbyterians of Hollywood and the socialites of Pasadena, all motion-picture people were vagabonds and outlaws. As a Californian, Anita Loos was under no illusion about the status of the picture colony. "In those days people were real," she told me in her midtown Manhattan apartment, laughing hard behind gold-rimmed pixie glasses beneath her jet bangs. "If they were trash, they were real trash and if they were ladies, they were real ladies. The Talmadges," she explained, "were class trash."

Loos complicated my search for the real amid the fake. If the colony as a whole were real social outcasts, they had devised a rigid class system of their own that put comedians at the bottom. Gloria Swanson remembered, in *Swanson on Swanson,* that she quit Keystone the moment Mack said, "I think I can make another Mabel Normand out of you." Mabel personified slapstick, and Gloria hated slapstick. Slapstick was vulgar. "I felt about it the way my mother felt about motion pictures in general — it was somehow not respectable."

By the twenties, when French journalist Robert Florey landed in Hollywood, the caste system was so extreme that the serious stars were as brahmins to the comedians' untouchables. The comedians were *"les 'parents pauvres' du cinema,"* Florey wrote, and no serious star would be caught dead with a Keystone starlet. By then, Keystone starlets were mostly bathing beauties whose sole attributes were dimpled knees, but Mabel was still the Queen of Slapstick and still scorned by ex-bathing beauties like Swanson who refused to spend "all their time having their skirts lifted and dodging flying bricks."

Within even the lowest caste, discriminations were refined. Minta Arbuckle thought Chaplin vulgar because he came from "a low-caliber family," wore "a race-track suit" and did "dirty things" like scratching his hair or armpit with a fork. Chaplin thought John Barrymore vulgar because he "had the vulgarity of wearing his talent like silk socks without garters," and cared less about fame than drink. Griffith thought Douglas Fairbanks vulgar because his comedies appealed "to a class of people I don't make pictures for."

Mabel was doubly vulgar because she was not only a comedian, she was a comedian girl. By the double standards of the time, a girl's vulgarity was measured by what she did in public. Mabel did openly what other girls concealed. With no stage mother to guide her, Mabel did what she liked, and she liked to run wild because it shocked stage mothers and delighted their daughters. Mabel liked to be the scandal of the town.

"You've got to understand the difference in the times," Adela Rogers St. Johns warned me. She also was motherless and joined Mabel to run around after dark, smoke ciggies, drink whiskey, and flirt with the boys. They worked like crazy and played like crazy at a time when having fun was a subversive act. "They thought we were hellions," she said. Mabel and Adela danced and drank with other movie trash at the Vernon Country Club out in San Fernando Valley. Vernon's was a saloon, dance floor, and boxing ring, and Mabel liked all three. The owner was unhappy serving the girls because they were underage, but Mabel always got round him, Adela recalled. "Mabel was always cold, so she took a little whisky and added apricot brandy to kill the taste." Then they danced the Turkey Trot, the Grizzly Bear, and the Black Bottom, and sometimes they danced all night and went straight to work, Adela to the *Herald* offices in downtown Los Angeles and Mabel to the studio in Edendale.

They drank and danced in the same spirit with which Adela took up baseball and Mabel prize fights. Whatever girls weren't supposed to do, they did. Mabel was a more ardent fight fan than Mack, Adela said, and Mabel made him take her to Jack Doyle's place in Vernon or to the Western Athletic Club above Barney Oldfield's saloon in Los Angeles.

Mabel played practical jokes for the same reason. Girls weren't supposed to. They became her "thing," like Mack's tobacco chewing, begun as an act of defiance and continued as a habit.

As Mack became more and more absorbed in the business end of being "the Old Man" at Keystone, he left Mabel to have the fun. "Mabel would do anything for a laugh," director Raoul Walsh told me in Hollywood. Walsh remembered going with Mabel one afternoon to one of the cheap movie houses where "all classes of people" would go in at 9:00 in the morning and stay all day. "By afternoon the place smelt like a menagerie," he said, "so the management would walk up and down the aisles spraying a pump gun filled with odor of magnolia or rose blossoms. Mabel would grab the gun and start to spray the piano player."

She was always doing tricks like that, Walsh said, only sometimes she'd go overboard. "When the studio car came to pick her
up at her apartment at 7:00 A.M., the driver would blow his horn
to get her out of bed and she'd appear in a window without a
stitch on but a picture hat and warble, 'I'll be right down.'"

One of the best film cutters in the business, William Hornbeck, once a boy on the Hornbeck ranch and now a dignified
gentleman in English moustache, remembered other jokes. Mabel
was always throwing firecrackers into the developing room at the
studio. "No one ever got hurt that I remember," Hornbeck said,
"but we were scared to death with all that nitrate film."

Slapstick was nothing if not violent, and Mabel often went
too far in slapsticking her friends. She nearly asphixiated one of
her favorite Keystone victims, Mack remembered, when he was
laid up in bed with a broken leg. She lit in his bedroom the
smudge pots used to protect orange groves from frost, hid his
crutches in the toilet, and forgot to call the fire department to put
out the smoke. King Vidor, who was determined to head for
Hollywood after falling in love with Mabel, recalled a story his
mother and aunts in Texas had told him to keep him home.
"When Sennett bawled Mabel out one day for being late," they
told Vidor, "she climbed onto his lap and wet her — and his
— pants for revenge. Sennett hit the ceiling." I asked Vidor
whether his mother and aunts were shocked. "They enjoyed it,"
he said.

Not everybody enjoyed Mabel's jokes. Many deplored them
for giving movie people a bad name. Hollywood was always divided between the Griffith girls and the Sennett gang and, as the
money increased, so did the split. "The Griffith Studio was very
careful that the girls were not seen around too much," another
Griffith star told me when I visited her in London's Bolingbroke
Grove. "They had to be very dignified and very fussy about what
they did," Bessie Love said. "What they did on their own, of
course, was nobody's business."

As a prat-faller, Mabel was all undignified flesh. The Griffith
girls, on the other hand, were epitomized by the fleshlessness of
the most spirituelle of them all, the still radiant Lillian Gish.
Lillian was "the Puritan in art," a contemporary scholar-critic

called her, "like nothing so much as a pure white flame." They were all fulfilling the destiny of their images, since life and art were one, and a fleshless flame could have little in common with a red red rose that withered. "We were very snobby at the Griffith Studio," is the way Bessie Love put it. The strictness of the Griffith castes caused complaints even within the ranks, as some thought Griffith thanked god too much for little girls, and some thought Lillian "too high-toned." Snobbery, I discovered, was as immune to time as the type of the spirituelle. "Miss Lillian remembers *absolutely nothing* about Mabel Normand," Miss Gish's male secretary told me on the phone. "Miss Lillian was one of the Griffith girls, of course, and they were *never near* the Sennett set."

MABEL AND FATTY

MAY 24, 1974, LOS ANGELES
Dear Steve:

This 'ecstacy'-like feeling has to be Divine. I entertain only thoughts that are spiritual. I have an all-consuming fire of love that I long to share with you because I feel you live close to God and understand me. There shall be no sin — thought, word or deed!!!

Knowing I spiritualize my thoughts I like to say as a mother I love you and I mean it in the very cleanest sense of the word.

Julie

AUGUST 25, 1977, HOLLYWOOD

Not far south of Edendale, I knocked on the door of a stuccoed duplex where a broken sofa rested on the porch and a broken car on the lawn. I was looking for a shy soft-spoken man in his late forties, who came to Hollywood from the Midwest to become a photographer and archivist of the past that Hollywood trashed. His name was Don Schneider, and he taped every word of Minta Arbuckle's last garrulous years. I wanted to know what Minta had said about Mabel. But nobody answered the bell at the Heliotrope Street address Don had given me, and the place looked abandoned. Paper tape masked completely every window and glass door, and I was about to give up when the door opened a crack. A man in thick spectacles emerged from the darkness with a carton of files. The files were the final remains of Minta Durfee Arbuckle.

They were all that Don could save of "that old movie junk"

which Minta's companion had heaved into the trash when Minta died. Her companion was a manicurist whose sense of history was slighter than Don's. That old movie junk included all the costumes Minta and Roscoe had worn in their Gilbert and Sullivan days in the Far East before they found Edendale. The junk included all the letters Roscoe had written Minta during the bad days of the trials in 1920 and '21. Don had managed to save a few of those letters when he found Minta's retarded brother sitting in the back yard of her little bungalow on Coronado Street, tearing stamps off their envelopes for his collection. Minta was a special loss to me because she had been so much a part of the Sennett set. "I worked with Mabel four solid years, six days a week and eight hours a day, and I knew her backwards," she said to Don. "They worked the panties off her, dear."

When Roscoe "Fatty" Arbuckle took the trolley out to Tropico in April of 1913, dressed in a white suit with blue tie and white shoes, and stepped off into mud "pretty near to his waistline," he changed Mabel's image as radically as he changed movie slapstick. Mabel remembered standing outside Mack's office, quarreling with Nappy, when "the fattest thing I'd ever seen" came up the stairs and introduced himself as "the fat laugh in the Long Beach Stock Company." To show what he could do, he plunged headlong down the stairs, landed on his neck, and bounced back up to ask for a job. Minta remembered a different scene that had Arbuckle wandering onto an empty stage and being hollered at by a man with a cheek full of tobacco juice: "You be here tomorrow morning at 8:00." He was, and Fatty and Mabel created the most popular boy-and-girl team in silent comedy.

When Roscoe came to Keystone, he was twenty-six, 5'10" tall, and weighed 266 pounds. "Not soggy fat," Minta said, "but hard as nails." Like Mabel, Fatty was a skilled athlete — a swimmer, acrobat, and tumbler — and as light on his feet as Zero Mostel. Dancing with Fatty, actress Louise Brooks remembered, was like dancing with a floating doughnut. With his blue eyes, blond hair, and wide sunny grin, Fatty played the big overgrown all-American boy that he was. For the first time, Mabel had a male partner as young-looking and innocent as herself, and together they developed a style of kid comedy a decade before Laurel and Hardy or the real kids of Hal Roach's Our Gang. Typically, Mack was blind to Fatty's virtues and didn't want to keep him. Typically, Mabel talked Mack into it. It was a pattern they would repeat with Chaplin and with anyone else whose comic genius differed from the "Old Man's."

Over the next three years, Keystone's Fatty and Mabel films became the most popular and profitable of all the Keystone shorts. From June of 1913 to May of 1916, of the sixty-six films Mabel shot thirty-six were with Arbuckle. Mabel's relation to Chaplin was brief by comparison. During Chaplin's year at Keystone, from January to December of 1914, Mabel teamed with Chaplin for a mere eleven films. For the curious, I've listed Mabel's films in order with the Arbuckle ones in bold type and the Chaplin ones starred.

Passions, He Had Three, *The Hansom Driver, The Speed Queen,* **The Waiter's Picnic, For the Love of Mabel, The Tell-tale Light, A Noise from the Deep, Love and Courage, Prof. Bean's Removal, The Riot,** *Baby Day,* **Mabel's New Hero, Mabel's Dramatic Career, The Gypsy Queen, The Fatal Tax-icab, When Dreams Come True,** *The Bowling Match,* **The Speed Kings,** *Love Sickness at Sea, A Muddy Romance, Cohen Saves the Flag, The Gusher, Fatty's Flirtation, Zuzu the Band Leader, The Champion, A Glimpse of the City of Los Angeles,* **A Misplaced Foot,** *Mabel's Stormy Love Affair, Mabel's Bear Escape, Won in a Closet, Mabel's Strange Predicament*, Love and Gasoline, Mack at It Again, Mabel at the Wheel*,* **Where Hazel Met the Villain,** *Caught in a Cabaret*, Mabel's Nerve,* **The Alarm,** *The Fatal Mallet*, Her Friend the Bandit*, Mabel's Busy Day*, Mabel's Married Life*,* **Mabel's New Job, Those Country Kids,** *Mabel's Latest Prank, Mabel's Blunder, Hello Mabel, Gentlemen of Nerve*,* **Lovers' Post Office,** *His Trysting Place*, Tillie's Punctured Romance*,* **Fatty's Wine Party, The Sea Nymphs,** *Getting Acquainted*, How Heroes Are Made,* **Mabel's and Fatty's Wash Day, Fatty and Mabel's Simple Life, Fatty and Mabel at the San Diego Exposition, Mabel, Fatty and the Law, Mabel and Fatty's Married Life, That Little Band of Gold, Wished on Mabel, Mabel and Fatty Viewing the**

World's Fair at San Francisco, Cal., Mabel's Wilful Way, *Mabel Lost and Won,* The Little Teacher, *My Valet, Stolen Magic,* Fatty and Mabel Adrift, He Did and He Didn't, Bright Lights, Gaumont Graphic Newsreel #39.

The appeal of Fatty and Mabel was their innocence. Unlike Bunny and Finch, Fatty and Mabel were cute. Instead of battling marrieds, they were kid sweethearts, like the Campbell Soup Kids based on Rose Latham's kewpie dolls. They were absurd and lovable cartoons of the small-town rural America drawn by Mark Twain, country kids fighting and courting over the milking pails. Their violence punctured nostalgia. When big Fatty kicked little Mabel in her rear, Mabel kicked back. She kicked back with a symbol of small-town rural American womanhood, the American pie.

The birth of the pie-throw is another of those movie legends, but most sources concur that Mabel was the first to throw and Fatty the first to receive a pie in the face in *A Noise from the Deep,* released July 17, 1913. Minta recalled the first throw as originating in one of Mabel's practical jokes. Mabel had brought to the studio a fresh raspberry pie in a paper bag from Greenberg's Bakery across the street. When some studio hand made a wisecrack about what Mabel might have in her bag, she showed him. The works. Sennett yelled, "What the hell's going on?" and Mabel replied, "I'm just giving Joe a piece of my pie." It was like a pratfall of the face, good for close-ups, that substituted a visual whack for the sound of stage slapsticks.

Although pie-throwing became standard funny business for male comics, Mabel began it in the ongoing battle of the sexes that Mabel and Fatty parodied as kid comics. Their knock-about spooning, marriage, adultery, and divorce burlesqued the violence of real social change and restored sex to innocence. In *Mabel and Fatty's Wash Day,* they commit adultery in the park by running off to share a soda pop: one bottle, two straws. In *Fatty and Mabel Adrift,* they pretend to be newlyweds, but they sleep in separate beds in their little doll's house, Mabel curled up with Fatty's dog Luke instead of Fatty. They portrayed puppy love for a public nostalgic for love without sex, and they did it so well that when Arbuckle was later charged with rape, the public felt betrayed.

Away from the studio, Mabel formed a threesome with the Arbuckles because they were her kind of folk. Roscoe, she called "Big Otto" after an elephant in Colonel Selig's Zoo, and Minta "Mintrattie" after a mouse. Roscoe and Minta had grown up in California, had met and married on the stage of the Byde-a-Wyle Theater in Long Beach, and had trouped the country before getting steady work at Keystone. Minta had grown up between the railroad tracks, where her father was an engineer, and a row of prostitutes' cribs, where her mother was a dressmaker "for society and the sporting trade." As a girl Minta had admired the bright red satin dresses of the girls "who hung their busts out the window," and she remembered how upset her mother was when the Friday Morning Club ladies wanted to shut the cribs down. That would scatter the girls all over town, Mrs. Durfee said, and you wouldn't know who you lived next to anymore.

Minta remembered how lonely Mabel was and how glad for friends. She would come to dinner at the Durfee house and curl up in Father Durfee's lap. She would come Sundays to the Arbuckles' Santa Monica house and swim with Roscoe (and a dolphin, Minta swore) to Venice pier and back. They got rich together and moved from rented apartments to classier houses at the same time. A 1914 *Photoplay* charts their rise with a photo of "Chateau Normand" under the rubric "What comedy has done for Mabel Normand." The Arbuckle mansion points the same moral: "Fat is a dreadful calamity but see what it has done for Roscoe Arbuckle." They were movie trash displacing the establishment together. And when the Arbuckles bought a mansion on West Adams Street with butler and cook and two-way iceboxes opening on the porch, they bought it from a society matron of impeccable credentials, Mrs. Huntington Randolph Miner. The establishment wouldn't forgive that, either, in the troubles to come.

Minta, like Mabel, had wanted nice things, and comedy got them for her. The Arbuckles' marriage didn't last but their loyalty did, and Roscoe supported Minta in style in New York until the scandal broke him. Even after, Minta lived like a lady until the crash of '29 when she lost everything, everything but her dresses, lingerie, stockings, and gloves. "I couldn't part with those," she said. "But I had to sell my diamonds and emeralds and furs, all of my first editions, all of my paintings and my Rolls." I thought of the thesaurus in Mabel's trunk and the consolations of poetry.

MABEL AND CHARLIE

Nine months after Arbuckle bounced into the Sennett lot, a scroungy little newcomer changed the course of movie history, although nobody guessed it at the time. Later on, of course, Mabel like everybody else took credit for uncovering his genius. "I like him," Mabel remembers telling Mack when they went to see "the little Englisher" in Fred Karno's *A Night at the Club;* "he needs movie technique but he's got the stuff." Mack remembers that Mabel refused to play with him when the Englisher showed up on the lot: " 'I should say not, Mack,' she told me, 'I don't like him so good now that I've seen him.' " Most memories were like actress Marie Dressler's: "I knew that boy had genius." But in fact most of those who worked with him were repelled by the intense dark-eyed Cockney who was vulgar in his manners, filthy in his person, and totally lacking in self-humor. Dressler complained to Sennett on the set of *Tillie's Punctured Romance* that the Cockney had the same piece of banana on his collar for sixteen days running. Minta complained about his smell. "He was a clever man," Minta told her interviewer Don Schneider, "but he was plenty dirty."

Charles Spencer Chaplin hated the Keystone lot. He felt like an exile surrounded by savages and saved only by pretty Mabel, "lighthearted and gay, a good fellow, kind and generous; and everyone adored her." Chaplin adored her and wanted romance. He made a pass at her late one night after Mabel, Charlie, and Arbuckle had done a comic turn at a charity benefit in San Francisco. "She looked radiantly beautiful," Chaplin remembered, "and as I placed her wrap over her shoulders I kissed her and she kissed me back." When he later tried to follow up the moment, she turned him down. "I'm not your type, Charlie," she said. "Nor are you mine." She was not his type because Chaplin saw women only as projections of his own need for romance. Recalling his first teenage love, Chaplin said, "It had little to do with sex; more important was her association. To meet elegance and beauty in my station of life was rare." Chaplin yearned for elegance and beauty to lift him from the reality of the Cockney gutter that shamed him. As Chaplin hated the vulgarity of Keystone, so he hated the vulgarity of the tramp he created there until, he said, "I thought of the tramp as a sort of Pierrot." Throughout his life, Chaplin wanted a Columbine, not a pie-throwing tomboy. Mabel was far too real and far too American for Chaplin.

If they couldn't be lovers, they could be friends. Mabel was the only one on the Keystone lot to befriend him. "Mabel made them all," Minta said, meaning that she mothered all the comics and stood in the way of Mack's wrath. The little dressing room she called her "igloo" stood just inside the studio gate, and Mabel remembered how she used Pepper, the fat studio cat, as a barometer of Nappy's mood. Would Mack scratch Pepper's ears or squirt them with tobacco? "Pepper and I got several raises for Fatty Arbuckle and Charlie Chaplin," Mabel recalled. Chaplin recalled fleeing to Mabel's dressing room for tea and comfort and the warmth of her kerosene stove during his year of misery at Keystone.

Chaplin's music-hall drunk was wrong for the camera. His first picture, *Making a Living*, directed by his chief hate, Pathé Lehrman, was bad. Sennett "screamed that he had hooked himself up with a dead one," Mabel recalled, but she begged Mack to give Charlie another chance. "I was alien to this slick tempo," Charlie recalled. Mabel was in fact the only one to recognize the value of Charlie's different tempo and different style, because it was much closer to her own than to the frenzy of Sennett's menagerie. But Charlie was a sensibility without a character until he saw on the screen the image of a little fellow, in pants and boots too big for him, twirling a little cane. "The moment I was dressed, the clothes and the make-up made me feel the person he was," he said of the birth of the tramp. But Chaplin's memories, by the time of *My Autobiography*, were processed by a mythology that had long ago displaced fact, history, and person with the fiction of somebody who had to call an autobiography "My."

Chaplin's memories crucially distorted his relation and indebtedness to Mabel the comedienne. Chaplin was a solo performer whose strength lay in recreating the world, like a comic narcissist, in his own image. There was only the one reality. Even other comics were figments of his imagination — especially girl comics. Chaplin wanted a pretty foil, like Edna Purviance, who became Chaplin's stock heroine and Mabel's pal. Mabel encouraged Chaplin to develop his own tempo, but teamwork was not part of it. Contemporary critics of *Caught in a Cabaret*, one of the Chaplin-Mabel films most often shown today, spotted the newcomer: "Charles Chaplin was the leading funmaker. Mabel Normand, with several of the actors, furnished the show artistically." Small wonder that Chaplin was never popular among the Keystone funmakers he despised. Other existing films, however, show how funny Mabel could be with Chaplin when she played a scrungy fishwife equal in size and scrunge to his drunken tramp. In films like *Mabel's Married Life* or *His Trysting Place*, she kicks back by socking him with whatever is at hand in their tenement ghetto — her iron, his pants, her ironing board, their baby.

Given Chaplin's sense of himself and his view of women, it's not surprising that he believed that he created himself full-blown from the Medusa-head of Keystone. The films show otherwise. One film historian who studied Mabel's films before Chaplin arrived at Keystone saw "entire routines, gestures, reactions, expressions, that were later a part of Chaplin's characterizations." Sennett, later on, credited Chaplin with first taming the beasts of slapstick comedy but in fact Chaplin was indebted to Mabel — not the other way round. Only Mabel was a girl, and girls didn't count.

Chaplin's sexual bias has obscured one of Mabel's brightest achievements. When women directors were unheard of, unless like Pickford they were in a position to run the whole show, Mabel fought for and won the right to direct her own films. Sennett announced the fact to the trade papers on December 13, 1914: "Mabel Normand, leading woman of the Keystone Company, since its inception, is in the future to direct every picture she acts in." In practice, Mabel directed only those pictures in which she starred, but in the world of comedy, that was another first. It was a testament both to Mabel's competence and to Mack's respect for it.

But few today are aware of that achievement because of Chaplin's story starring himself. Mabel remembered that when she begged Sennett to give Charlie another chance, "Nappy turned him over to me and I directed several of his pictures." "This nettled me," Chaplin said in his memoirs, "for charming as Mabel was, I doubted her competence as a director." Mabel had proved her competence in over 121 comic films made in the three years before Chaplin made his first. It was not Mabel's competence that nettled Chaplin. It was her sex. He admits that he could not take orders from a woman, so that when Mabel directed him to do a bit of business with a hose and a skidding car, he refused. "I don't think you are competent to tell me what to do," he told her. Mabel was bewildered and hurt, he remembered, and that bothered him — a little. Chaplin confessed that he was soft on her, "but this was my work."

Ironically, those who know Mabel today know her largely because of her work with Chaplin in Sennett's first feature-length comedy, *Tillie's Punctured Romance*. The film was to be the apotheosis of Keystone.

"The 'Impossible' Attained — A SIX-REEL COMEDY!" Sennett wanted to do for comedy in *Tillie's Punctured Romance* what Griffith would do for melodrama in *The Birth of a Nation:* elevate the status of movies as junk food for the masses to gourmet art. Sennett's feature comedy in six reels instead of one-half, one, or two reels, marked a beginning and an end. It marked the beginning of silent comedy as a serious form but the end of slapstick's first, fine careless rapture. With the release of *Tillie's Punctured Romance* on November 14, 1914, comedy rose to big money, and the big money boys took over.

To capture the status of stage comedy for his movies, Sennett hired the great comedienne Marie Dressler for $2500 a week and purloined her stage success *Tillie's Nightmare* for the screen. When the fourteen-week filming was over (an unprecedented stretch for a comedy), Dressler sued Sennett for $50,000 because he'd cheated her of her distribution rights, or so she claimed. At the time, Chaplin and Mabel were still being paid $175 a week with control over nothing but their own funny business. Mack was not called 'Nappy' for nothing, and his rule was both authoritarian and totalitarian. When Chaplin, at the end of his first year, asked Sennett for a raise, Mack offered him $400. Chaplin demanded $750. Mack refused. In January of 1915, Chaplin signed with the Essanay Company in Chicago for $1250 and complete artistic control. Nobody was sad to see him go but Mabel. They had a weepy lunch together at Pop Levy's Cafe, Mabel said, before he shuffled off to Chicago and Mt. Olympus. Mabel was stuck with her old salary because she was stuck on Mack. But it was a new ball game, and the big-league money that the movies were now commanding altered the rules at Keystone as it would alter Mack and Mabel's romance.

The film of *Tillie* was in fact about the power of money to puncture romance by altering class. Tillie, played by Dressler, is a caricature of a nouveau-riche yokel straight off the farm. Chaplin caricatures a city slicker out to con the yokel of her cash. Mabel, in cahoots with Chaplin, is simply an ordinary girl who puts the audience into the scene of comic extremes. Tillie's progress from country to city, as she throws off gingham for harem pants, caricatured the nation's "progress" from a rural to an urban culture and to new-money prosperity. The film was about itself in that money and the movies were in cahoots to con the nation into an entirely nouveau class of celebrities.

In the fall of 1914, Chaplin, Arbuckle, and Mabel Normand were a comic triumvirate, celebrated by *Photoplay* in a comic menu that listed "Chaplin Supreme, Stuffed Arbuckle, and Normand, Scrambled." When each eventually left Keystone, each developed a line of comedy expressive of his own sense of class. That Chaplin outlasted the other two was not only a matter of talent and luck but partly a matter of Cockney smarts. In contrast to Fatty and Mabel, Chaplin was in fact a city slicker out to con the hicks. Fatty and Mabel were so innocent, so young, so American. Their comedy sprang from the energy and spontaneous hijinks of youth. Generous and naive, exactly what Chaplin was not, neither Fatty nor Mabel understood the virulence of class envy any more than they understood deception and betrayal. They were Americans. They believed in the goodness of man and nature and of Eden without the fall.

Chaplin was wiser. He understood cruelty and injustice and envy and betrayal because he had experienced them as a child, and he practised them as an adult. His knowledge helped him to survive and to transform the dark and nasty interior studios of his memory into an imaginary world where the last shall be first, the poor rich, the humble famous, the tramp a king. He survived so long that he lived decades as an exiled king in his Swiss castle, self-banished from the country that had made him rich and famous and royal. While Fatty and Mabel died young, Chaplin lived on to take his revenge as *The King of New York*.

MABEL AND MACK

Dear Steve:

Since Mabel died you coming into my life has been an unusually fantastic thrill!! Of course you give me credit for realizing all about the generation gap, etc., however my body remains quite nice. I wear a little bigger 'bra.'

God is very good to me — I have no scars — no sickness ever kept me from working as a nurse and when with Mabel I kept myself immaculate — still do. How come I want to be so near you? Steve I promise to entertain only the most spiritual thoughts ever — you too?

Love,
Julie

JULY 4, 1915, EDENDALE

On July 4 the entire Keystone crew was celebrating America's "national orgy of self-justification," as it has been called, with beer and Keystone bombs. Beside their new 18′ × 35′ swimming tank, they gnawed barbecued spareribs and guzzled boilermakers and exploded firecrackers to celebrate the third and last anniversary of Keystone and the beginning of a new company, Triangle Corporation.

They were celebrating the fact that their gambling had paid off and they had arrived. They had arrived in America's symbol of success, the racing car, and Mack and Mabel had arrived at the lot that day in racing cars of equal horsepower, Mabel in her 120-horsepower black Stutz Bearcat and Mack in his 120-horsepower red Fiat. By their efforts, comedy had arrived on equal terms with Griffith's melodrama and Ince's westerns in the new triumvirate of Sennett, Griffith, and Ince that gave Triangle its name. Movies as a whole were in the process of arriving as the ten million Americans who spent one million dollars every day on the movies were abandoning the nickelodeons for Samuel "Roxy" Rothapfel's new "Temple of the Motion Pictures — Shrine of Music and the Allied Arts."

All work had stopped at Keystone on July 1, so that the enlarged studio and its improvements under Triangle could be completed. Triangle was the brainchild of two big money boys, Harry and Roy Aitken of Waukesha, Wisconsin, who had taken over and taken in the bookies Kessel and Baumann. The Aitkens thought and spent big. They paid for the new tank that held 85,000 gallons of water and for the heating apparatus to warm it in winter. They paid for the new 70' × 155' stage where fifteen crews could work at once. They paid for the seventy-five new dressing rooms and for a company of one hundred and for a garage of bought, not rented, cars. They paid Sennett $100,000 to upgrade the studio, known later as the Pig Sty because of Sennett's fondness for raising pigs and chickens on the lot. Soon they would pay vaudeville stars from New York three times as much as Chaplin had asked and failed to get from Sennett. But Chaplin had quit six months before Triangle took over.

Except for Mabel, every one of the original Keystone gang had quit Mack for more pay and more control. Some, like Sterling and Mace, had quit and come back. Producers who knew that Mabel had no legal contract with Mack tried to woo her away, and one claimed that he missed signing Mabel "by a cat's whisker," but Mack got wind of it and raised her to $500 a week. The producer overlooked a simple fact. In July of 1915, Mabel was still Mack's girl.

July 4 of 1915 was the date they had set for their wedding, or so Mabel and Mack remembered. The date was mythical, but a wedding *was* planned. What happened was a mystery as puzzling as the Taylor murder mystery, where everybody told conflicting stories for reasons of their own. "This is the most difficult part of my story to tell because I can't explain it, even to myself,"

Mack confessed in *King of Comedy*. Under a covering fire of wisecracks, Mack tried to explain the immediate cause of their break-up, but he could not explain why Mabel made it permanent. Nobody could. Mabel was silent.

That Mack and Mabel were in love nobody doubted. That they meant to get married nobody doubted. Mabel was still Mack's girl after all the upheavels of those five years during which they went, as Mack said, "unsteady." Marriage was in the cards. What happened to end the true-life romance of Mack and Mabel? At first I thought the answers lay hidden in Mack's ghosted autobiography behind the layers of hedging and of guilt. He confessed so much. "This story would be different," he confessed *if only* he had asked Mabel to marry *him* in July of 1913 instead of asking her to marry his new company. With hindsight, he confessed that maybe money had outrun sex and business had outrun romance.

Their affair, he confessed, had been "a series of fractures and refractures." He meant it literally. He was crazily jealous. Mabel was flirtatious. He was not above spying on her, he confessed, or above breaking her and other people's bones. He once made a fool of himself with Mabel and a handsome Irish leading man, Jack Mulhall, Mack confessed, when Mulhall took Mabel out to Vernon's to dance. Mack hid in the shrubbery and slugged Mulhall when he took Mabel home. Mack denied, in his confession, that he had slugged Mabel. He claimed that the sling she wore on her arm the next day was "for effect." Besides, Mack confessed, it was all the fault of Pathé Lehrman, who egged him on because Lehrman was in love with Mabel himself.

Mack was a good story teller, and his confessions, I learned, carried as much weight as the eye-witnesses who said, "I know. I was *there.*" Mack changed his story about the wedding each time he told it, using his confessional voice with the engaging con of a Huck Finn. But the essence of his story was this. Mabel was sulking after Mack hit Mulhall, and she forbade him to come near her on the lot. To make amends, Mack bought a $5000 diamond ring to replace the cheap ring she had worn since the Staten Island ferry, and he told her to find a Justice of the Peace. But Mabel wanted "orange blossoms, a wedding gown and a honeymoon, damn it." Mabel set July 4 as the date and ran out to buy a $5000 trousseau at Madame Frances's exclusive dress shop. The $5000 was as formulaic as the date.

The night before the wedding, one of the Keystone couples threw a dinner for the bride and groom and asked other members of the company, among them a girl named Mae Busch. Mabel had known Mae in New York where she had modeled some and acted some. When Mae sought her fortune in Hollywood, Mabel talked Mack into hiring her at Keystone. So far so good. Then Mack begins to cloak the facts in metaphor, as he did for Fowler in *Father Goose*. He went to the apartment of "an actress" after dinner, Fowler says, and "leaned on her upright piano, muttering bass notes, while she played a little night music." Later, Mack came right out with it. "I made a boob of myself," he told his ghostwriter. "I made a play for Mae Busch." Mabel burst into the apartment, he went on, "put her hand to her forehead, stared for an instant, then turned and fled." Mack chased after her, broke down the door of her apartment to find her kneeling at her hearth with a hammer, ready to smash all the diamonds he'd given her over the years. "Don't do that," Mack yelled. "Honey, we can make up like we always do, *but you can't make up those diamonds.*"

Mabel's pride took over, he claimed, and she played sick to get newspaper headlines. "Mabel was staging a thriller to get even," Mack said. "Mabel's headlined illness was a phony we never discussed." He couldn't discuss it because Mabel would not see him or talk to him, or to his mother when she came down from Canada to negotiate. In desperation, Mack bought a piece of land, built Mabel her own studio, set her up in her own producing company, and gave her the film of a lifetime, *Mickey*. But Mabel, stubborn, proud, ungrateful, never forgave him. Mack spent the rest of his life trying to figure out why.

Mack told a damn good story that was full of fiction but not fact. Where it mattered, Mack lied. Mack lied about what happened after Mabel found him with Mae Busch. I turned to the story Adela Rogers St. Johns told in *The Honeycomb* about Mabel's attempted suicide after Mabel found Mack cheating on her. When I visited her in Desert Hot Springs, she elaborated.

"I was with her on the Nat Goodwin Pier in Santa Monica where there was a big restaurant called the Sunset Inn," she told me. Adela had gone with Mabel to the inn a couple of days after Mabel found Mack in bed with Mae Busch. At the inn, Mabel said, "Come on, let's get out of here where I can breathe." Adela remembered that she didn't want to go because she was sitting with matinee idol Wally Reid, whom she was stuck on, but Mabel insisted.

> *All of a sudden Mabel said, "This is doing nobody any good. If he loved me he wouldn't have gone to bed with Mae." Then Mabel jumped off the pier. It was pitch black and I knew I wouldn't be able to handle her in those waves. So I ran to a couple of life-guard boys and they jumped in and hauled her out.*

Adela said she wished they hadn't. Mabel went into a coma, and nobody thought she'd work again. While Mabel did recover eventually, Adela thought the blow to her skull permanently changed her personality and made her a bit crazy. Adela blamed Mack.

But Adela was also a good story teller and cited the reporter's creed: "If it didn't happen that way, it should have." Not until I read Minta's story in Don Schneider's files was I convinced that the story matched the event as nearly as I would ever know. Minta said that when she returned with Roscoe from a trip East, Mabel told her in secret that she was going to marry Mack. She was getting her trousseau together and having a satin wedding dress made. Mabel threw a party at her apartment for a few friends, including Ann Luther and Mae Busch. The girls wound up at the Arbuckles' Santa Monica beach house. Mack drove over in a studio limousine to take them home and dropped Mabel off first, then Ann, then Mae. Later Ann telephoned Mabel to tell her that Mack was at Mae's apartment. Mabel slammed her jockey cap over her curls and went flying over to check. Mack had sent out for liquor and sandwiches and when the bell rang Mae thought the bell boy had brought them. Mae opened the door and saw

Mabel. Mabel saw Mae in a nightgown and, behind her, Mack in his B.V.D.'s. Mae instinctively picked up a large vase, smashed it over Mabel's head and slammed the door. "What a wedding gift!" Minta commented.

Mabel told her what happened, Minta said, when Mabel arrived at the Arbuckles' doorstep covered with blood. Minta and Roscoe had been sleeping on a side porch when they heard the sound of animal moaning. "I opened the door and saw a man carrying Mabel in his arms, with blood all over her hair and face and streaming over her body." It was a cab driver whom Mabel had directed to the Arbuckles. Minta called a doctor who said Mabel would have to go to the hospital immediately. "Mabel went into a coma which lasted for weeks and weeks." Minta went every day with the wife of Tom Ince to divide up the hours. "Finally the doctor said they would have to perform an operation to bring the blood out of her head or she would die." After the operation Mabel rested for several weeks and when she was able to work Mack said he would do anything in the world for her and gave her *Mickey.*

Mabel felt doubly betrayed, I realized, because Mae belonged to Mabel's gang, "the Dirty Four." Since the principal male comics at Keystone — Sennett, Sterling, Mace, and Swain — called themselves "the Keystone Four," Mabel declared equal rights for the girl comics. The Dirty Four declared war on the exclusive right of men to talk dirty. Talking dirty was like playing practical jokes. Girls didn't, so Mabel did. It was a way of kicking back against the moral and sexual double standards of guys like Nappy when he came on as Aunt Prue. It was a way of kicking against the pricks. Only girls like Mae were cynical and played dirty to get ahead. About sex and people and double-dealing, Mabel was always naive. She never quite understood that the roles she invented like Dirty Mabel were a form of double-dealing that was natural to movies, but that also betrayed one's self.

I looked for Mack's newspaper headlines but couldn't find a one. I found instead a notice in *Motion Picture World* for October 9 that put the date of the wedding at the end of September and added the fictions of press agentry to the fictions by which people live.

OCTOBER 9, HOLLYWOOD

Mabel Normand, the popular Keystone girl, has been dangerously ill during the week past — in fact, her condition was so alarming that for several days she was not expected to live. Her illness is the result of injuries sustained while working in a Triangle comedy picture. She was accidently struck by a heavy shoe in a burlesque wedding scene. Roscoe Arbuckle was the bridegroom and the happy pair was given an unusual ovation of rice and shoes. One of the shoes was thrown with considerable force and hit Miss Normand on the head, knocking her senseless.

In unconscious condition she was removed to her suite of rooms in the Baltic apartments and a physician called in. He found her suffering with a concussion of the brain. For several days she remained semi-conscious and developed a high fever which made her recovery a matter of doubt. At the time of this writing her condition has improved and, unless new complications arise, she will soon be out of danger.

A week later, the magazine followed up with a second report: "Mabel Normand, our intrepid Queen of the Movies, who came so near death a week ago, is rapidly recovering and will be back soon on the Keystone screen in a short time." The report was adjacent to an ad for a new film called *Damaged Goods,* and I remembered that Mae Busch had played the lead in the stage play of that title before she came to Keystone. What went through Mabel's mind, I wondered, when she saw the page, as she surely did, and the ad copy for the film, "No Girl is Safe While the Double Standard of Morality Exists"?

Mabel never referred to the real cause of her concussion nor to the deeper wound it occasioned. Only twice did she mention an accident of any kind and when she did she upheld the studio's story. Once was in December of 1915, when she had recovered her health and was ready to leave for the East with Arbuckle to

Roscoe "Fatty" Arbuckle with Mabel and dog Luke in *Fatty and Mabel Adrift*, shot at Keystone Studio in December 1915, just before Fatty and Mabel escaped Mack by going East.

Mabel the Goldwyn Glamor Girl in 1918.

make films at Fort Lee. She said she was now ready for anything, "though a wedding with 'shoe-showers' might still make her nervous." The other time was in February when a *Photoplay* reporter interviewed her at Fort Lee and, after watching Fatty drop her headfirst over a bannister, asked her, "Why have you never been killed?" "Why haven't I? Why — I have," Mabel answered. She had been unconscious for twelve days, she said, and laid up for three months after an accident where Roscoe "sat on my head by mistake." To the same interviewer, she let slip an oblique reference to the real story. "What's the use of making plans to go places or marry people," she said, "when like as not you will have to write a note saying, 'Excuse me, I did want to become your blushing bride today, but it's no go. I was killed yesterday doing a high dive into a tank of brick bats.' "

Mabel was covering her real hurt with the fakery of her art, the clown's art of taking falls painlessly. Buster Keaton, who was taking falls at age three in vaudeville, said that kids don't get hurt when they take a fall because they don't have far to fall. Mabel was twenty-three when she took a fall that hurt all her life and hurt so much that she couldn't admit it. Mabel ended her *Photoplay* interview by calling herself an "I-Don't-Care Girl" for real. "I just live along from day to day," she said. "I never make any plans. Nobody in the world lives up to the literal instruction, 'Take no thought for the morrow' like I do." Something broke inside Mabel, and she decided to live up to her name.

None of her friends at the time could understand why she took it so hard. Blanche Sweet remembered her own puzzlement because she had thought Mack and Mabel sophisticates, to whom one affair more or less wouldn't matter. Blanche found out she was wrong. Mabel grew more and more depressed, she said, and to keep her busy Blanche would drive her around town in her car. "Sometimes we'd talk and sometimes we'd just drive." Minta remembered that Mother Durfee tried in vain to tell Mabel that Mack was simply a man "having a last fling." Mack remembered his mother telling Mabel the same thing with the same results. Mabel wouldn't talk to her or to him. She sent back his letters and gifts unopened. She shut him out. For good.

I too wondered why and remembered that Mack called Mabel "the most naive person that ever lived." Adela called her "unusually pure," with "no desire, no sex, no nothing" for anyone but Mack. But Adela also said something that stuck with me: "You see, she had this passionate streak in her." A passionate innocence would go far in explaining Mabel's wound that would not heal. But Hollywood had other explanations that were simpler and more worldly.

One was Mother Sinnott, Mack's mother. "She was a big bustling Irish woman," Minta said, "and you knew immediately who ran the big ranch." Mack said that his mother was always pushing him to marry Mabel. After Mabel broke off their engagement, she pushed him toward one of the other Keystone girls, "Marie Prevost, Mae Busch, Gloria Swanson, and Phyllis Haver, for instance." Minta was sceptical. Minta believed that Mother Sinnott never wanted Mack to marry anyone, and others agreed. One of the researchers for *King of Comedy* described her to Stephen as "a powerful, even domineering woman. . . . Sennett would have married Mabel at the beginning," the researcher felt, "had it not been for his ambivalent feeling toward his mother." Mack seemed naive himself when he boasted that his mother "came to the studio almost daily during the 21 years she spent with me in California" and that she came to *all* the parties. "When I went," Mack said, "I was accompanied by Mabel and Mother." After Mabel left him, Mack vowed that he would always remain a bachelor because his old Mother was his fiancée, and so she was.

Other friends of Mack and Mabel gave other reasons. Mack's production manager in the twenties was a man named Lonnie D'Orsa, who lived with him in the mansion on 140th Street that Pickford and Fairbanks vacated when they moved to grander quarters at Pickfair. D'Orsa told me that while Mack was in love with Mabel, Mack didn't want to marry anybody. He was "a man's man," a health nut, and a chronic athlete. He got his kicks by walking to work every morning over the top of his 300-acre mountain, from the "Hollywoodland" sign to the far side of Griffith Park. Or by sailing every weekend to Catalina on his 63-foot cabin cruiser "The Ding" to fish for swordfish he never caught.

The director Allan Dwan told me that it was Mabel who

didn't want to marry anybody, let alone a vulgarian like Mack. Dwan recalled a moment in the back seat of a car with Mabel when Mack leaned out the front window to spit his wad and the wind pushed it back in. "He blacked us out," Dwan laughed. "She never loved any man, maybe, and not even Mabel loved tobacco chewing." Another Sennett contemporary, now in his nineties, assured me that Mack didn't marry because he was "queer as a coot," just like William Desmond Taylor. Mabel, of course, was a well-known lesbian. Hadn't she lived with a nurse all those years?

Mack, I found, offered the best reason himself, although he shied away from understanding it. He was sorry, he told his ghostwriter, that he had not taken time to know Mabel better. "That is what I mean: *know* her better. . . . I was not thoughtful. . . . I was too busy to be kind and understanding." Only in his seventies did he discover that he had not taken time to know himself better either: "I am not sure that I knew it then, but I think that all along I wanted to marry a wife, not an actress."

July 4 was a symbolic date to Mack and Mabel because its fireworks were appropriate to a celebration that blew up. The blowup of their wedding foreshadowed the speedy blowup of the whole Triangle balloon. Although Mack occupied Edendale for another fifteen years, the romance and delirium of the pioneer days were over in the summer of 1915, when it seemed they were just beginning. Behind the success story of Keystone and the team of Mack and Mabel was a nastier tale of cannibalism. Mabel spoke of the camera as "an insatiable Minotaur demanding youth and beauty." Mack spoke of the speed with which their films were "immediately consumed, the reels actually worn out, scratched and destroyed, in the grind of small movie houses." The camera ate actors alive, the projector ate film, and the audiences ate both at once. Film speeded up their lives, and the faster they ran, the faster they were consumed. Their moment was as fragile as the nitrate film that recorded it.

As long ago as 1933, Gene Fowler had visited the Keystone lot and found a graveyard of memories. "It was as though a lost civilization lay buried beneath the kitchen-middens of Edendale," he wrote. "The old pool seemed a sacrificial pit of a weird and vanished race." I found other vestiges of that weird and vanished race in Mabel's own studio, just over the ridge of Silver Lake Reservoir, nestling in a hollow below Sunset and Hollywood boulevards. At that junction, the mighty towers Griffith built for *Intolerance* in 1916 for years put Mabel's little building in the shade. But today only an asphalt parking lot marks the fall of Babylon. There were other falls. I found the Hotel Alexandria on a squalid corner of the inner city of Los Angeles. Its Palm Court, where Mabel had danced, was clogged now with plastic palms and signs reading *"Inglese parlate aqui."* I found Echo Lake and its Japanese arched bridge just as it had been in so many films like *A Muddy Romance,* but the boaters now carried transistors instead of movie cameras, and the picnickers wore sombreros instead of top hats. I could still see Mabel doing her stuff among the picnickers at Echo Park, but I think she would have turned away from the bleakness at Edendale. When I first drove to the old Keystone lot, just before I reached Effie Street, I saw a real coyote lope in front of me across four lanes of traffic. Was it a sign?

ARTISTE

MAY 30, 1974, LOS ANGELES

Dear Steve:

I dislike people unless they place 'love' on a higher level than sex. Because of your genuine sincerity, your great understanding, I dare discuss this thing called 'love' with you, Steve.

I told you I never allow myself to think 'old'. . . . the feeling of youth is always there. 'Praise Him!'

Julie

DECEMBER 31, 1915, NEW YORK CITY

When Fatty and Mabel stepped off the Twentieth Century Limited at Grand Central Station on New Year's Eve, they were greeted by the heads of the New York Central Railroad and of Triangle Corporation and by a host of press photographers. There was no time now for interviews. The railroad and movie barons whisked the pair into their limousines and drove them to the Lexington Opera House for the evening performance of a Christmas pantomime, *Peter Rabbit in Dreamland.* Fatty and Mabel were ushered into the royal box, and as a spotlight picked them out, the audience rose and applauded. In the words of *Motion Picture World,* "The white lights beamed merrily for them, the cup of joy effervesced; in plain vernacular, Fatty and Mabel are on the job in New York."

Mabel had come East for the first time since she had left four years before. She returned rich and famous as laughable, lovable *Keystone Mabel,* "The Sugar on the Keystone Grapefruit." With "The Keystone Fat Boy" she had come East to make a new series of two- and three-reel comedies for Sennett at Triangle's Fort Lee

87

Studios. Triangle announced publicly that "Director Sennett of the Keystone Company has consented to her Eastern appearances before the camera, largely that she may have the proper locale for Keystone scenarios written for an Eastern setting." In fact, Mabel wanted to get as far away from Mack as possible, and both Mabel and Fatty had threatened to quit. In fact, Mabel's quarrel with Mack was as professional as it was personal, and behind the dirty story of sex was the dirty story of money.

"The worst predicament of all," Mack confessed, "is to fall in love with an actress with whom you are in business." The war between Mack and Mabel was a war between the sexes over power, and if their marriage had come off, it would have turned their cold war hot. "Nappy and I battled more and more," Mabel told Sutherland. She wanted better pictures, better pay, and more artistic control. "Mack accused me of being temperamental and hard to control, both in and out of the studio," she said. "I accused him of experimenting with new faces and names, giving them fine pictures, while using me to keep the cash rolling in." She felt exploited. Mack admitted that she *was* exploited. "That was how we got along and made money." Mack complained that Mabel wanted "longer and deeper and more romantic parts" because she thought she was a great star, but he was in the business of comedy, not romance.

When Triangle first took over, Mabel believed the Aitkens' ballyhoo and thought her moment had come. Triangle advertised "CLEAN PICTURES FOR CLEAN PEOPLE" in order to tap the market of the respectable middle classes. As stock manipulators, the Aitkens were skilled in exploiting cultural snobbery. They remodeled legitimate theaters for "the Triangle program" of a full evening's entertainment, two dramas and a comedy, and upped ticket prices to an unheard of two dollars to keep out the riffraff. For comedy films they hired vaudeville headliners Eddie Foy and the Seven Little Foys for $1200 a week, Raymond Hitchcock for $2000, and Weber and Fields for $3500. Since the top pay for Keystone veterans like Mabel and Fatty was still $500, Mabel was none too pleased. She had her revenge when the vaudevillians discovered that their timing was off for the camera, and they came to Mabel for help. Mabel tried to explain to a desperate Lew Fields how "to space his stuff" and slow it down for movie audiences, but it was hopeless, and the stage comics left as fast as they had come.

All but the romantic comic Raymond Hitchcock, better known to Broadway as "Hitchy-Coo." Before he left, he made the initial two Triangle comedies opposite Mabel, as a romantic comedy pair, with Mack playing the fool. *My Valet* and *Stolen Magic*, shot in August and September, were to inaugurate a new era for comedy with Triangle's premier on September 23 at New York's Knickerbocker Theater, at Forty-second Street and Broadway. To show Hollywood its class, Triangle kicked off on September 5 with a formal dinner-dance, "the first formal affair ever given in the city exclusively for the people of the screen." Mack and Mabel attended. Mabel was scheduled to attend, with other Hollywood stars and New York socialites, Triangle's New York premier, that would introduce the public to Douglas Fairbanks in *The Lamb*. But by September 23, Mabel was in a coma and already disillusioned with the promise of better parts. *Photoplay*'s influential critic Julian Johnson noted that Mabel had been "a vicarious *sacrifice* for Hitchcock's success." And when the critic pondered who had delivered the most distinguished performance of the year, he wondered if it wasn't "Mabel Normand's bulwarking of all the Keystone comedy with her own slender shoulders."

Mabel had real grounds for discontent. In July of 1915, *Motion Picture World* ran its first movie popularity contest, and the winners of "The Great Cast Contest" were Pickford for Leading Woman, Chaplin for Male Comedian, and Mabel for Female Comedian. That same year Mabel saw Chaplin go from $1250 a week at Essanay to $10,000 a week at Mutual. She saw Pickford renegotiate her contract with Zukor for $700,000 a year, plus 50 percent of the profits, a $300,000 bonus, and a $10,000 a week drawing account. Under Mack, Mabel was going nowhere: $500 a week and no control. It made sense only to Sennett. Hal Roach was not the only one to say that Mack was stubborn as an Irish-Canuck and impossible to do business with. He never put anyone under contract, Roach told me, "I mean what the hell, he had Arbuckle, Chaplin, Keaton. . . . But he had the cockeyed idea that he was bigger than any of them, that it was all Sennett, that another Chaplin would come along, another Arbuckle."

And another Mabel. When Mabel left Sennett, he tried one by one to make Gloria Swanson, Louise Fazenda, Marie Prevost, and Mae Busch into another Mabel Normand. When Mabel and Fatty both rebelled against the Sennett dictatorship, Mack openly took revenge and announced to the trades, "Now that Mabel Normand is in the East, Miss Busch is getting the cream of the straight feminine roles at Keystone." Eventually Mae too left Sennett to end with Laurel and Hardy at Hal Roach Studios.

Before she fled East, Mabel made one more old-style slapstick with Keystone's Chester Conklin that ended in an accident that could have been far worse than "getting beaned with a wedding shoe." *Dizzy Heights and Daring Hearts*, filmed early in December, put Chester and Mabel in a monoplane with Chester at the controls. He was supposed to taxi on the ground, but he got excited, opened up the throttle by mistake, and the plane took off. Fortunately it hit some trees and fortunately Mabel jumped before the crash, but *Triangle News* reported that she would be "confined to her home again for several days."

Mabel recovered fast enough to film at Santa Monica the first of Fatty and Mabel's final trio of films before the pair hopped on the train just after Christmas. Fatty was as discontented as Mabel with Sennett's stubborn fear of change in the business of comedy. The demand of the newly refined audiences was for "Clean Comedy," which meant less physical humor and more comedy of situation. Away from Mack, Fatty and Mabel could work in a more sophisticated vein, and some of their best work as a team is in the two surviving films, *Fatty and Mabel Adrift* and *He Did and He Didn't*. Away from the tiresome ogling of Ford Sterling, Fatty and Mabel could break through Keystone clichés. Critics praised their "higher" style in which Mabel "set the standard" for funny-girl heroines and in which the pair provided "action for the 'Hee-Haws' while offering an abundance of amusement for minds not primitive." Mack must have spit a wad over that one.

After finishing *Bright Lights*, Mabel took sick with one of her respiratory ailments that were worse every year. This time,

Mack admitted, Mabel was genuinely sick. This time, Mabel announced, she was quitting Mack and his cheap-Jack comedies for good. "No more slapstick, flour-barrel, custard-pie, aeroplane, water-stuff comedy for Mabel Normand, who is now to play light dramatic roles." Those were the headlines in the trades when Mabel announced in April of 1916 that she was leaving Sennett for Tom Ince, who had promised her her own studio at Inceville, as well as her own plays and her own directors. Mabel may have been bluffing, but if so her ploy worked. Mack negotiated fast and promised Mabel everything she had always wanted — her own studio *and* her own film company. That would put Mabel on a par with Pickford. Mabel accepted graciously and announced that her first film would be a romantic comedy not yet named. Her second would be *The Little Minister* in "a part I've always longed to play," the double role of Lady Babbie and the Gypsy that Minnie Fisk had made popular on the stage and that a later lady-gypsy, Katharine Hepburn, would make popular on the screen.

Refined tastes had always sniffed at the coarseness of "rough-house" comedy, but at the beginning of Keystone they were outnumbered. As far back as *A Strong Revenge* a critic had complained, "The vaudeville acts contain coarse touches, which are unfortunate, and the 'rough-house' ending will not appeal to a refined audience." Certain subjects were automatically dubious: milking scenes, kissing and spooning, death. Admitting that the funeral in *Heinze's Resurrection* was "excruciatingly funny," the critic suddenly had second thoughts, "if people can be made to see the funny side to a burlesque funeral."

As the masses rose, so did their refinement. The raw stuff was out, the genteel was creeping in, and all the comedians were caught in the bind. Chaplin elevated his tramp to an aesthete that Oscar Wilde might have recognized. Arbuckle elevated his fat boy to an Arrow-collar batchelor and man-about-town. Mabel was elevating her tomboy to an elegant lady of fashion. When she posed for the 1915 *Who's Who in the Film World,* she wore rich brocades and a plumed diadem. Chaplin credited himself with redeeming slapstick from the primitives, but Mabel had civilized the brutes before Chaplin arrived. In her last Fatty and Mabel films, critics discovered that "by an infinitude of tiny movements and shifting changes of facial expression, she lays bare the state of mind of a woman struggling between primitive emotion and acquired self control." Farewell to the Hee-Haws. Hail to Mabel, "Dramatic Artiste."

Mabel's mixture of the dainty and the coarse had always defined her unique virtue and her problem. Her popularity lay in the fact that she appealed to the refined, on the one hand, and to the vulgar on the other. In the context of Mack's gorillas, she was a redeeming social influence. In the context of Griffith's girls, she was a subversive joker. The combination of sweetheart and buffoon upset tidy minds then as now. Even a feminist critic like Molly Haskell calls Mabel "an irritating blend of seductress and practical joker," although she confesses that the prejudice against a woman being both "may lie in us and our conditioning." Haskell conveniently forgets three recent generations conditioned by Lucille Ball.

But there is no accounting for laughter or tastes when the submerged issue is class. When Mabel had set off to seek her fortune, she had wanted nice things. Now that she had them, she wanted more. Like other Hollywood migrants, she wanted class. Hollywood was the most class-conscious enclave in the country for the simple reason that it had none. "You know what our problem is, Gloria?" an actor asked Gloria Swanson. "It's that nobody around here except you and me has any class." Class was one more thing they had to invent, like their names and identities.

When Mabel returned to Hollywood and to Sennett on May 1, 1916, she returned in triumph as "America's Premier Comedienne of the Screen — Star of the Mabel Normand Feature Film Company." She returned to make *Mickey,* a new kind of comedy that would show her off as a dramatic actress and turn her tomboy into a glamor girl. On the screen, she wanted less clowning and more sexiness. In her personal life, she wanted no clowning and no sex at all with Mack. From now on, it was strictly business. I noticed, however, that in a photo essay of "Mabel Normand at Home," in which she sexily lazes about a bedroom in silk pajamas and peignoir, there was a framed photograph on her bed table in the background. It was an old photo of Mack.

MICKEY

MAY 31, 1974, LOS ANGELES

Dear Steve:

Can you really understand this great magnetic force
connected with the person and name of Normand?
Your yearning since a child to seek more and more
about Mabel, surely God brought us together. God
help me first to love 'Him' above all else, then to
make me happy with Steve the one I love.
Also it must be mutual!!!

Love,
Julie

SEPTEMBER 10, 1978, HOLLYWOOD

You would hardly notice the little white stuccoed building
at the junction of Bates, Fountain, and Talmadge streets except
for its triangular shape. In the sunshine, Mabel's studio looks like
a white hot iron. A small sign indicates a scenic shop within. Not
a sign of Mabel anywhere, except for the capitols of nine pilasters,
each of them a grinning mask.

Mack built Mabel's studio to order in the spring of 1916. She
ordered rose and cream wallpaper for her dressing room, with
matching chintz curtains and an oriental rug. Someone gave her
a canary in a wicker cage. Mabel added a built-in kitchen and a
Japanese chef who specialized in chicken and canned pineapple.
Mabel's studio was just over the hill from Keystone and therefore
out of sight but close enough to holler. It seemed ideal.

Mack gave Mabel the script she wanted. This was the script
he had offered earlier to "another comedienne" to punish Mabel
for her rebellion. Mabel had got angry, got sick, and quit. Now

93

the script was hers. It was for the feature-length dramatic comedy called *Mickey* that for the next two years, from 1916 to 1918, became the battleground in the ongoing war of Mack and Mabel. What really happened to *Mickey* was yet another puzzle, like what happened to Mabel. Mack spun another story of Cinderella romance, but in fact it was another farce of sex and money, as I discovered, that ended bitterly for Mack and Mabel alike. The story did not end until January 22, 1921, when the Aitken boys were charged before the New York State Supreme Court with conspiracy to defraud the stockholders of Triangle and were found guilty. By 1921, a lot had happened to Mabel.

Mabel called *Mickey* an "historic picture" and it was. Both Mack and Mabel claimed that it made more money in proportion to cost than any before it. While figures were unreliable (Mack claimed $18,000,000 gross from an outlay of $150,000), *Mickey* did make million-dollar profits for a number of people. Mabel was not one of them. Nor was Mack, but Mabel never knew that. Mabel was certain that Mack had betrayed her a second time, this time with money rather than sex. When she finished filming *Mickey* in the spring of 1917, she quit Mack for Sam Goldwyn. "I decided I'd had enough of the Keystone Company," Mabel said.

Mickey was historic because it was a model of the modern film which is marketed before it is produced. *Mickey* was marketed by saturating the media with publicity and by promoting "selling tie-ins" of merchandise over a period of two years *before* the film was released. *Mickey* was also a model of modern corporate fraud. The Aitkens, reaping windfall profits from *The Birth of a Nation*, were certain that a comedy could double the box-office success of a serious drama. They would make *Mickey* a smash hit, and they did. They made Mabel for a decade "The Little Girl You Will Never Forget," but Mabel didn't make a cent.

Just ten days before the murder of William Desmond Taylor, the directors of Triangle Corporation learned in court that the Aitken brothers had set up a number of phony companies with *Mickey* as the capital. The result was a $3,000,000 bilking of Triangle stockholders. Harry Aitken's sole defense was "I do not remember." He settled out of court for $1,375,000, but it was far too late, and Triangle went into bankruptcy. One cameraman remembered the Aitkens as "pretty slick fellows," who "shook the world for awhile and then, all of a sudden, they just went ka-flooey." The truth of *Mickey* was buried in another morass of lies. For Mabel, the only certain fact about *Mickey* was that it was the first, last, and only production of the Mabel Normand Feature Film Company before it too went ka-flooey.

For Mabel, *Mickey* was a bad-luck film all the way. Mabel quarrelled with Mack over three directors before Mabel fought for and got F. Richard Jones. Although Dick Jones had been directing shorts for Sennett for a year, Mack thought him too young and inexperienced. "But Sennett was on the run," Mabel said, "and I had my way." She picked her cast from old friends — Minta Durfee, George Nichols, Laura LaVarnie, Wheeler Oakman, and her future husband Lew Cody. Lew was fresh from a film called *The Grinning Skull of Respectability,* which might have given the wary a clue to the Aitkens.

Then filming stopped when Mabel got sick, again, with sinus and a hacking cough and "hemorrhage after hemorrhage," Minta said. That Mabel's obvious symptoms of tuberculosis should have gone unnoticed is not surprising. Mabel never took care of herself, and she hated doctors, or what Hollywood knew of doctors. Typical was Dr. Raymond A. Sweet, known as "a surgeon, automobile salesman and man about town." This surgeon-salesman tailed Mabel in the hope of blackmailing her, until Mabel called in a detective who nabbed him. At first the doctor claimed that "someone" had paid him $610 to shadow Mabel for sixty-one days, then confessed that he was broke and hoped simply "to make money out of someone who was well known to the public." Mabel suspected Mack and declined to prosecute. But she also declined medical treatment. Minta recalled that Mabel would take a swig out of a bottle, saying, "I better take my goop because I feel like I'm gonna have a little hemorrhage." Her cough syrup was laced with opium and heavy use of her goop led to her later addiction to cocaine. Arbuckle, in the same fall of 1916, became addicted to morphine and heroin when he was treated by a medical hack who allowed a superficial leg wound to become gangrenous and who then wanted to cut off the leg.

Mack began an intensive publicity campaign on *Mickey* for

reasons of his own. Mack wanted to break loose from Triangle by busting the system of block-booking that tied Sennett's comedies to the complete Triangle program. *Mickey* was to be the first of all blockbusters. He would sell Mabel as a "super-star" and her film as a "super-special" to independent exhibitors. While Mack was in New York throughout the summer and fall negotiating with the Aitkens, his publicists were turning Mabel into a media event. Featurettes on Mabel as Mickey appeared in all the trades. She was named Queen of the San Diego Exhibition. She was suddenly a stylish horsewoman, receiving a pair of polo ponies from "Lord Tweedmouth." She was a collector of snazzy automobiles, who had just bought a grey Mercer roadster built to her own design — "a dream of a car" — with Goodrich Quick-Detachable Tires and a custom dressing table and makeup mirror that folded into her car door. She was a fashionable duck hunter who spent her weekends bagging game. She was the pet of "Indian Minnie" or "Minnie Ha-Ha," a real Canadian Indian named Minnie Devereaux who was part of the *Mickey* cast and who showed her devotion by embroidering Mabel a pair of beaded moccasins. She was the idol of Japan, whose admirers sent hundreds of mash notes: "Joe saw you in films which acted by you so many times and pleased by your nice eyes, mouth, hairs and other ones."

During the winter Mack stepped up the publicity because he was stalling for time. The first *Mack Sennett Weekly* on January 1, 1917, announced Sennett's new plans for distribution side by side with Miss Normand's new character in *Mickey*. A photo of Mabel shows the "quaint little mountain girl" dressed in an oversized man's vest, baggy pants, and laced boots so long they look like Chaplin's. But she also has masses of hair loose to the waist, and she is smiling at us like a wild rose. Mabel will create a new kind of picture play, the copy reads, "no rough comedy, no flying pies, no innocent heroines seduced, no buckets of blood, and no padding." *Mickey* would have all those things and more when the film finally released, but the releasing was the whole point. *Mickey* would be released after the first of the year, the *Weekly* announced, method and date to be announced later.

Much, much later. Every month for the next six, Sennett

announces that Jones has "just completed production," that *Mickey* is "almost ready and certain to make a hit," that despite previous costs, more and more money will be spent until "every frame sizzles" and the action "doesn't drool along." By March, Mack admits that "this great multiple-reel drama has been a strain." The film has been so long gestating that Mamie, the Keystone kitten, has produced a litter. By April, Mack is finishing the cutting, he says, while Mabel says goodbye to the Keystone menagerie of geese, squirrels, burros, ponies, and dogs that performed with her. Mack did not announce that in April Mabel also said goodbye to Mack and the whole Keystone enchilada. She wired Sam Goldwyn in New York to meet her at the Hotel Muelhenbach in Kansas City, where she signed a five-year contract, took the next train back to California, and told Nappy. "He went wild."

Mabel was fed up because her film had become everybody's pawn in the struggle to conceal the "dull sickening thud," as the trade magazine *Wid's Daily* said, of Triangle's collapse. Neither Mabel nor Mack knew the Byzantine intricacies of the struggle. In January the Aitkens and a fellow conspirator from the South, aptly named Stephen A. Lynch, conned Kessel and Baumann out of their Triangle stock by the simple device of hiring an actor to impersonate a Wall Street tycoon. The "tycoon" lent the bookies money with stock as security. The Lynch-Aitkens bought up the stock. The trio then set up two phony companies, W. H. Productions and Western Imports, to sell "Super-Triangles" on the open market at extra-high rates. *Mickey* was the only Super-Triangle in the offing, and they would use *Mickey* to break their own block-booking contracts with their own theaters. No wonder Mack was conned.

Mack thought he was the one using *Mickey* to break his contract with Triangle. But Mack was out of his class. Mack gambled with *Mickey* for nearly a year, and at the end, he lost both *Mickey* and Mabel. He could admit to the loss of the girl but not to the loss of the property. One of the most bizarre and touching of Sennett's lies is the story he invented to salvage his pride. He convinced himself of the story's truth, and then he convinced others, so that even today his fiction stands as film "history." He admitted that he lost in June his Keystone trademark and his entire stock of Keystone film to the Aitkens, but he outsmarted them all, he said, by retaining the Mack Sennett name, the Keystone lot (which became Mack Sennett Studios), and *Mickey.*

Mickey was his but *"Mickey* was a failure." After a year's work and an investment of $125,000 plus all his personal assets, no exhibitor would touch the thing. "I tried again and again and again to induce somebody to show *Mickey."* No luck. It was a full year later, in 1918, when a two-bit exhibitor from Long Island came into Kessel and Baumann's office desperate for a picture that hadn't arrived, that Mack induced someone to show *Mickey.* The bookies groaned, Mack said, but Mack persisted, and overnight the dud became a hit. "I told you so," Mack yelled while the money rolled in, and *Mickey* became "the greatest Cinderella story in the history of pictures."

It was also a bald-faced lie. The truth was revealed in a handful of telegrams I found in the Sennett Collection in the American Motion Picture Academy of Arts and Sciences in Beverly Hills. The telegrams were exchanged between Sennett in New York and his business manager J. A. Waldron in Los Angeles, from June 6 to July 3, 1917, after Mabel quit. While selling the rest of his Keystone interests, Mack was trying to retain control over *Mickey,* but a telegram from Waldron on June 7 indicates that Mack had never seen the full seven reels. Waldron wired that he and two others had looked at the reels the previous night: "NO SUBTITLES AND LOOSELY ASSEMBLED," but they had no question about its quality once Sennett reassembled, subtitled and edited it to give the story its missing snap. The men agreed that "PRESTIGE, PERSONALITY AND ACTING OF STAR WILL PROVE DRAWING CARD."

On June 27, Sennett wired Waldron, "MICKEY PICTURE BELONGS TO PATTERSON." Patterson was head of the new Triangle management, and Sennett believed that Patterson "WANTS ME TO HELP TITLE AND ASSEMBLE IT." Then a new complication. Waldron wired that director Dick Jones had just put a lien on *Mickey,* or as Mabel said later, "kidnapped and hid" a couple of *Mickey* reels in lieu of unpaid bonuses totalling $16,000. Sennett told Waldron to threaten Jones, "INSTEAD OF GIVING HIM A BONUS THEY WANT TO GIVE HIM PRISON." But Mack also asked Waldron to do some kidnapping for himself: "IF YOU HAVE OPPORTUNITY TAKE REEL OR SO OF THRILLS FROM CUTTING ROOM AND PLACE IN PRIVATE CAMERA VAULT UNDER MY ROOMS AND YOU KEEP KEY." In the end, Sennett kept Jones by promising to make up lost bonuses by a salary increase and for awhile he even kept a share in the rights to *Mickey.*

But Mack had lost control over the film, and Triangle would not release it. For months the trades asked regularly, "What happened to *Mickey?* Who knows?" I discovered the answer in another telegram in the Sennett file. This was from a man named Winnik, head of the phony company Western Imports in New York, to Sennett in Los Angles. Winnik claimed that he was trying to make a deal with Triangle to buy *Mickey* outright, but Triangle demanded $200,000 by July because they'd have to buy out Mack. Winnik complained that the film couldn't make that kind of money anywhere near that fast. Then he came to the point: "WILL YOU SELL ME YOUR CLAIM OF TWO HUNDRED THOUSAND FOR ONE HUNDRED AND FIFTY THOUSAND CASH AND I CAN THEN DO BUSINESS WITH DAVIS?" Mack sold without knowing that both Winnik and Davis were front men for Harry Aitken. Mack was the fall-guy in a sting.

When Mack lost the film, he lost any right to edit it. But he couldn't admit that, either. He always claimed credit for assembling and editing *Mickey* but, in fact, an obscure cutter in New York finished the job, cutting it to its "present 7000 foot length" and reordering scenes "to make the story more logical and convincing." Western Imports finally released *Mickey* on August 11, 1918, just two years after its inception, in the midst of a national epidemic of Spanish flu. Since the government had ordered theaters closed except for a couple of days a week, that might have been the end of *Mickey.* Instead, the film earned back Mack's selling price in a matter of weeks and was so clearly a winner that exhibitors called it the "mortgage-lifter." But in this Cinderella story, nobody lived happily ever after. Winnik was arraigned along with the Aitkens in the 1921 conspiracy suit, and Winnik countersued. He claimed that Triangle's directors owed him $250,000 because he had never received, as he said, the "complete" reels of *Mickey*.

A "complete" *Mickey* was a fiction. From the print we can see today the story is about as logical and convincing as any Keystone madness. Triangle publicists tried to cover its weak structure by crediting Sennett with "a new 'epic' form," one that combined "humor, pathos, thrills, adventure and heart." But it wasn't Mack, it was Mabel who had in fact created a new comic epic simply by being Mabel. She hadn't dropped the custard-pie pratfalls of slapstick after all. She had simply added pathos and heart to the old formula of sex, spills, and thrills to create a unique genre of "slapstick romance." While *Wid's Daily*, the sheet exhibitors used as their Bible, criticized the mixture of burlesque with romance in *Mickey*, they predicted, "Mack Sennett has here concocted a peculiar type of popular appeal subject that is going to make a lot of money." *Mickey* made a lot of money because its concoction appealed to the new family audiences who were deserting vaudeville for movies in the search for refinement and who demanded the same entertainment values of "wholesomeness" and "variety."

Mabel must have burned when she read *Wid's*. Mabel had battled Mack on just this issue of romance. Mack wanted no part of it. He was in the business of comedy, not romance, and comedy was burlesque as it had always been. He had a bank account to prove it. Mule-stubborn as always, Mack was the last to sense the changing tastes of changing folks. Mabel had quit Mack once over the issue, and she came back only on the condition that she could have her way.

Her way was to take a Cinderella story and give it her own comic twists. If Cinderella is an orphan, Mickey is a tomboy of the West, raised by a grizzled prospector and Indian Minnie. If Cinderella makes trouble for her uppity relatives, Mickey turns their parlors into bomb sites. If Cinderella wins a Prince,

Mickey wins a handsome but dumb hero whose wooing is upstaged by a squirrel that runs up Mickey's leg. Because Mabel is Mickey, she adds adventure to farce and turns the victim-heroine of melodrama into the New Woman as spunky American Girl. Mickey attracts her man by diving nude as a water nymph (in flesh-colored "fleshings" this time) into a woodland lake. She saves her man, when he has gotten himself into a money mess, by disguising herself as a jockey in a horse race. She wins her man by giving *him* a pot of gold (from a lucky strike at Tomboy Mine). And she carries off her man to live happily ever after in *her* kingdom of the West. Mabel's Mickey is a Cinderella who kicks back.

Mabel thought it her best work. Of the films that remain, it comes closest to capturing her infinite variety. Her instinct was to play "the moment," and *Mickey* is an anthology of movie moments bursting with life. "There are mad races between trains and motors," a contemporary critic wrote, "rattling chases on horseback, an eye-filling ballroom scene, and everything else that is known to filmdom, even to having some 'eats.'" Unconditioned by the stage, Mabel helped liberate movies from the structure of the stage by replacing coherence with speed and variety of action. Mabel had no sense of story but a strong sense of scene, and in 1916 she created the kind of movie entertainment that would become a formula for decades. It was the formula prescribed in 1922 by one of the most successful of photodramatists, who called for action, thrills, romance, suspense, human interest, a tear, a smile — "then you've got a story."

Mabel became Mickey for the public the way Topsy became Eva Tanguay. The public was sold Mabel as Mickey in the first big movie tie-in campaign in history. The Aitkens were conmen of vision who saw that the future of Hollywood lay in publicity. They hired a song-writing team to sell *Mickey* by the first "song exploitation" in movie history. They saturated the country with sheet music, vaudeville lantern-slides, arrangements for band, orchestra, and player piano, with Columbia gramophone discs "to reach every city, town, and hamlet in the United States before the release of the picture." They also saturated the country with merchandise. "We have 'MICKEY' shirts, sox, flowers, sundaes, phonograph records — 'everything that's loose,' " the syndicate boasted. They urged exhibitors to drive their town "MICKEY-MAD!"

Mickey madness caught on because the timing was right. In 1918, the Great War had made Americans nostalgic for an innocence they had always symbolized by the American Girl. The simple-minded lyrics of "Pretty Mickey, pretty Mickey, Can you blame anyone for falling in love with you," had the tone of a best-selling novel during the war called *Carolyn of the Corners,* in which Americans were urged to "Look up! . . . Look at the sunshine. . . . Read how a little girl, with this simple philosophy, changed the world into a happier place for any number of interesting people who had grown a bit grouchy and gauche." While a number of Europeans had grown a bit grouchy and gauche in the trenches of Verdun, Douglas Fairbanks was urging Americans in a moral essay of his own composition to *Laugh and Live.* Fairbanks's remedy for grouchiness was to *"Get out in the air and run like a school boy. Jump ditches, vault fences, swing the arms!"* The mood was cheery. Success was simple. *Mickey* celebrated the energy and gaiety of "the will to do" that automatically won success. In Fairbanks's words, "The thought of *success,* the courage that comes with *success,* leads to *more* and *more success."* Mabel was not prepared for what might happen *after* success. There was no script for that. There was no script for Arbuckle either when he was asked "What's the worst thing that can happen to an actor?" and he replied, "To arrive."

GOLDWYN GIRL

JUNE 2, 1974, LOS ANGELES

My dear Son:

It is a special gift from God that you have the fortitude to practise "celibacy!"

Pray for me as I hold you close to my heart as any dear mother would do.

I cannot think of destroying your letters.

Affectionately,
"Judy" Mama.

JULY 23, 1917, NEW YORK

Mack wrote a novel once, never published, now lost, and gave it a title that was the imperative of his life, *Don't Step on My Dreams.* Mabel stepped on his dreams by running off to Goldwyn, so Mack dreamed up another story to soothe his hurt. While Samuel Goldfish was four years younger than Mack, he was street-old and street-smart the way Chaplin was. Goldfish had fled the slums of Warsaw and Liverpool for the chance to laugh and live in America. His own will to do had won success automatically, first by selling gloves and then by selling stars.

Goldfish, too, lived on dreams, and when they got stepped on, he was as resourceful and far more resilient than Mack. When Adolph Zukor purged Goldfish from the combine of Famous Players-Lasky, Goldfish joined the Selwyn brothers to reinvent himself with a new company, a new name, and a new identity. As head of Goldwyn Pictures Inc., his first act in February of 1917 was to woo a "mystery" star. By this time, Zukor was distributing the new Mack Sennett productions and by June, both Goldwyn and Zukor had announced an "exclusive" new contract with Mabel Normand. *Wid's* reported, "Injunctions, suits, litigations of all sorts seem to be in sight."

Injunctions were never in sight because Mack knew he could never handle Mabel by waving a mere legal document in her face. But in his dream, Mack was always in control of his irrational, irresponsible, impossible girl. So he made up a story. He said that he followed Mabel to New York to get her a better contract with Goldwyn. He said that Mabel then gave Goldwyn the same treatment she'd given Mack, sassing her boss, not showing up for work, then running off to Paris to buy clothes at outrageous prices and to create scandal by outrageous behavior. He said that after two years of this Goldwyn was glad to get rid of her and to give her back to Mack. That was Mack's story, and it again became film "history."

I began to unravel Mack's story when I found more telegrams in the Sennett file. These were exchanged between Mack in Los Angeles and his lawyer in New York, covering a couple of weeks between July 11 and July 23, 1917. On July 3, Mack had returned to Hollywood to hand the Keystone stock over to Triangle's new management. While Mack went West, Mabel packed her bags and came East to rent an apartment on Seventy-first Street near West End Avenue. Mabel had retained the same lawyer as Mack, Arthur Butler Graham, to complete her negotiations with Goldwyn. Mabel said that she won a five-year contract with Goldwyn that would begin at $1000 and increase to $4000 a week in the fourth year, with a share of profits in the fifth. When Mack told his story, he said that Goldwyn was going to pay her a pittance, so he argued with Sam and got Mabel raised to $1500 a week. The telegrams said different.

The telegrams showed lawyer Graham caught in the crossfire between his warring clients. Graham, violating Mabel's trust, as he told Mack, wired Mack the terms of Goldwyn's contract. Sennett wired back that Mabel should stall: "IT IS ONLY NEC-ESSARY FOR A LITTLE MORE TRADING AND DICKER-ING TO BOOST THAT UP." Sennett also wired the old producer Baumann to get him to outbid Goldwyn and buy Mabel back. Baumann wired that Mabel was "ABSOLUTELY UN-

MANAGEABLE AND UNALTERABLE." She refused, in fact, "ABSOLUTELY TO HAVE ANYTHING TO DO WITH ME OR YOURSELF IN CONNECTION WITH ANY BUSINESS PROPOSITION."

The message would seem to have been absolutely clear, but not to Mack. Graham was forced to pull his legal rank. In a long telegram of July 13, he told Sennett that after ten years of negotiating and matching wits in the picture business, the lawyer ought to know his business and he knew that he had gotten Mabel the best possible deal. "BUT IF THIS IS NOT TRUE I AM NEVERTHELESS UNABLE TO STALL OR BARGAIN BECAUSE CLIENT WILL NOT PERMIT IT." Graham did not even dare show Mabel Mack's telegrams.

The final telegram, on July 23, was sent by Mabel to Mack:

SIGNED TODAY. . . . GRAHAM VERY
SATISFIED. SAID MUCH BETTER THAN
EXPECTED. START WORK SEPT. 1.
COMPANY SAID I DIDN'T LOOK WELL.
MUST REST AND GO AWAY UNTIL THEN.
WINTER STUDIO FLORIDA. SO I WON'T BE
ABLE TO PEEP AT YOU EVER AGAIN.

Mabel's final sentence must have been a killer for Mack: "I WANTED YOU TO KNOW I SIGNED ALTHOUGH YOU NEVER WIRE." Mack wired no more. Instead, he rented Mabel's studio on September 1 to William S. Hart Productions for Hart's cowboy pictures.

In the new age of advertising, Goldwyn was a supersalesman with a genius for packaging. Goldwyn's dream was to package the classiest of "Eminent Actresses and Eminent Authors" in order to attract to movies "the carriage trade." Mabel became the first of his "Five Glamorous M's" of stage and screen: Mabel Normand, Mary Garden, Maxine Elliott, Madge Kennedy, and Mae Marsh. He soon added authors Rex Beach, Rupert Hughes, Gouverneur Morris, Mary Roberts Rinehart, Sir Gilbert Parker, and Elinor Glyn. As his dream grew, he wooed Maurice Maeterlinck from France and tried to woo Sigmund

Freud from Vienna. Goldwyn's dream of culture coincided with entrepreneur "Roxy" Rothapfel's in his self-appointed mission to elevatetaste.RoxyspokeforSamwhenhesaid,"Thepeople,Ihope,are beginningtorealizewhatisbeingdoneforthem."

Goldwyn's first mission was to transform, like Pygmalion, the vulgar pie-thrower into a lady. Soon after he hired Mabel, Goldwyn hired Norbert Lusk to direct publicity and to give Mabel "the Goldwyn touch." The Goldwyn touch conferred the gold of glamor when glamor was still a new word, a new idea, a new look. Glamor was the way to upgrade sex from the vulgarity of burlesque to the chic of high fashion and to transform flesh into art. In Goldwyn ads, Mabel now appeared in titillating glamor-girl poses, sanctioned by their "artiness." In a 1918 *Photoplay*, Mabel leans on a pillar, her head wrapped in a silver lamé turban, eyelids drooping, lips parted, her body nude beneath some artful drapery. It was all very sexy but dignified by the artfulness of Lusk's prose. Mabel's eyes are "the color of autumn leaves glimpsed under a swiftly moving brook." Lusk quotes Gautier, they are "stars rayed with black lace." Lusk, desperate, coins a new word. Mabel is . . . "mabelescent."

Mabel reveled in her new image. It was her revenge on Mack. The author of *Film Folk* in 1918 contrived a Movie Queen Comedienne named "May Chapin," who was Mabel thinly disguised. When May explains her transformation from "a sort of female Charlie Chaplin" to a serious comedienne, she says, "I find myself at last cast in comedy dramas that call for something approximating intelligence and offer a chance for more subtle comedy than cyclone and cataclysm." She wouldn't have to fight Goldwyn for serious comedy because Goldwyn himself thought slapstick vulgar.

Mabel's first film for Goldwyn was to be a serious drama that would contribute to the war effort. *Joan of Plattsburg* (originally *Joan of Flatbush*) sounded like a burlesque of Geraldine Farrar's *Joan the Woman*, but ads suggested its serious intent: "This Picture Will Silence the Whispering Campaign of Slander Directed at the Mothers of America." Photos showed Mabel in helmet and sword crying, "Stand Fast, America!"

Immediately Mabel was in trouble. The style was all wrong.

Goldwyn shelved the film in November for "military reasons," he explained, and hired the prestigious director George Loane Tucker, who had made *The ManxMan* and *Traffic in Souls,* to direct Mabel in her "first" Goldywn comedy, *Dodging a Million.* When *Joan* finally appeared in May, largely reshot by Tucker, the critics were not impressed. Mabel was miscast. While *Wid's* called her "a likeable 'she-ro'," they added, "Mabel's too darned plump and easy to gaze upon to be considered one of those ethereal spiritual gooks who imagine things." Mabel was no Lillian Gish.

Goldwyn continued to publicize himself as the Midas who would "realize Mabel's beauty and artistic capacities in a manner that will astonish her millions of admirers." In fact, Goldwyn and Mabel returned to the successful formula of *Mickey* and worked it to death. Over the next three years, Mabel made sixteen features for Goldwyn. One year she made as many as nine, plus a short for the U.S. Fourth Liberty Loan Drive. They were all slapstick romances, hung on a Cinderella plot in which tomboy or shopgirl overcomes obstacles of birth and circumstance to win success. Of the fifth such, *Back to the Woods, Wid's* commented, "Well, they took old Formula 56 off the shelf, dusted it off a bit and jazzed it up to fit Mabel." Titles were as interchangeable as plots: *Dodging a Million, The Floor Below, Joan of Plattsburg, The Venus Model, Back to the Woods, Peck's Bad Girl, A Perfect 36, Sis Hopkins, The Pest, When Doctors Disagree, Upstairs, Jinx, Pinto, The Slim Princess, What Happened to Rosa?, Head Over Heels.*

They were all "Snappy hokum farce with a fast meller finish put over by atmosphere and characters and speed," as *Wid's* wrote. Speed covered the cracks. They made Mabel's pictures quickly and never worried about the stories, one of Goldwyn's first production managers told me, "because we could fix it up with sub-titles." Another production manager told Sutherland, "Why we didn't even have to buy great pictures for her. Her personality made any picture a success with the booking agents even before it was started."

Mabel quickly discovered that she'd left one treadmill for another. Goldwyn quickly discovered that it was Mabel's comedies that paid the bills. Unfortunately, Goldwyn's bills were mounting as high as his ambition "to draw to the screen the most finished histrionic ability, the names of deepest import in the world of art." He drew opera stars to the silent screen and novelists to the wordless one. "To this ambition," he confessed in *Behind the Screen,* "may be traced the great disasters of my professional career." It was an understatement. Finally not even the profits from Mabel's comedies could float Goldwyn's sinking enterprise, and he lost control of Goldwyn Pictures Corporation to a swindler as disreputable as Harry Aitken, F. J. Godsol. The only pictures that Goldwyn had turned to gold were *The Cabinet of Dr. Caligari* and the comedies of Mabel Normand.

Mabel gradually became disenchanted with the Goldwyn touch. Goldwyn drew opera divas like Geraldine Farrar to the screen by paying her $15,000 a week. When Goldwyn moved his studio from New York to Culver City, Mabel "launched a campaign of ridicule" against Geraldine Farrar, Norbert Lusk wrote. Mabel would parade around the lot loaded to the gills with Madame Geraldine's feathers and pearls, demanding silk panels for her dressing room and a jazz band to drown out the sound of Madame G.'s string orchestra. When Madame G.'s favorite gentleman caller came to her dressing room and sang out, "My beloved, where are you?" Mabel would sing back, "In the toi-let." Or so Hollywood said.

Hollywood began to collect Mabelisms as it collected Goldwynisms because, true or invented, they made good copy. Lusk was the source of many, and he complained about the difficulty of getting printable quotes from Mabel for press releases. "You want me to be dignified and act like a star, like your Geraldine Farrar," she teased him and called him by the name of a recent W. D. Taylor hit, "but I can't Bunker Bean, I *can't,* because I'm shanty Irish." When he pressed her for some idiotic publicity feature to describe her ideal man, she replied, "A brutal Irishman who chews tobacco and lets the world know it. If anyone wants to know what I enjoy most, say I love dark, windy days when trees break and houses blow down; and what I like best to do — don't say 'work,' that's like Mary Pickford — just say I love to pinch babies and twist their legs." Hollywood added a Mabel-ism, "Don't say 'work,' that's like Mary Pickford, that prissy bitch." Mabel, however, would not have leveled that kind of shaft at Mary but at another Goldwyn girl, Madge Kennedy, whom Mabel thought an awful prude and called "Goody-goody Madge."

Mabelisms grew as she kicked harder against the hypocrisies of promotion and show-biz. When Goldwyn began Goldwyn Pictures, he promised a national advertising campaign that would "imitate the success of the best commercial enterprises like Pack-ard Automobile, Royal Baking Powder and the Victor Talking Machine." He made good on his promise by making marketable commodities of stars. Mabel wanted the stardom, but she hated the fakery of press agentry and the discipline of commercial display. For *Joan of Plattsburg*'s opening, Goldwyn arranged a premiere in Washington D.C., in which the President's wife, Mrs. Woodrow Wilson, would appear on stage with Mabel. Lusk was in charge, and Mabel gave him a hard time. She dawdled in her bath and drank champagne and demanded a larger hotel room. "I *had* to have a suite because Mae Marsh got one when they sent her to Buffalo," she explained to Lusk. "You can't wait for justice from the bastards that make pictures, dear."

Goldwyn's manager Abraham Lehr added to the Mabel-isms by detailing her rebellion against his "businesslike princi-ples." "What a little devil she was!" Lehr told Sutherland. "What a glorious, loveable, unmanageable minx!" Everyone at the Fort Lee Studio was her slave, Lehr recalled, including the boss who "refused to help me keep her in line." Mabel was chronically late and teased Lehr with outrageous excuses: she had picked up a load of soldiers in her limo' so they wouldn't be AWOL at Camp Merritt; she had to wait at the bakery for a cookie Lehr liked "though she never saw me eat a cookie in her life." If he scolded her, she sprayed him with perfume and told him to take *that* home to his wife. If he was firm, she burst into tears and promised to buy him a car. When he rebuked her for too much night life, she accused him of spying and sent him a ritzy watch for his birthday with a note misspelling his name:

Dear Mr. Leer:

*Wishing you many returns of the day. And now,
damn you, you and your dicks can tell just what time
I come in.*

*Love,
Mabel*

At the same time, the girl who called herself shanty Irish yearned for learning and culture. She grew studious, Mack complained, and took up books. But she did it in true Mabelese. She ploughed indiscriminately through Schopenhauer, Brander Matthews, Francois Coppée, Montaigne, Heywood Broun, Conrad, Baudelaire, Freud, working-girls' confessionals, and socialist pamphlets. She loaded her secretary Julia with a bag of Great Books while her chauffeur carried her furs and dogs, and her maid her perfume and bags of cookies. "She does not take her reading like a sponge," said one interviewer, assuring readers that Mabel was no highbrow, "but like an electric motor." When Louella Parsons asked Mabel how many of the books in her library she had actually read, "Not a one," Mabel said, "but I've read the reviews."

Mack sneered at Mabel's "doses of culture," but Goldwyn admired her seriousness and called her a real reader, "not a phony." Of course Goldwyn was the real reader who liked *The Wizard of Oz* so much that "I read part of it all the way through." Publicist Lusk was closest to capturing the mixed results of Mabel's electric-motor approach to learning. When he asked Mabel to autograph her picture for him with something personal, she said, "I know, I'll write something from Swinburne." Swinburne was her favorite, even if his first name *was* Algernon. And she scrambled a couplet from "Erontion" into Mabelese prose, "I shall remember your friendship, loyalty and kindness while the light lasts, and in the darkness I shall not forget."

If her reading was without rhyme or meter, her need to know was as intense as Chaplin's when he said, "I wanted to know, not for the love of knowledge, but as a defense against the world's contempt for the ignorant." As long as she knew her, Julia said, Mabel's first question always was "What have you brought me to read?" That she cut through Pierre Louÿs's *Aphrodite* and Olive Wadsley's *Sand* at the same speed was irrelevant. Mabel's point was immediate and personal. Mabel's point was that neither Mack nor Sam had read anything at all.

!STAR!

In 1918, Mabel achieved the star status symbolized by Gloria Swanson in the twenties, when stardom conferred, as Gloria said, a "dizziness of freedom" that only the strong willed could resist. Mabel arrived at stardom just as America, celebrating the war's end in 1918, wanted to be free, as William Shirer said, "to make money and whoopee." In making plenty of both, Mabel embraced rather than resisted freedom, and her stardom became synonymous with its dizziness. When she signed with Goldwyn, her biographical data-sheet read

Name: MABEL NORMAND
Occupation: STAR

In November of 1918, Mabel was at the peak of her stardom. *Mickey* had just opened in August in a glare of publicity. Goldwyn had just launched his promotion of Mabel as a glamor queen. Mabel's photos were everywhere, and Mabel spun dizzily because nothing could stop her. She was exempt from silly war-time rules, rules of sex or rules of propriety. Mabel's attitude toward rules of any kind was typified in a story of Lusk's about Mabel during the war. Lusk had begged Mabel to entertain a member of the Serbian delegation visiting New York. Mabel took him to the Savoy Hotel dining room and ordered nine martinis, one Baked Alaska, and one hundred melachrinos, to be served all at once. When the horrified waiter reminded her it was against the law to serve men in uniform, Mabel retorted, "Law, my eye! — Send the captain here — Miss Normand calling. Put them in a straight row and *go away.*" One straight row later, Mabel and her Russian buddy weaved into a carriage in Central Park where Mabel taught him Indian war whoops. Lusk's friend wrote from Moscow, "Mees Mobble have beautiful heart."

Everyone agreed about Mabel's heart, but people were divided on the whoopee. Before the flapper of the twenties, there was the sport, and Mabel was the idol of the sports. In 1918, Mabel set the style for a new generation of sporting girls. "To be like Mabel" was the goal of comediennes Dorothy Gish and Constance Talmadge. To be like Mabel the younger girls would buy a box of cigarettes and down a teaspoon of gin before splurging on a dinner at the Angelus Hotel. To be like Mabel they would tell dirty jokes. "Mabel wanted to be smart," Allan Dwan remembered, "and being smart meant doing what wasn't done. Mabel would tell jokes like

Question: What was the slipperiest day in Jerusalem?
Answer: When Saul went through on his ass.

" 'Tell that one,' they'd say to Mabel and die laughing at a three-letter word."

Mabel could get away with it, Blanche Sweet said, because "we all granted her the license of an enchanted princess, like Carole Lombard. When she spoke, toads came out of her mouth, but nobody minded." Some did. Comedy producer Hal Roach minded. When I found him in his Bel Air mansion, surrounded by stills of Laurel and Hardy and Our Gang, the genial round-faced Irishman told me that Mabel was "the wildest girl in Hollywood" and "the dirtiest talking girl you ever heard." Roach was not amused, however, because he felt that Mabel and her Dirty Four had helped destroy younger girls like starlet Clarine Seymour. When Roach rebuked them for their foul language, the Dirty Four would walk just behind him and talk even dirtier for revenge. "Clarine ran around with these gals for about a year," Roach explained, "and then kicked the bucket in 1920." Some said she'd died of drugs. Roach blamed Mabel.

Trying to curb Mabel was counter-productive. Goldwyn, like Mack, had the misfortune to fall in love with the actress with whom he was in business. "Goldwyn had a real case on her," one of Goldwyn's managers said, "but I don't know if he ever caught her. She spent most of her time trying to avoid him." Or insult him. Most remembered her insults to Goldwyn because they made good stories. She treated his Napoleonic delusions the same way she treated Mack's. "She knew how to handle him," Mack's biographer Fowler described the Mabel treatment. "She fought with him. He seemed to like resistance. It focused his mind." Because Sam had more mind to focus, he challenged Mabel to greater resistance. He was a tyrant, and people who knuckled under his tyranny enjoyed recalling the way Mabel would mimic Goldwyn a foot or two behind his back and, if he turned, right to his face.

Hedda Hopper remembered Goldwyn's vain pursuit of Mabel in the fall of 1917 at the Raymond Hitchcocks in Great Neck, Long Island. Mabel had been vacationing there after she signed with Goldwyn in July. Hopper remembered her as a mermaid among goldfish. Speeding on a surfboard behind Caley Bragg's speedboat in a man's sweater, and seemingly nothing else, "she'd come in with her long eyelashes braided with spray." Sam would motor out from Manhattan in his Pierce Arrow to take Mabel to dinner, Hedda said, but Mabel would dawdle upstairs and after midnight send a message down, "Tell him to go home."

One of Goldwyn's scenarists, Frances Marion, recalled the way Mabel handled Sam when he tried to mend her manners.

> *The lessons pleased her at first, then they began to irk when he curbed her natural instinct to stand spraddle-legged, rocking with laughter, and tossing in a few words usually scrawled on fences.*
>
> *"I'm mad at him now," she said to me one day in the studio as we watched Sam stalk across the stage. "Look at him," stabbing her finger in his direction, "that stuck-up bastard! That . . ." and she let fly a string of cuss words that no longshoreman could improve on. Finally, out of breath, she turned to me apologetically: "Excuse me, Frances, for pointing."*

Anita Loos also recalled a Mabelese moment, at a Christmas Eve party in New York. Mabel arrived late with torn stockings, with disheveled hair and without "her permanent escort of the time, Sam Goldfish." Mabel told the girls that she'd gone to St. Patrick's Cathedral and got roughed up in the crowd. She'd gone to pray to St. Anthony, she said, to please give Sam a good nose job for Christmas.

Goldwyn never mentioned his pursuit of Mabel, but he made *Behind the Screen* a valentine to her. In 1923, she was the only one of his Five M's he remembered with awe instead of vituperation. Mabel was as mysterious as a force of nature because she was immune to money. He told how she would give away a $100 bill or a $1000 check to some little waitress or needy extra girl. How she wouldn't bother to cash her paychecks and consequently threw his books out of whack to the tune of $44,000. How she threw $50,000 worth of Liberty Bonds on his desk when she learned his company was going bust. He compared Mabel to Pickford, who concealed behind her little-girl mask "the mind of a captain of industry." He compared Mabel abroad to Pickford and Fairbanks abroad. The Fairbanks were prisoners of their own images even to themselves, Goldwyn observed, and when they traveled in Europe they seemed lost without their pictures. Mabel, by contrast, was an adventurer, in Europe as elsewhere, and she gave herself entirely to the scene. Mabel's real generosity, Goldwyn said, was not in giving money but in giving herself.

Mabel's generosity was one of the attributes of the "I-Don't Care Girl." While Eva Tanguay had tucked $1000 bills in her purse to give away at random, Mabel's spending went beyond notoriety or charity. The wife of Mabel's favorite Goldwyn director, Victor "Pops" Schertzinger, was often the recipient of Mabel's need to give gifts. After a long day at the studio, Mabel would insist that "Pops" pick out a jewel for his wife from the little chamois bag she wore around her neck. "Mabel wanted to give everything away," Mrs. Schertzinger said.

It was almost as if she wanted to get rid of herself. Lusk spoke of her urge to "exhaust the incandescence that set her apart from the ordinary." Making whoopee seemed to relieve the guilt of money and the guilt of fraud. Other shanty Irish suffered the pangs of superstardom in just that way. Maybe the same passion for honesty that kept Mabel from forgiving Mack kept her, too, from forgiving herself as she experienced the shams stardom enforced. Maybe she needed to give more and more of herself away as she felt less and less self to give.

On the screen, Mabel was a prisoner of her little-girl image in the same way Pickford was. And while Mabel could step up the glamor, she couldn't alter the age. She was stuck with Topsy as Mary was stuck with Little Eva. They were both stuck with the sexual double standards of their audiences. Chaplin could develop the character of his tramp because he was old, no matter how childlike his vision. Mabel could not develop her tomboy because the function of a tomboy was to revert to a girl, not a woman. Not until Mae West did a full-blown voluptuous woman get away with clowning adult sex on the screen.

As Mabel grew older, her parts grew younger and more stale. While Goldwyn advertised *The Pest* in April of 1919 as "the great American public's conception of the Ideal Normand Picture," *Wid's* noted that the film was about kids and for kids. In December of 1919, Mabel appeared Christmas day on the stage of the Capitol Theatre at Broadway and Fifty-First streets, accompanied by society leader Mrs. William Randolph Hearst, at a matinee of *Jinx* to benefit 5300 orphans. Mabel said, "This is the first time I've seen an exclusively child audience watching the movies." Unfortunately, *Wid's* review of *Jinx* warned that it was only "good for patrons under 12 years of age." Mabel was supposed to be not much over twelve herself in the story of a circus orphan who jinxes a number of circus acts and finds refuge in an orphanage.

The comedy seemed as dated as a waltz in the context of the Capitol's opening show in October of that year, with George Gershwin's "Sewanee," Mae West's shimmy song, "Oh, What a Moanin' Man," and Douglas Fairbanks's *His Majesty, the American.* Under Goldwyn, Mabel sought to legitimize her art just as Goldfish sought that same December to legitimize his name by a legal change to Goldwyn. Just as movies sought to legitimize their medium in theaters that now "Hopelessly Out-Classed, Out-Dollared and Out-Illuminated" the so-called legitimate stage. And just as Americans sought to legitimize democracy by usurping monarchy in films like *His Majesty, the American.* But instead of authenticating her astral identity, Mabel found herself mired in clichés, and the more she struggled, the faster she stuck.

"Mabel in a Hurry," a *Photoplay* interviewer had called Mabel in November of 1918. She was a madcap, the journalist said, who loved ice cream for breakfast, purple flowers, black-lace stockings, and dime piggy banks. She was a wilful adorable child, who in one picture was too plump from ice cream and in the next too thin from exhaustion. "Someone told us once," the reporter said, "that Miss Normand reminded them of a dancing mouse, whirling madly all the time, but without purpose."

Mabel was still whirling in the spring of 1920 when she filmed *What Happened to Rosa?*, the only one of her Goldwyn features to survive. I could see from the film what was happening to Mabel. I could see it in her thin face, baggy eyes, and frantic tempo. After manic bursts of energy she collapses, like a rag doll. The story is incoherent beyond anything in *Mickey,* and often the humor seems forced and uncomfortable. Goldwyn also saw what was happening to Mabel and didn't release *Rosa* until a year later, after Mabel and his company had collapsed. *Rosa* followed *The Cabinet of Dr. Caligari* at the Capitol Theatre, and the conjunction was ominous. While critics hailed the German film as "a radical departure" in photo-dramatic art, they were tired of Mabel's same old story. The star, they said, provided the only "glint of redemption from utter trashiness."

The star was in need of redemption herself. The Rosa Mabel was playing appealed to her because it allowed her to play a double character, like the tomboy-lady of *Mickey* or the lady-gypsy of *Little Minister.* It was the same character that would appeal to her again in the story of "Rosa Mundi" by Ethel M. Dell, one of the two books William Desmond Taylor bought Mabel on the last day of his life. In the Goldwyn film, Mabel plays a little hosiery clerk who believes that she is the reincarnation of a famous Spanish dancer, Rosa Alvaro. The delusion allows her to dress as the dancer for a masquerade ball on the yacht of the millionaire-doctor hero. But this Cinderella is schizophrenic, "gone dippy," as the subtitles say, in one of her "Spanish spells." Instead of the New Woman, rescuing and buying up her man, the little clerk is a comically pathetic victim, driven to self-mutilation to put herself in the hands of the doctor she loves. Mabel is often very funny, fluttering her hands and lashes in a wicked parody of the Gish girls, or farcically trying to snap her arm or crush her hands by stepping on them to do herself doctorable damage. But Rosa is much closer to the sweet pathos of Chaplin than to the boisterousness of Mickey. If *Mickey* was a story of Cinderella success, *Rosa* was a story of failure.

As early as the spring of 1919, Mabel's health was failing and her image showed it. The trades warned exhibitors of *When Doctors Disagree* that Mabel was not photographed to best advantage and advised, "Be honest about its defects." First Mabel was too fat and then too thin. Her fluctuations of weight charted her unhappiness. Everybody noticed that something had happened to Mabel, but what? Being honest about defects was a logical impossibility in a business based on concealing defects to sell illusions. "Mabel Normand was one of the baddies," Anita Loos assured me, "but of course only insiders knew." An insider like MGM publicist Howard Strickling knew everything that had ever happened or could happen in Hollywood, but he summed up industry attitudes toward defective merchandise when he told me that he couldn't talk about the past nor could he write his memoirs because he didn't want "to tell all that dirt."

A French critic observed unkindly that "there are two things the American heroine will never lose, her innocence and her back lighting." By 1920, no amount of back lighting could conceal the wasted image of Mabel, who looked like innocence lost. She had changed, Lusk wrote, when he saw her in Culver City after the war-time energy crisis of October, 1918, forced the Goldwyn company to move West. There Goldwyn revamped the old Ince Studio owned by Triangle into an English country estate. He rolled an English lawn over the sand and planted an English rose garden. Mabel trampled on the lawns and picked the roses because Sam put up signs saying not to. But her old energy was gone. "The only crumpled rose leaf in this Eden," Lusk said, was Mabel.

Lusk was providing Mabel with the back lighting of his prose, but the camera was less kind. Still photographs for *The Slim Princess,* made a few weeks before *Rosa,* show Mabel haggard. Her final Goldwyn film, *Head Over Heels,* was so bad that it was not released until 1922, without publicity. Goldwyn had hired a newcomer to Hollywood to codirect this film. His name was Paul Bern, and he promptly fell head over heels for Mabel. Bern, however, had a more compelling rival than his boss. During the spring and summer of 1920, another director, working on *Anne of Green Gables* with the girl star Mary Miles Minter, had fallen for Mabel when she fell in another sense. William Desmond Taylor was the man who stepped in to rescue the crumpled Rosa.

The trouble with Hollywood's eyesight is that back lighting is its only "truth" and all the rest is "dirt." I knew by now that what had happened to Mabel under Goldwyn was drugs. But I didn't know how or why because of all that back lighting. Once again the villain-hero was Mack, who once again made up a story in his own peculiar mode of gallantry and self-interest. Mack had his own need to keep Mabel innocent, so he made up a story that made Mabel a pawn. Mabel had given Sam so much trouble, Mack said, that Sam was glad to get rid of her.

> *Mack: If you want to get out of this deal with Mabel*
> *I'm willing to take her off your hands.*
> *Sam: You're right, Mack, take her.*

The closest Mack ever gets to mentioning a health problem as a euphemism for drugs is when he says he was "amazed and upset" when Mabel arrived at his studio. "She was unhappy and ill and she looked it," Mack says, confessing that he didn't know how badly she had been photographing. But that was under Goldwyn. Goldwyn didn't know how to handle her, Mack says, but Mack will now rescue the crumpled Rosa and give her another chance.

As usual, Mack's fiction concealed a money fact. In 1920, Goldwyn's dream went ka-flooey the way Mack's had with the Aitken boys. Goldwyn was glad to get rid of Mabel for the simple reason that Goldwyn had already been gotten rid of by the ace swindler Godsol, who stepped in and kicked Sam out. In August of 1920, rumors were rife. Mabel was rumored to have signed with theatrical producer Al H. Woods to do a stage play. Goldwyn was rumored to have signed Mabel for a new Goldwyn company in Europe. Goldwyn was also rumored to be contemplating a tour of the world "for an indefinite period." In fact, Goldwyn Pictures

Corporation was finished, and Mabel and Sam were both out of a job.

Nineteen-twenty was a bad year for dreams. The Armistice that was supposed to herald peace eternal and "put a quietus on sham," as *Wid's Daily* proclaimed, had instead polarized conflicts and institutionalized sham. So many dreams were stepped on. So many of Mabel's generation were lost. That fall Olive Thomas, the beautiful violet-eyed wife of Jack Pickford and a friend of Mabel's, was found dead in her Paris hotel room of "accidental poisoning." Bobby Harron, Mabel's old friend from Biograph days, was found dead in his New York hotel room of an "accidental pistol wound." Clarine Seymour, Mabel's satellite, was dead in a Hollywood hospital after unspecified "emergency surgery." So many images broken.

Puzzling over the change in Mabel, Lusk said that she was like "a worldly sophisticated child" who couldn't "reconcile what she feels with what she knows." She had dropped out of Edendale into the Wasteland where feeling and thought were numb. Mabel withdrew and gave even her closest friends, Lusk said, "the Staten Island treatment." When Mabel wanted to be elusive in New York, a caller would be told that Mabel had left for Staten Island and if he called Staten Island, Mabel had just left for Manhattan. Lusk said that when he quit Goldwyn to work in England and made a farewell call to Mabel, he didn't even get the Staten Island treatment. In the summer of 1920, a strange voice answered the phone and said coldly that Mabel was out. I guessed that the voice was Julia Benson's and was certain of it after I learned that Julia was concealing more than drugs.

DOPE FIEND

AUGUST 8, 1974, LOS ANGELES

Dear [Steve]:

The time is so fast approaching now, I am more than 'excited.' God grant the Normands peace and quiet and rest. You have all suffered long enough due to publicity and unscrupulous writers who commercialized on a great genius.

Lee is making all our plans for stay at Hotel Ambassador.

Your other 'Mama,'
Judy.

AUGUST 17, 1974, LOS ANGELES

Stephen's search for Mabel reached its climax when he met Julia for the first time in the lobby of the Ambassador Hotel on August 17. Stephen had flown to Hollywood for the opening of David Merrick's production of *Mack and Mabel* in Los Angeles. Six months before, Stephen had talked to Julia on the phone when he first got wind that the script of the musical portrayed Mabel as "a dope addict." Stephen wanted to sue, but his lawyer warned that he would have to prove Mabel had not been so addicted. "What I mean to say," Stephen said to Julia, "is that they say Mabel was on dope when Taylor was killed." "Oh the idea!" Julia replied. "They'll say anything."

When Stephen set out from Staten Island, he was determined to prove Mabel's innocence. He did not know what was in store for him. He kept a diary of his trip that he showed me when we first met. Only later, when I was well launched into my own search, did he disclose a second diary that he had kept back.

121

In the first, he described in detail his feelings when he at last met Julia and Lee in the "20's-but-not-tacky" Ambassador Hotel.

Arriving at the Ambassador I felt the same excitement I was sure Julia felt the afternoon she was summoned to MN's home when she was sick with flu. I began searching the lobby and saw an old man standing next to a tiny lady, hunched up and lost in the plush settee. He was maybe 5'8", burly, hair closely cropped, a narrow white moustache. That must be Lee. He wore a plaid shirt, beat-up shoes and held a crumpled cowboy hat.

Julia had on wire-frame glasses and her grey hair was wound in a bun. She wore a beige housedress with a jacket my grandmother used to call a "topper." On her feet were blue flannel slippers with pom-poms.

"You must be Steve Normand, I can tell that plain as hell by those big eyeballs of yours! Jesus Christ, Julia, isn't he a miniature of Mabel!"

Lee bellowed this and I wanted to crawl behind a palm. Julia began wiping tears from her eyes and complimented me on my pale blue striped Palm Beach suit and my glossy white shoes.

"You're every inch a Normand. You dress so beautifully."

So, after all, I did have a legacy to continue. The elevator took us to the third floor and to room No. 325. There were two Hollywood beds in the room, which was sort of run down and had no drapes. Lee came out of the bathroom with the noise of the toilet flushing.

"The toilet's okay. Other than the bed it's the only thing important in these flop houses," Lee said. "I guess I'll leave you two now for the night. I've got to get back to the house and to Cody."

Is he going to leave me here with Julia, I wondered?

*"Okay, Steve, you take good care of Julie and I'll
give you kids a call in the morning."*

*I nearly died. Julia went into the bathroom with
her big brown pocket book, which was evidently her
suitcase. She reappeared in a white peignoir set like a
bride would wear. She scurried to the foot of the
nearest bed and knelt down.*

*"Thank you, dear God, my sweet Jesus, for
Stephen's safe journey."*

*Then she got into bed and asked me to get into
bed with her.*

*"Do you think it would be sinful if you were to lie
beside me, the real flesh and blood of Mabel
Normand to keep me warm?"*

*I nearly threw up, but just said I wouldn't like to
and went into the bathroom and changed for bed. It
was a terrible sleep for me. And when I woke up at
6:30 A.M., she was looking in my eye.*

Stephen asked if they couldn't stay in her house instead of
the hotel, but that did not solve his unease. Lee picked them up
in a fifties Cadillac, and when Stephen arrived at the Ingraham
Street bungalow, he "nearly collapsed." "The place was a dump,"
he wrote, "ripped-up papers on the floor, boxes of junk, beat-up
furniture like a slop house, an unmade bed, the smell of cat poop,
a broken bathroom sink so that one had to fill a pan from the tub
to wash. . . . Julia said she hoped I wouldn't get fleas from the
cat. I was mortified."

That evening Stephen decided to wear his beige suit rather
than his rented tuxedo to the opening, because he was "just not
up to dressing up." He thought the musical a lovely play with
catchy music, but the scenes with Taylor and dope were "too
much to comprehend." Julia's response was blunt. The star Bernadette Peters didn't look at all like Mabel, she said, and Julia was
outraged when she saw Mabel in corset and stockings singing
"Wherein He Ain't." "What baloney," she whispered to Steve.
"Mabel couldn't sing and if she ever tried, it would never be in
her underwear."

The Mabel of *Mack and Mabel* was but one of a series of reinvented Mabels. In the fifties, Paramount had wanted to cast Betty Hutton as Mabel opposite John Lund as Mack. In the sixties, Warner Brothers had wanted to cast first Natalie Wood and then Carol Burnett as Mabel, in a film they wanted to call *The Delinquent Angel*. Neither film got off the ground, partly because Mabel was hard to cast and partly because the facts of her story were awkward. Merrick faced the same problems in his musical. Before he cast Bernadette Peters opposite Robert Preston, he had announced so many Mabels for the show that wags began to call it *Mack and Maybe*. Merrick admitted that the story line was troublesome and that they had added a dream sequence of Mack and Mabel's wedding "to alleviate the gloom of Mabel's death." But the fiction of a wedding didn't quite do it. As Loos commented after its New York opening in October, "A musical comedy in which the heroine is carried off by drugs in the prime of her youth and beauty put the audiences into low spirits, and the show flopped." Actually the heroine was entirely a creature of Broadway rhyme without reason,

> *She was plain little Nellie*
> *The kid from the Deli*
> *But Mother of God look what happened to Mabel.*

The musical perpetuated the legend that Mabel lived and died a dope fiend. But Julia was ready to take an oath that she had not. Stephen asked Julia to sign a notarized form to that effect, witnessed by Lee, on August 30, 1974, that read in part:

> *To my personal knowledge as Miss Normand's*
> *confidante and in my professional opinion as her*
> *nurse I firmly state that Mabel Normand was never*
> *treated by any physician for drug addiction nor did*
> *she ever show any symptoms of being addicted to any*
> *drug.*
> *I swear that this statement is the absolute truth*
> *and that it is made without prejudice and that it is*
> *the truth as I know it to be.*
> *Julia B. Benson, R.N.*

It was easier for Julia to attest to the "absolute truth" of this statement after she had unburdened herself of a truth she confessed to Stephen at the Hotel Ambassador. Stephen left out her confession from his first diary, which was devoted largely to his enthusiasm for Hollywood sites — the Avenue of the Stars, Aunt Mabel's Mausoleum, her memorial plaque at C.B.S.'s T.V.-Studios, and Pickfair, where Mary Pickford waved to him from her bedroom window, "in a beautiful flowing peignoir set." Stephen returned from his Hollywood trip with Julia's testimony in hand to write a biography clearing his Aunt Mabel's name.

To find out what had happened to Mabel, I would have to look into the Hollywood drug scene at the end of the teens. Some said drugs were as common then as now, among show people and the fast set. Others, like Loos, said that drugs were extremely limited before 1920 and that Hollywood had only two famous drug takers, "Wally Reid and Mabel Normand." The pairing was ominous since Reid's death by drugs in 1923 caused a national scandal and a number of Hollywood antidrug crusades.

I soon learned that drugs were one of those many postwar changes that crept in almost unnoticed in the general desire to laugh and live. The date of the first federal report on drugs, 1919, was a turning point. Before then, "dope" usually meant opium and suggested either Yellow Peril exoticism or English eccentricity. Either way, dope was largely comic. Typical of Hollywood's earlier attitude was an ad run in 1915 by a manufacturer of motion-picture screens. "Are you a 'dope' fiend? Take the cure," the manufacturer advised theater owners. "Install a Day and Night Screen and you'll lose your taste for 'dope.' " Also typical was a Douglas Fairbanks's spoof of a Sherlock Holmes mystery called *The Mystery of the Leaping Fish,* in which the detective jabs himself with opium syringes while chasing opium smugglers.

But with the war, the hop-smokers in Chinatown began to move out and the coke-sniffers in. At first coke was shocking, then chic. Adela Rogers remembered her shock when C. B. DeMille handed some stuff around at luncheon parties. "It was HMC," Adela said, "a combination of hyacine, morphine and cactine." Mack's pal Lonnie D'Orsa confirmed that it was easy enough to get "a little nose candy" from the doctors around. Keystone actor Eddie Sutherland had named Hughie Faye at Sennett's studio as the pusher who put "Mabel Normand on the junk, Wallie Reid, Alma Rubens." Since Alma was another star who died of drugs, the Mabel linking was not encouraging.

I learned from the current husband of Gloria Swanson, William Dufty, the writer who had to know about drugs for *Lady Sings the Blues* and for an unpublished biography of Waxey Gordon, "The King of Dope," that the war had institutionalized drug traffic along with liquor traffic. In 1915, Waxey had organized from his prison cell a corporate network of criminals and federal agents that made Waxey a multimillionaire after October 28, 1919. That was the day the war-time restrictions on alcohol were made permanent. I also learned that the Godsol who bought out Goldwyn was related by family and profession to Elie Eliopoulos. By the end of the twenties, the Eliopoulos family ran, according to Gertrude Jobes in *Motion Picture Empire*, "the central bank and clearing house for the biggest share of the world's illicit trade in opium, morphine, and heroin ever organized up to that time into one system." Big money brought in big crime.

But in 1918 – 19, as Dufty said, Mabel would have "had no botheration from the law." And for a girl like Mabel, if it was smart to drink gin and talk dirty, it was a helluva lot smarter to sniff coke. I felt that Mabel as a rebel would take the stuff on principle. The real question was how much did she take and how bad did she get? Hedda Hopper had described vividly a scene at the Ritz in New York when she visited Mabel there with Zabelle Hitchcock sometime in 1918. They found her in bed, a wraith, surrounded by twenty-five boxes of dead flowers like a burlesque funeral. "The stench was unbearable," Hedda wrote. They looked for "the white powder we knew Mabel had been using." When they found it, they flushed it down the toilet, installed a nurse, and left.

If Hopper was worldly wise, Griffith-girl Miriam Cooper was innocent. Yet she too described a Mabel drug scene at the Ambassador Hotel in Hollywood. Miriam had visited Mabel with Mae Marsh and Norma Talmadge because Mabel was down with the grippe. Mabel went into the bathroom, stayed awhile, and when she came back, she flipped up her skirt with her back to a mirror and whooped, "My ass is open to the world." Miriam was puzzled at the sudden change in her, and Norma had to explain that Mabel had given herself a shot in the bathroom.

Sennett's accounts of Mabel's wild extravagance in Europe at Goldwyn's expense led many to believe that Mabel's nuttiness was the result of drugs. Sennett reported that she left Goldwyn in the middle of a picture, spent thousands on clothes and jewels, hobnobbed with dukes and sheiks, dived naked into swimming pools on English country estates, wrecked Goldwyn's schedule, and cost him a fortune. But Mack's story was another fake. Mabel made her first trip to Europe in 1922 with the full approval of Mack. His story was part of his attempt to cover up the truth of Mabel's illness, when he and Dick Jones found that "Mabel wasn't the same."

I was confused about Mabel's chronology. Lusk had said that Mabel was sick with "a pulmonary complaint" during much of 1919 and worked twice as hard to make up for it. Until that fall, Mabel was turning out a feature every two or three months. Then there were long stretches between films until her last film a year later, completed in August of 1920. In January of 1921, the *Mack Sennett Weekly* announced "THE RETURN OF MABEL NORMAND." What happened to Mabel in between?

My only real clue was a *Photoplay* feature published by Adela Rogers the following August, 1921, in which Adela welcomed her old pal back to Hollywood after her long absence in the East. Hollywood welcomes back "the same old Mabel," Adela wrote, "just as she looked when you first saw her on the screen." Adela had last seen her on the Goldwyn lot at Culver City, looking drawn and grey, Adela said, as if "she were eaten up inside by something that was bitter to her spiritual digestion." Then she disappeared, Adela wrote, and retired to a small New England village in order to rebuild her "wrecked nervous system." Now that she was back with Mack, however, Mabel looked "as though the hands of the clock had turned back." To prove her point, Adela printed contrasting photos on facing pages. There was Mabel, before and after. On the right was a sad-faced, drooping, bulging-eyed Mabel who tried and failed to smile. On the left was a grinning, effervescent Mabel who posed in a powdered wig and ball gown for her new role in *Molly O'.*

The reference to a "small New England village" was the closest I came to locating the sanatorium where Mabel went to take the cure. Only later did I learn that William Desmond Taylor had sent her there. At the time, I was merely struck by the phrase about Mabel's inner pain, eaten up by something "bitter." "She haunted me," Adela wrote, and I wondered whether Mabel's bitterness had something to do with Mack or with Goldwyn. I had no idea that I would find the answer in Stephen's second diary.

Julia told Stephen that she had first come to look after Mabel in the winter of 1918 in the midst of an epidemic of Spanish 'flu. When Goldwyn moved his studio West in October, Mabel was the last to move. She didn't want to return to Hollywood and Sennett territory at all. But she did, because she had to. Julia Brew, as she was then, had just graduated from St. Vincent's Hospital and was assigned her first case, "the great comedienne, Mabel Normand." "It was a priviledge!!!" Julia wrote Stephen. She remained on the case twenty-four hours a day because Mabel had developed pneumonia on top of 'flu. She had a temperature of 104° and became delirious. Her first sight of Mabel, Julia told Sennett once, was of "a little girl just over five feet tall, weighing only 99 lbs., in pigtails and a flannel nightgown, and that is how I thought of Mabel from then on."

That was how she wanted to think of Mabel from then on, so that is how she did. Not until she found Stephen, Mabel's own flesh and blood, did she admit that the truth was different from her willed image. Stephen scrawled his second diary in the form of rough notes after his night at the Ambassador, and he labeled it "Julia's Confession." Lee referred but once to the substance of that confession when he wrote me, "Nobody knows but me and J. and it won't do you any good to know either." I don't know that it did Stephen any good to know, but he wrote it down.

> *After Julia knelt by the bed she got up slowly and said, "Steve, I am so happy you are here I must lighten my heart this night with a most tormenting memory. I have held it deep within my soul all these*

128

years and swore to your Aunt Mabel never to reveal it to anyone."

I was dumbfounded. She lay back on the bed and asked me to lie down next to her. Then she grabbed both my hands and held them to her breast.

"Steve, you remember I told you that I came to work for Mabel during a 'flu epidemic. Well it didn't happen quite that way. St. Vincent's called one afternoon and told me to go immediately to the home of a movie star at 7th and Ventura where Miss Mabel Normand was confined to bed. The case was confidential and I was to speak to no one about it.

"So I hurried to the house and knocked with a brass knocker shaped like the mask of comedy. A middle-aged woman let me in. This was Mamie Owens, Mabel's personal maid for all her life. She led me upstairs to a hall where a young balding man with wire-rimmed glasses sat on a chair. He looked pale and quite nervous.

"Miss Owens opened the door to a bedroom and there was Miss Normand in bed. She was in child labor and was moaning quietly. She looked pale and helpless. Her large eyes closed with pain and then opened again. Her time had come and the baby was delivered — dead. It was a premature five-month old boy. Miss Normand was in a terrible state. She had lost a lot of blood.

"The man outside the room came in awhile later and kissed Mabel on the forehead. He whispered, 'I'm so terribly sorry, Mabel!' Mabel did not answer and he left the room for Mabel didn't want to see him."

Julia was crying now and trembling and she grasped my hands tighter. "Oh Steve you don't know what I went through those ten years with Mabel. It took the strength out of me and left a terrible scar on me. Come lie down next to me and hold me tightly to you as Mabel did to me and keep me warm."

Holy Christ, I thought. She fell into a deep sleep

and I thought about the poor thing keeping that story locked in herself all these years.

Among the photographs Stephen had shown me, I remembered one of a young balding man with wire-rimmed glasses sitting in Mabel's open touring car. It was the young Sam Goldfish. I also remembered what Lee had said once to Steve, "You see, Julia went through hell so many years keeping Mabel clean for the public."

When I visited Hollywood, I telephoned Julia, although Stephen warned me that she wouldn't want to talk. She spoke in a high thin voice, and she had trouble breathing. They had called her "The Movie Nurse," she told me, because she had taken care of so many stars after Mabel — Douglas Fairbanks, Mary Pickford, Charles Boyer, Maureen O'Sullivan, Mia Farrow. Her only real problem was high blood pressure, she said, for which she'd been taking vitamin B_1 shots for twenty-five years, but sometimes the sisters wouldn't give them to her. Then abruptly she didn't want to talk anymore. When I called a day or so later, Lee answered and told me not to call again because any talk upset Julia. Soon after, I received a note:

At this time I am unable to see you due to a situation with me of H.B.P. Truly I tried.

Most regretfully,
Julia Benson

I never spoke to Julia again. At ninety-four she is now in a nursing home where Lee visits her every day. I spoke often to Lee, however, and began my own unlikely correspondence with the cowboy protector of the protector of Mabel Normand.

RAPE MOLL

AUGUST 29, 1978, LOS ANGELES

Box 76294
Sanford Station

Dear Betty:
   Time changes everything. Now you can call me
from 8:00 P.M. until 5:45 A.M. and if I should forget
the phone in Julia's room and she should answer it,
just say, 'Is Tony there?' and if I should answer it in
her room I will say, 'You've got the wrong number,'
and then I'll call you back.

Lxx

To write Lee was to plunge into conspiracy, but I thought that Lee, twelve years younger than Julia and then a mere seventy-eight, might be more approachable on the subject of Mabel. I knew nothing about him except for Stephen's descriptions in his diary and for Julia's in her letters to Steve: "When he comes in the room, it's like God walked in." I wrote him when I returned East after my initial Hollywood trip, and he replied with his business card, "Garden Enterprises," stamped in purple "RETIRED." I was to write to his post-office-box number in Sanford Station and never to his Pacoima address lest Julia see my letter. When I returned to Hollywood the following summer, I could telephone him according to the instructions above.

By that time, I knew that he had been born with the century and had come to California in 1927. "I'm just an old Swedish Baptist," he wrote me, "born in Great Falls, Montana, where the Catholics were bad, the Presbyterians were bad, and even other Baptists were not too good." Before he reached Los Angeles, Lee had been a cowpuncher, gambler, railroad worker, waiter, masseur, landscape gardener, and cook. Somewhere he had taken a correspondence course in "pen and ink" and signed his letters with a cartooned cowboy next to his name of kisses, "Lxx."

Lee had come to work for Mabel on July 31, 1929, sent by Melruth's Employment Agency to be a general helper and handyman. He carried Mabel about when she was too weak to walk and, after Mabel died, he went to work for Cody as his masseur and cook. After Cody died, he teamed up with Julia, although as she was to say many times, "There is *no marriage* relationship between us." I hoped that Julia had not burned all of Mabel's diaries or had forgotten some letters somewhere. As Julia's health and watchfulness declined, Lee would send me what he called his "stuff and stuff and stuff," salvaged from buildings and garages in Greater Los Angeles for half a century. He had salvaged lumber once from St. Vincent's hospital to build himself a garage. "I've got the wood that Julia walked on for my floor and sides," he said. Sometimes he would send me a recipe, like the corned beef and cabbage recipe for "Cody's Stinky Dinners." Othertimes scandal sheets from the past like *Midnight Close-Up*, with stories titled "We Need a Nudist in the White House," "Thugs Hang Man from Meat Hook and Rip His Guts Out," or "He Slices Off His Wife's Ears and Feeds Them to His Dog." And once in a while a scribbled note in Mabel's hand tucked in a book or an envelope of snapshots. Whatever else he was, Lee was some kind of real.

SEPTEMBER 11, 1921, NEW YORK

Mabel was sleeping late in her Ritz-Carlton suite, hungover from a Saturday night celebration at Delmonico's. She was celebrating the completion of *Molly O'* that marked her return to Hollywood, to Sennett, to health and sanity and hope. She had made the last chase shots in a blimp at Pensacola, Florida. While the rest of the company returned to Hollywood, Mabel skedaddled to New York to rest up after ten months' hard work. She was to return in time for the grand premiere in Los Angeles on October 9 at the Mission Theater, the Theater that Mack had bought and revamped as a showcase for his star.

Mack had advertised *Molly O'*, "A Drama of Youth and

Optimism," as a born-again *Mickey*: "The creator of MICKEY, the star of MICKEY and a picture bigger than MICKEY!" He had invested $40,000 to make it "the most costly production that has been produced in the world." He had promoted a plugger song just like the *Mickey* song, in "Molly O', I love you." Mabel, like a prodigal sheep, had "returned to the fold," and he couldn't help rubbing it in a bit in the "Prepared Reviews" sent in advance to lazy newspaper critics: "Frankly, Miss Normand was a disappointment to us in all of her vehicles since MICKEY until we saw her in MOLLY O'."

With Mabel in *Molly O'* Sennett was turning back the hands of the clock in every way. His publicists maintained that Mabel "retains all the charming youth and pep of the days Mack Sennett 'found' her and made her a star." Molly O' Dair was an Irish Cinderella, "Happy, sincere, unaffected Molly O' rose from obscurity in the slums to the heights of affluence and happiness." To Mack, it was the reality of his dream that, in 1921, he saw actualized in owning a mountain top, a theater, a yacht, thousands of dollars worth of stocks, 500 prime hogs, a quartz mine called "The Normandie," and a star called Mabel Normand. Despite the fact that Mabel had told him she would return to Mack the producer but never to Mack the lover, Mack did not believe that time changes everything. Mack believed in the timelessness of fairy tale and reworked its plot irrespective of change. In 1948, Sennett was still reworking the plot of *Molly O'* for television, under a new title, *When Grandma Was a Girl.* "It deals with a more gentle and simple time," Mack wrote, "with the hope that its re-telling may capture some of the nostalgic charm of that earlier day when a good five-cent cigar was not a rarity."

Even in 1921, it dealt with a more gentle and simple time that audiences hungered for and had never had. In 1921, as Griffith exploited America's nostalgia for prewar innocence with *Way Down East,* so did Mack with *Molly O',* which hearkened back to the ethnic class comedy of *Peg O' My Heart* of a decade before. Mack reworked the old battles between the poor and the swells, where ditchdigger O'Dair embarrasses his womenfolk in a pair of "Comedy Meals." And he reworked his subtitles, rejecting

"The Charity Ball — where the classes mingled with the masses" in favor of the more poetic, "where Rosie O'Grady and the Governor's Lady joined hands for the good of the cause."

The result was a box-office hit that was *"funny, thrilling* and *sentimental,"* said the *New York Times,* despite a story that was "pure hoakum." The actor and playwright Albert Hackett, whom I found at Central Park West, had played Mabel's younger brother in the film, and he recalled the whole film as surreal. Of the climactic chase scene, he remembered, "Lowell Sherman got her up in the blimp and tried to seduce her, but you couldn't really tell whether he was seducing her or just taking off her clothes and putting them on himself." Sequences were even more chaotic than *Mickey's,* and Mack floundered in his chronic inability to edit a feature-length film. This time he was saved by the incompetence of his film cutter, an ex-prize fighter named Al McNeil, who inadvertently left one reel behind in the studio when rushing *Molly O'* to its first preview in Santa Barbara.

Molly O' did not open on October 9 as planned. Mack delayed the premier until December because of what happened on September 10. In Hollywood memories, that was a day that would live in infamy, although no one had a clue at the time to the extent of the peril or the nature of the betrayal. No one had a clue because America, like Mabel in *Molly O',* was turning back the hands of the clock to a time of youth and optimism, when "the will to do" made time stand still. At the dawn of the twenties, Mack said, "We made big pictures, made big money and thought it would last forever."

September 11 was a Sunday, and when Mabel woke with her hangover, she asked Julia to order up a gallon of chocolate ice cream and a copy of the *New York Times.* Mabel was feeling good about her work in *Molly O'* and about her personal comeback from drugs. If she owed her professional comeback to Sennett, she owed her personal one to Taylor. Taylor was the only man who had ever really cared about her, Mabel thought, cared about her as a person instead of as a commodity. There was his daily telegram on her bedside table and a hotel room full of flowers to prove it. Mabel would have been astonished to learn that the owner of

Delmonico's, where she'd had too much gin, was married to the former wife of William Desmond Taylor when he was known as "Pete" Tanner. Mabel didn't know that Taylor had ever had a wife, or another life and another name and another occupation in New York City.

Mabel opened the paper to look for a Sunday afternoon movie, but a headline caught her eye:

ROSCOE ARBUCKLE FACES AN INQUIRY
ON WOMAN'S DEATH.

The dateline read September 10, San Francisco. It seems that a girl Mabel knew in Hollywood as the current girl friend of old Pathé Lehrman had died during a weekend party given by Arbuckle at the St. Francis Hotel. The girl's name was Virginia Rappe (pronounced Rap-pay, accent grave over the "e," as W. C. Fields would say). There was no charge, detectives said, but Arbuckle was being detained for questioning. Mabel picked up the phone and called Minta Durfee's sister on Ninety-seventh Street. Mabel knew that Minta was visiting friends at Martha's Vineyard that weekend where there were no phones. Minta's sister said that she had just seen the paper herself and was about to send a telegram. Minta had been living in New York for the last three years, ever since she and Roscoe had separated. But they'd remained good friends, Roscoe had sent her a new automobile for Christmas, and Mabel knew that Minta would defend Roscoe to the death.

The first report did not suggest that sort of crisis, but it was worrisome. Any publicity not put out by the studio was worrisome. Mabel knew something about that from two years of drugs. Mabel knew nothing about the San Francisco party except what Lowell Sherman had told her when the *Molly O'* company finished shooting in Pensacola. Sherman told her he was going to vacation in Hollywood's playground, San Francisco, where easy booze and sex had always been traditional come-ons for Calvinist Los Angeles. From the paper Mabel learned that Sherman had driven North on September 4 with Freddie Fischback and Roscoe Arbuckle in Fatty's brand new $25,000 custom-built Pierce-Arrow with foldaway cocktail bar and toilet. Roscoe had reserved a twelfth-floor suite at the St. Francis over Labor Day weekend "to renew his pep." He needed to, Mabel knew, because he had just completed three films at once in a grueling but profitable schedule under Adolph Zukor. Now Mabel learned that the boys had had a two-day binge as planned and had returned to Los Angeles on September 7 on the "Harvard" car-ferry. On September 10, Arbuckle had volunteered to drive back up to San Francisco to help investigators discover the cause of Virginia's death at the Wakefield Sanatorium the day before. His arrival at the courthouse was social news, and reporters described Fatty's chic driving costume of "dark green golf breeches with stockings to match." Fatty flashed reporters his big grin.

Morning headlines on the twelfth were a shocker. In the *New York Times* Mabel read, "ARBUCKLE IS JAILED ON MURDER CHARGE." Arbuckle had been quizzed for three hours by the Deputy District Attorney and then locked in a jail cell overnight. Next day, District Attorney Matthew Brady announced, "We have evidence that shows conclusively either an assault or an attempted assault was perpetrated. The evidence disclosed beyond question that Miss Rappe died of internal injuries caused by Arbuckle." Brady charged Arbuckle with murder in the first degree.

Mabel was stunned. She knew there must be some terrible mistake. She phoned Minta, who was about to leave for San Francisco, and Mabel saw her off at Grand Central, where she pinned an orchid on Minta's mink. For luck. In New York, Mabel followed the developments of the case in the papers with shocked disbelief. Anyone who knew Roscoe knew a rape and murder impossible. "Why he is just a great big lovable overgrown boy who is really very shy with women," Minta told reporters. Only three days after the first headline did Mabel sense what was really at stake. She read her future in adjoining headlines:

ARBUCKLE INNOCENT DECLARES HIS WIFE
600 THEATRES HERE EXCLUDE ARBUCKLE

"Audiences Hiss Films," the subhead ran. The moment Arbuckle was charged with a crime, Sid Grauman withdrew *Gasoline Gus*, starring Fatty Arbuckle, and substituted the latest film of Mary

136

Miles Minter. Within five months, Grauman would repeat the process with Minter's and Mabel's films. Mabel saw the handwriting on the wall in Pathé Lehrman's pronouncement, "There are some people who are a disgrace to the film business. . . . They are the kind who resort to cocaine and opium and who participate in orgies of the lowest character. They should be driven out of the picture business." The day newspapers credited the words of a fink like Pathé they were all in trouble, the trouble instantly headlined by Hearst,

PLAN TO SEND ARBUCKLE TO DEATH ON GALLOWS.

The public was out for blood, and Mabel could not understand why. Arbuckle, just thirty-four, was so popular that he was until that moment the highest paid star in the world. In eight months, he had made seven features for Paramount at a salary of $3000 a *day*. He had recently made his first trip abroad to the acclaim of the crowned heads of Europe. He had just bought the Vernon Tigers baseball team, which had just won its first league championship. He had just bought his fifth luxury car, the specially designed "superautomobile" with "cellerette." Like Mabel, he was as generous as he was innocent, and he gave the most lavish parties in town. He too seemed to want to give everything away.

Mabel tried to piece together what had happened from the papers, but facts were scarce when even the sedate *New York Times* broadcast headlines like "ARBUCKLE DRAGGED RAPPE GIRL TO ROOM, WOMAN TESTIFIES." The woman who testified was a woman Mabel had never heard of, a woman named Bambina Maude Delmont, a friend of Virginia Rappe's. Virginia and Maude, with a seedy character named Al Semnacher, were staying in another hotel when Arbuckle's friend Fischback ran into them and said, "Join the party." Arbuckle had begun to dispense the usual bootleg gin and juice around noon on Labor Day to a dozen or so guests, one of whom was the daughter-in-law of temperance preacher Billy Sunday. It was that kind of party. By mid-afternoon, the party was rolling, and the girls were dancing drunk. Maude had slipped into a pair of men's pajamas to be comfortable. Fatty was in pajamas and bathrobe because he had burned his butt on a hot stove on the last day of shooting, and pajamas were more comfortable than trousers. By three o'-clock, Virginia was violently sick in one of the bathrooms. Ten minutes later, she was trying to rip her clothes off and was scream-ing hysterically with pain. Arbuckle called the hotel doctor, and the house detective checked in, but everything seemed to be in order except for a girl freaked out on gin. Maude called another doctor later in the evening, who gave Virginia a morphine injec-tion for pain. Maude was sufficiently unworried to go to bed with the house detective.

Before the morphine, Maude and others had tried a number of home remedies on Virginia without success, sure-cures like immersing her in a cold bath, pouring bicarbonate of soda down her throat, putting ice cubes on her nude body. Nothing worked but gin and morphine. Next morning, when Virginia had not improved, Maude called more doctors and hired a nurse to stay on while Arbuckle, Fischback, and Sherman took the ferry back to Los Angeles. The combined doctors never publicly diagnosed anything worse than too much booze until three days later when Virginia died of peritonitis.

What Mabel could not know because nobody knew except District Attorney Brady was that his sole "evidence" against Ar-buckle was the perjured testimony of the woman named Bambina Maude Delmont. What not even Brady knew was that Maude was not only a prostitute, she was also a bigamist and a con-woman, whose "duty," as she said, forced her to accuse Arbuckle of rape and murder. "Virginia was a good girl," she told reporters. "I know that she has led a clean life, and it is my duty to see this thing through." She did not tell reporters or other investigators that her duty to her profession and to her accomplice Al Sem-nacher had forced her to play the old badger game. Two days before Virginia died, Maude sent identical telegrams to a lawyer in Los Angeles and a lawyer in San Francisco: "WE HAVE ARBUCKLE IN A HOLE HERE. CHANCE TO MAKE SOME MONEY OUT OF HIM." Nor did Maude tell reporters the facts of good girl Virginia. At twenty-seven, Virginia was not the saintly victim depicted by the press. She had had an illegitimate baby at sixteen, had undergone several abortions since then, was suffering from gonorrhea at the time of her death, and was once again pregnant. She had also suffered from chronic cystitis for a decade and had been forbidden alcohol by her doctors. Whenever she drank, her bladder caused her such pain that she often screamed and tore off her clothing. Reporters failed to tell their readers at her death that the sanatorium where she died was a maternity hospital.

Reporters did not know that the night before her death, her attending doctor had called in a Stanford University surgeon, who said that the peritonitis made surgery impossible. After she died on the following afternoon, however, both doctors performed an illegal post-mortem in which they removed and destroyed all of her reproductive organs. They then announced that the cause of death was a ruptured bladder. By mere chance a deputy coroner got wind of the illegal autopsy and started snooping. By evening, reporters had located Maude, who was only too ready to claim that Arbuckle had attacked and raped Virginia. Attorney Brady was all too ready to fabricate a case that would make him famous overnight. He quickly discovered that Maude was lying, but the stakes were far too high to let facts interfere with fiction. The complexities of Brady's fiction were not uncovered until 1976 when David Yallop in his *The Day the Laughter Stopped* accused the doctors of covering up a botched abortion. Today, few even in Hollywood believe what Lonnie D'Orsa told me, "Fatty got a dirty deal because this Virginia Rappe, she was a bum." They don't believe because fiction is far stronger than fact, and Arbuckle, as Yallop said, "walked right into a myth in the making and gave it form."

Myth, the noted mythographer Roland Barthes has said, is not defined by truth but by alibi. Today, Fatty Arbuckle is remembered not for his hundreds of comedies but for having raped a girl with a Coke bottle. Fatty gave form to the myth of the monster rapist. And because Mabel was paired with Fatty in the minds of the myth-makers, she too was caught in a myth that was an alibi for everybody's lost innocence after the Great War.

At first, Mabel seemed to have escaped. Lowell Sherman was the one Mack worried about in delaying the premier of *Molly O'.* Sherman eluded police and reporters and had more or less disappeared until Albert Hackett ran into him in New York shortly before *Molly O'* was to open at the Strand. Sherman had dispensed tickets to friends for the opening, and they cheered him when he entered the theater, Hackett recalled, but when cast credits appeared on the screen, "Sherman's name had been wiped clean off." The purge of comedy had begun, and Mabel would be caught in the purge. I discovered that the need for alibi was so strong in the craziness of the twenties that Mabel's entrapment seemed inevitable, given time. Mabel would furnish the opportunity. The public, conditioned by and responding to a decade of faked images, was now taking revenge by inventing mythic images of its own.

From the beginning, factual evidence had almost nothing to do with the three successive trials of Arbuckle. At his first trial on September 22, the judge recognized the paucity of evidence and reduced the charge from murder to manslaughter. On December 4, Arbuckle's first trial ended in a hung jury, ten to two for acquittal. On February 3, his second trial ended in a hung jury, ten to two for conviction. And on April 12, his third trial ended after one of the shortest jury sessions in history. The jury returned after five minutes, just long enough to compose their statement of exoneration:

> *There was not the slightest proof adduced to connect*
> *him in any way with the commission of a crime. . . .*
> *We wish him success, and hope that the American*
> *people will take the judgment of 14 men and women*
> *who have sat listening for 31 days to the evidence*
> *that Roscoe Arbuckle is entirely innocent and free*
> *from all blame.*

But Arbuckle was not innocent of the success they wished him nor free from the blame of money and fame. It was the American success story that was on trial. Judge Lazarus had instructed the jury at Arbuckle's first trial, "In my opinion we are not trying Roscoe Arbuckle alone. . . . We are, in a sense, trying ourselves, our morals, our present day social standards." They were also trying the imagery by which America projected its pursuit of happiness.

Proof, judgment, evidence were powerless against the power of images. Hollywood brought in Presbyterian elder Will H. Hays to purify its image, and the public cheered when Hays in April of 1922 banned Arbuckle and his works from the screen. When Hays rescinded his ban eight months later, the public howled and enforced their own. Under the pseudonym "William Goodrich," Roscoe attempted to direct comic shorts during the next few years, but it was no go. Keaton gave him a directing job in *Sherlock, Jr.*, and Hearst did the same in Marion Davies's *Red Mill*, but his broken image broke the man. During the trials, close personal friends like Mabel and Keaton were powerless to help him and were persuaded not to testify on his behalf because Hollywood testimony could only hurt him. Adela Rogers's father, Earl Rogers, refused to represent him because his status as Hollywood's finest criminal lawyer would imply Arbuckle's guilt. Industry moguls were powerless to help him because their own necks were on the block, and the good of the business community was at stake.

After the trials, Arbuckle tried performing stand-up comic routines in nightclubs and vaudeville. In 1928, he opened his own nightclub in Culver City, "The Plantation Club," and Mabel sent a giant replica of him in flowers for opening night. But he was finished the moment he was accused. He died broke and in debt on June 29, 1933, in the Park Central Hotel in New York, after too many wives and too much booze and too much publicity. What's the worst thing that can happen? To arrive, Roscoe had said.

"They kicked the hell out of Arbuckle because the Hays organization was looking for somebody to pin something on and Arbuckle was the unlucky guy," Hal Roach told me. Arbuckle was unlucky because he stood for the crime of new money, which was a crime of class that condemned Hollywood as a whole. "Hollywood as a moving-picture colony must go," an Eastern theater owner announced, because Hollywood was parvenue: "The minority, who have made money quickly, persons with little character and less morals, have had their heads turned and have cast aside all restraint." Threatened, the minority was as quick to name names as later, when accused of a crime of political belief. Lehrman, an ex-barboy himself, cast the first stone when he called Arbuckle a low vulgarian: "This is what comes of taking vulgarians from the gutter and giving them enormous salaries and making idols of them. . . . He was a barboy in a San Francisco saloon. He washed the dishes and cleaned the spittoons. Such people don't know how to get a 'kick' out of life except in a beastly way." Even Anita Loos attacked Arbuckle in *Hollywood Goodbye* when she learned that the star King Alphonse of Spain wanted most to meet, when he was visiting the Fairbanks at Pickfair, was Fatty Arbuckle. "I couldn't see much culture where a king wanted to associate with Fatty Arbuckle." The moment Arbuckle was accused, the Theatre Owners Association of California resolved to remove Arbuckle from the screen because "California people are bitter over the undesirable notoriety the state has received," announced the Association Secretary, Glen Harper of Corona. That name rang a bell. Glen Harper was my black-sheep uncle whom I had met only once because Uncle Glen was not respectable. He was divorced and, for his sins, ran a movie theater.

Arbuckle had lowered the moral tone and class standing of the entire state. Arbuckle was less a victim of industry greed than of its moral sentimentality. Hollywood believed its own publicity as "public benefactors, . . . earnestly endeavoring to bring enlightenment and enjoyment into weary and dreary lives, laboring loyally to contribute their share to human progress and human happiness." Hollywood believed in its political mandate: "We are part of every American home, not through any selfish desire, but because it is the will of the public." Hollywood believed in its moral responsibility and seconded the resolution of the Women's Clubs of Hollywood that "Hollywood shall become a strictly moral residential district" and that "the stain attached to Hollywood by reason of the alleged immorality of the picture people must and shall be wiped out." Hollywood even believed in its racial redemption. After an attack by a Los Angeles reformer — "When the Jews get together to say what my boy and girl shall see on the screen, then I am going to fight" — Hollywood applauded a DAR member who came to its defense. "The Jew magnates," she said, "agreed among themselves to appoint as the absolute arbiter of the motion picture industry, in all its branches, a Gentile."

From such spoor the monster rapist was born. Adela's father had predicted that the public would crucify Roscoe because of his fat. A fat rapist was monstrous, and actress Miriam Cooper projected the image as fact when she wrote, "Fatty had raped her, falling on her with his huge body." But it was less Arbuckle's fat than his baby fat that crucified him. With their kid comedy, Fatty and Mabel had cashed in on the vogue for baby innocence by publicity shots that put them in baby carriages and baby clothes. An ad for *Brewster's Millions,* Fatty's last film before his arrest, showed "Baby Fatty" in an out-sized high chair, being spoon-fed by a real baby. The majority of Fatty's fans were not kings like Alphonse and Al Capone (who kept a pin-up of Fatty when he moved around), but women and girls to whom Fatty was a living doll. As one fan wrote to *Motion Picture Magazine,*

> *When I'm tired of watching "vamping" by the mile*
> *And I wish to clean my mind out and to smile,*
> *I go where that dimpled "Fatty"*
> *Makes me laugh until I'm batty*
> *With his innocent and cunning baby smile.*

"Mothers loved Fatty best of all," Minta said, "because he never did anything dirty." The myth of Fatty brought to a head the war between the "dirty" and the "clean," headed by the mothers of America. As early as 1916, in the midst of the Fatty and Mabel films, Arbuckle had said, "My pictures are turned out with clean hands and, therefore, with a clear conscience. Nothing would grieve me more than to have mothers say, 'Let's not go there today. Arbuckle is playing and he isn't fit for the children to see.'" In 1921, the Women's Clubs and their Vigilante Committees insisted that Arbuckle be permanently banned: "What we do object to is having him paraded before little boys and girls to be idolized and emulated. . . . Let's have our fun and our fun-makers clean." When Arbuckle was first brought from his jail cell for arraignment at the courthouse, the head of the Women's Vigilante Committee of San Francisco was appalled when she saw some of her members automatically applaud the appearance of their favorite star. "Women of America, do your duty!" she cried, and they covered him with spit. With his innocent and cunning baby smile, Fatty had betrayed the mothers of America. Worse, said a Methodist preacher, "Roscoe Arbuckle had betrayed the innocent childhood of America."

UNCLEAN

By 1921, a generation of moviemakers had betrayed the innocent imagination of America and, like other professional virgins, America cried, "RAPE!" Since a baby could not rape without aid, what could be more monstrous as his tool than a bottle of soda pop, symbol of youth and refreshment? When Al Semnacher described the ice-pack treatment applied to Virginia Rappe, he claimed that Arbuckle had pushed ice "in her snitch." One of Virginia's nurses had testified that Virginia in her pain had asked, "What could be broken in my insides?" What else but a Coke bottle wielded by the filthy against the clean?

On the very day that Virginia Rappe was buried in Hollywood Cemetery, the new head of the Motion Picture Directors Association, William Desmond Taylor, announced to the Public Welfare Committee of Los Angeles that Hollywood was "cleaning house" and henceforth would produce only "the cleanest of films." Arbuckle himself had predicted, in August of 1919, "Now that the war is over the public will desire 'clean comedy' more than ever." Postwar America engaged in a purge of the body politic by a program of personal cleanliness.

The camera had made man's flesh visible as never before, and new products were invented daily to decontaminate, deconstipate, and deodorize it. The camera closeup had filled the screen with dirty flesh ever since the first movie kiss in 1896 appalled the clean. The "prolonged pasturing" of May Irwin and John Rice in *The Kiss* was beastly enough when life-size, clean viewers cried, but "magnified to Gargantuan proportions and repeated three times over it is absolutely disgusting." The camera had created a world of Gargantuan flesh in comic Fatty, who all along had performed the role of classic scapegoat. Now, to get rid of Fatty was to get rid of all the sins flesh is heir to, like offensive body odor. An editorial in the *New York Times* drew exactly that analogy: "It will do the picture business no good to have [Arbuckle] tottering back into the parlor, bringing his aroma with him. An odor clings to him and it will cling no matter how he sprays himself with Biblical analogies." In the metonymic nostrils of the reformers, the images themselves stunk of sin and of the corruption of the flesh. The Reverend John Roach Stratton, who became the Scourge of Hollywood in the name of Christendom, proclaimed Roscoe Arbuckle a stench and a disease beyond the remedy of high colonics: "You cannot purify a polecat, you cannot denature a smallpox epidemic. . . . You cannot cure the organic disease of film corruption . . . with soothing syrup."

The Reverend Stratton's denouncements were fueled by the industry's own efforts to purify itself of moral, religious, and racial charges of UNCLEAN. In 1920, King Vidor had taken "A Creed and a Pledge" as pure as Baden-Powell's: "I will not knowingly produce a picture that contains anything I do not believe to be absolutely true to human nature, anything that could injure anyone nor anything unclean in thought and action." UNCLEAN covered a multitude of sins named now by the new Hays Code: smoking, drinking, stomach dancing, shimmying, spooning, jazzing, belching, "and all sordidness." UNCLEAN was a matter of class. The base-born were dirty by nature, the upper classes by art. Only the middle were clean. The Hays Code paralleled the Volstead Act in confusing social norms and manners with moral imperatives and criminal law. Famous Players-Lasky soon amplified the Hays Code with their own to guarantee the CLEAN that the following subjects would all be "treated within the careful limits of good taste": "CRIMES AGAINST THE LAW, SEX, VULGARITY, OBSCENITY, DANCES, PROFANITY, NUDITY, NATIONAL FEELINGS, RELIGION AND REPELLENT SUBJECTS such as HANGINGS or SURGICAL OPERATIONS."

Before the Hays Commandments, the industry had ridiculed the absurdities of movie conventions dictated by public mores in *Photoplay*'s "Commandments of the Films":

> *Item: Smoking is a practice indulged in only by*
> *vampires, adventuresses, pleasure-loving ladies of the*

Top Mabel with Sam Goldwyn, left, Chaplin, right, in 1919 at Goldwyn's new studio in Culver City.
Bottom Goldwyn's Eminent Artists and Writers in 1919: (*l. to r.*) Grace Kingsley, Margaret Ettinger, Mabel in her *Jinx* costume, Rupert Hughes, Sam Goldwyn, Geraldine Farrar, Rex Beach, Florence Lawrence.

Top   Mabel and her director of *Mickey*, Dick Jones, on the
set of *Molly O'*.
Bottom   Mabel with Mack and Dick Jones at the premier of
Molly O' at the Mission Theater in Los Angeles, December 1,
1921, three months after the Fatty Arbuckle scandal.

ensemble and callous leaders of the haut monde.

Item: No gentleman may confer a kiss upon a maiden unless they are engaged. No woman may shoot a man — not even in defense of her life or her virtue.

Item: No wife may inform her husband that he is about to become a father. No lady who prizes her good name has breakfast in bed, for it is a sign of fast living and spiritual indolence.

Item: Anyone who gives or attends a party where there are cocktails, jazz music, confetti-throwing and shimmying is an apostle of evil headed straight for perdition.

Now the industry through Hays' "morality clause," better known as the "Arbuckle clause," legislated such conventions into law dictating private behavior. Any performer "tending to shock, insult, or offend the community or outrage public morals and decency" was subject to immediate firing.

Mabel's Topsy character, on and off the screen, based as it was on shock, insult, and outrage, was automatically outlawed by the "morality clause." Worse, Mabel's entire career as a comic voluptuous was outlawed by the "impurity clause" that stated, "Impure love must not be the subject of *comedy* or farce or treated as material for *laughter.*" The new Puritanism that forbade the showing of udders in a milking scene could hardly tolerate the exposure of man's animal nature that was the basis of Old Comedy since the Greeks. Slapstick was now UNCLEAN and therefore perverse. A Philadelphia journalist who had compared Arbuckle's "orgy" to a Roman bacchanal accused slapstick of sadism worthy a Nero: "Arbuckle was a master of slapstick comedy — the fall, the kick, the shove, the thumb in the eye." Suddenly the public found itself guilty of complicity in a new crime, the crime of buffoonery. "We have here a criminal with millions, which was built by the cheapest kind of buffoonery," said a spokeswoman of the Women's Vigilantes. "We have been responsible for that buffoonery for we have countenanced it and laughed at it." The buffoonery of Fatty and Mabel had caused them to betray the nation's vulgarity, and for that there was no forgiveness.

The untouchables of comedy were now universally UN-CLEAN. The purge of vulgarity by the moral majority had unleashed a new virus, Gilbert Seldes warned in 1924. "The village virus of the Genteel" was undermining the vigorous masculine honesty of slapstick with the ladylike pretentions of "refined" comedy. The virus was emasculating the country with its shams, Seldes snarled. To enthrone earnestness and banish laughter was to banish Mabel. Mabel tried to refine her comedy, but laughter kept breaking through. The one thing Jack Mulhall remembered in his ninety-first year when I found him at the Motion Picture Country Home was her irreverence. "Mabel Normand? Unforgettable," he said in his Irish brogue, recalling their first days at Biograph. "She had a wit that was devastating. Oh god."

The public that wanted to purge the screen of flesh willed a return to the fleshless image of Little Eva. "Movie 'Vamp' Extinct," an editorialist declared in a 1922 *Chicago Tribune.* "Public Wants Little Eva Type Now." The Little Eva type meant "good little girls," he wrote, "with golden hair, blue eyes, sincerity and innocence." The public wanted the illusion of sincerity no matter the cost in sham. They wanted Mary Pickford at thirty playing a ten-year-old Eva. And when Pickford played her own age in *Coquette,* the public hooted her off the screen, a martyr to nostalgia when Little-Eva Christianity, as one historian said, began to function as camp.

As a bad little girl, Mabel had no place to go. The comic outlaw was outlawed by the changes of time. Mabel was twenty-nine in 1921 and too old to adopt the strategies of the new "Tom-girls" in getting around the ban on flesh. In *Molly O'* Mabel was still transforming a tomboy into the belle of the ball, but the style was as anachronistic as the plot. The new style was an androgynous "It." Asked to define It, Clara Bow said, "I think it must be my vivacity, my fearlessness and perhaps the fact that I'm just a regular girl . . . a Tom-girl." Mabel's Tom-boy, her Dirty Four, her band of Sports, had paved the way for the new band of rebels that left the old girls behind. Mabel's gang had looked like girls no matter how much they behaved like boys. The new gang neutered themselves and, in one of those reversals common to history, became sexy by being sexless. The Tom-girl purged herself of flesh *and* sex by bobbing her hair *and* her breasts to produce the Flapper.

The Flapper was simply a Tom-girl in galoshes. She put a boy's body on a girl's legs to create a third sex. The impact of the new Boy-Girl was as radical as surgery. Colleen Moore, with her bobbed hair, bobbed skirt, cupid mouth, and cartoon Ella Cinder eyes was about to flash that astonishing image on the screen in *Flaming Youth.* "No girl had ever appeared on the screen before with straight hair, bangs and a boyish figure," Adela told me. "It changed the rhythm, culture and even the moral tone of every generation up to now," Anita Loos told me. When I looked up Colleen Moore in Paso Robles, I was startled to find youth still flaming in her seventies, her hair as black, lips as red, eyes as bright, and wit as merry as that screen image of 1923. "Every college girl in America went to see me in *Flaming Youth,*" Colleen told me," and there they were, the way they thought, and after that the way they looked and dressed — sexy, sexless."

Mabel's type of sexy comedy returned disguised by sexlessness, but the Fundamentalists, aware of Calvin's preachment, were not fooled: "Sainte Paule meaneth that women must not be impudent, they must not be tomboyes, to be shorte, they must not be unchaste." Tom-boys were sexual perverts, who flaunted public morals and decency, were undependable, undisciplined and, as a Harvard psychologist "proved," were frivolous girls who don't "care to bother with burdensome mental problems." The bobbed-hair flapper was the latest I-Don't-Care Girl, whose creed was summed up by Clara Bow: "We did as we pleased. We stayed up late. We dressed the way we wanted. . . . *WE* had more fun."

Actress Leatrice Joy, now a radiant silver-haired grandmother in Riverdale, Connecticut, recalled the spirit of the Tom-girls in a game she played with her first husband, actor Jack Gilbert, called "Do You?" The game was a sexual dare. When Gilbert walked into Wellman's Barber Shop in Hollywood and said to Leatrice, "I want my hair cut, do you?" she replied, "I do . . . I do . . . I do." She played the game by the rules and had her hair cut as short as his. And when her Studio bosses saw her, they moaned, "My god, the only female star we had left."

The sexual battles were, as usual, money battles. Female stars in numbers were often making bigger money than men. Colleen Moore's pay after the success of *Flaming Youth* was higher than that of the President of the United States. "The whole domestic scene was wrecked," Colleen Moore told me, "when a movie actress was getting $1500 a week and her boy friend shoving props on a back lot was getting $150. . . . It killed romance."

A return to the simpler, gentler image of Little Eva was of course a return to the security of romance images based on simpler categories of money and sex. Mabel's next film was to be *Suzanna,* an exercise in pure nostalgia, in which she turned back the hands of the clock to 1835 in "a romance of old California." After the Arbuckle scandal, Mack said, "I needed a big one to throw in the teeth of the fools and harpies." But a public that needed the alibi of a monster rapist to explain its loss of innocence needed its sexual parallel, the alibi of a monster murderess. As Fatty gave form to one, within five months Mabel gave form to the other.

MURDERESS

SEPTEMBER 30, 1978, PACOIMA

[Lee telephoned me at 6:30 A.M. at the Montecito.]
*She can't hardly read her letters anymore. Has a radio
on twenty-four hours a day. She's about twenty-five
feet from me now, but she can't hear me. You see the
reason you can't find out much about Mabel in
Hollywood, Julia didn't let anybody get near her.
Reporters came after Mabel died, but she wouldn't
tell them anything. She was as jealous of Mabel as
she's jealous of me now. If she knew I was talking to
you she'd just die.*

*Now it's her pride too. She don't want anyone to
see her lying in bed.*

FEBRUARY 2, 1922, HOLLYWOOD

Mabel was shivering as she dressed in her apartment at
Seventh and Vermont because it was cold at 7:30 that morning,
so cold that orange growers had had to smoke their trees. Mabel
was struggling with a Spanish comb and mantilla for the day's
shooting on *Suzanna.* Mabel was feeling good. "The whole world
and my future seemed cheerful and promising," Mabel recalled
to Sutherland. "Not only was the picture a good one, but I felt
that at last I was coming into my own." Despite the Arbuckle
mess, the premiere of *Molly O'* on December 1 had been a grand
success, attended by a host of celebrities and city officials, including the mayor of Los Angeles. Reviews and receipts had been so
good that Mack had spent last night at Tom Ince's house plan-
ning foreign distribution rights for the film. To capitalize on
Mabel's return, Mack had also just released an old burlesque of

151

historical romance that they had made six years ago called *Oh, Mabel Behave.*

With *Suzanna,* Mack was really coming through on his promise of better roles and bigger productions. He built a complete Spanish town of the period on the Studio lot. He hired Madame Violet Unholtz, of the Art Institute of Chicago, as *coutumière* to create historically authentic costumes. From Colonel Selig's Zoo he hired a menagerie of "black bears, timber wolves, coyotes, fighting cocks, a Mexican bull, and ten thousand head of steer." Whatever Mabel wanted, Mabel got. Mabel had just got a new pedigreed German shepherd and a snazzy new English convertible coupé, black with Victor Cord tires.

Mack was still wooing Mabel even though Taylor had been squiring Mabel around ever since she returned to Hollywood. Taylor was the most formidable rival Mack had ever had. With Taylor, Mabel talked about Art and Philosophy and Ideas. "He was on the intellectual side and not exactly my style of man," Mack said, "not that I held that against him." But Mack did hold that against him because Taylor was exactly the opposite of Mack. "Mabel grew studious," Mack lamented, "and I couldn't follow her there."

In the context of Hollywood, Taylor was a soldier, sportsman, scholar, everything Mack was not. He was elegant, articulate, educated, cool. In 1922, he was forty-nine, seven years Mack's senior, stood 6'1", and was described as ascetic, "with thin wide lips, a thin aristocratic nose, high cheek bones and gray hair." Ulcers had left him with a bad stomach for which he took milk of magnesia. Smallpox had left him with a brownish skin. Adela remembered that he was "lean and deeply tanned" and that "he had a crooked smile." Julia remembered that he was "kind of cold-hearted and old." Mary Miles Minter remembered that he was "too much of a god to call him Bill, so I called him Desmond." George James Hopkins remembered that he was a "private silent man, who would have hated all the publicity about his death." Hopkins thought Mabel had been good for Taylor. "She made him laugh," he said.

Taylor had been good for Mabel. His discipline had steadied her wildness, and he took her aspirations seriously. To fulfill her dreams of being an artist, she had taken up music and painting and writing. She was penning little biographies of her friends, she said, and composing poems like "Poem."

> *There's a circle of gold in the sky*
> *And the sun's far out in the West*
> *It's that wonderful hour before dusk*
> *That hour we both loved best.*

She was also studying French with Georges Jaumier whom she called "Frenchy," a Hollywood tutor she shared with a younger nimbus rising in the East, Mary Miles Minter.

At the dawn of the new year of 1922, things were looking up generally. The morning papers of February 2 brought news that the Disarmament Conference had just taken a "First Great Step Toward Preventing Wars in the Future" and that Lenin "was abolishing Bolshevism and reinstating Capitalism." The jury of the second Arbuckle trial was still out, and no news was good news. Will Hays had vanquished "the day of the gloom spreader" and was inaugurating a new era of cleanliness in thought, word, and deed. Harold Lloyd was inaugurating a new era of comedy with *A Sailor-Made Man* at the Symphony Theatre and Edward Everett Horton with a timely drama, *Scandal,* at the Majestic. The president of the Motion Picture Directors Association was predicting a new era for the director, whose power would exceed the editor's and statesman's. "The reign of hokum has passed," proclaimed President William Desmond Taylor, "and a new honesty has begun."

At 7:45 A.M. the telephone rang. It was Edna Purviance, who had been Chaplin's star since Chaplin left Keystone, and who was a close friend of Mabel's. Edna lived in the duplex next to Taylor at the Alvarado Court Apartments at nearby Sixth and Alvarado. Edna was calling to tell Mabel that Henry Peavey, Taylor's black butler, was running around the court hollering that Taylor was dead. Seemed to be a stomach hemorrhage. Mabel couldn't believe it. She had seen him just last night, and he was supposed to have called her later in the evening, but she had gone straight to sleep. Edna called back a few minutes later to say that Taylor had been shot in the back. When they turned his body over they found a bullet wound between his neck and shoulder.

Mabel collapsed, but not for long. She had to deal with the mob of photographers, reporters, police detectives, and sensation hunters who rushed to Mabel's apartment after they had rushed to Taylor's. Mabel's image was all over Taylor's apartment. One photo of Mabel was tacked to the window frame above his desk, close to where the body lay. Another photo of Mabel was on the upright piano by the door. A third, inscribed "To My Dearest," was in a gold locket on the watch chain they found on his body.

When *Molly O'* had opened, *Wid's* cautioned its exhibitors, "You may have to do a little extra exploiting in connection with the star's name because it may have been some time since you folks have seen her." The Taylor murder took care of the star's name. "God, it is a fearful thing to see one's name smeared in huge letters all the way across the top of a newspaper," Mabel told Sutherland. That evening Mabel saw her name smeared across the top of the *Evening Express*, "MABEL NORMAND QUIZZED IN SCREEN CHIEF'S MURDER." She couldn't open a newspaper for a year after, she said, without trembling.

Since Mabel was the last person to see Taylor alive, Mabel at first was both chief witness and chief suspect. During the next four weeks, Mabel was quizzed intensively by detectives competing for information for the rival offices of police, district attorney, sheriff, and the city of Los Angeles, not to mention reporters competing for seven rival papers. The story Mabel told first to police Detective Sergeants Ziegler and Wallis she told again and again, because it was true. Witnesses could corroborate every movement she had made on the afternoon of February 1 when she saw Taylor for the last time.

That morning she slept late because she had the day off from filming *Suzanna*. Late in the afternoon, she told her chauffeur, William Davis, to drive her downtown to her two jewelers, Brock's and Feagan's. She took "Frenchy" George with her because she wanted to engrave a French inscription on a silver cigarette case she'd been given for Christmas, and she wanted to get it right. After the jewelers, she drove on to Hellman's Night and Day Bank at Sixth and Main to put the rest of her jewelry in her bank vault. She called Mamie Owens, her maid, to say that she would not eat dinner in because she wanted to see Lloyd's *A Sailor-Made Man.* Mamie reminded her that she had an early studio call next day and added that Mr. Taylor had phoned to ask her to stop by his apartment because he had found two of the books she had been looking for.

It was now around 7:00. On her way to Taylor's, she stopped by a sidewalk peanut vendor to buy two bags of peanuts and one of popcorn. Because the vendor couldn't change her ten-dollar bill, she ran across the street to get change at the drugstore in the Pacific Electric Building. There she bought the latest *Police Gazette* because the cover suggested a good publicity shot for *Suzanna.* Back in her Rolls, Mabel thumbed through the *Gazette,* ate peanuts, and tossed the shells onto a copy of Freud's *The Interpretation of Dreams* that lay beside her on the seat. "I had my Freud with me," she told Sutherland, "and I thought [Taylor'd] be pleased to know I read it in my car." When Davis parked on the steep hill of Alvarado, Mabel asked him to clean the shells from the tonneau while he waited for her.

Mabel heard Taylor talking on the phone when she approached his front door, which he often left open, and she waited until he hung up. As she entered his living room–study, with the piano on the left and the desk on the right, she handed him a bag of peanuts. Taylor had been talking to the tax accountant they shared, and he complained about the mess of canceled checks on his desk. He couldn't tell his own signatures from the ones Sands had forged, he said. Sands was Edward F. Sands, Taylor's former valet, chef, chauffeur, and personal secretary, whom Taylor had entrusted with all his affairs when he took a brief vacation to England the previous June and July. Taylor returned to discover that Sands had disappeared, along with Taylor's checkbook, jewelry, clothing, and car. Sands had also cashed large sums on the blank checks Taylor had signed for household expenses during his absence. When Sands ran out of signed checks, he forged them. On August 3, Taylor had charged Sands with embezzlement, and the district attorney had signed a warrant for Sands's arrest on two counts of grand larceny. But Sands had gone for good.

Or had he? During the past couple of months, there had

been disquieting signs of his presence. On December 4, Taylor's apartment had again been robbed, more jewelry taken, as well as his entire stock of custom-made gold-tipped cigarettes. A week later, Peavey had found the butt of one of these cigarettes on the front doorstep, and Taylor had found dusty footprints on his bed upstairs. Recently the phone would ring at odd hours, and when Taylor answered, the caller hung up. Taylor told Mabel that he was sorry he had made the charge against Sands, particularly after a disturbing message he'd received the day before Christmas.

He'd gotten an envelope in the mail with two pawn tickets in it from the Zematsky Loan and Jewelry Company in San Francisco. One ticket was made out to "William Dene Tanner" and the other to "Mrs. Tennant." Taylor didn't explain the first name but "Mrs. Tennant," he said, was the way Sands had always misspelled the name of Taylor's sister-in-law, Mrs. Ada Brennan, so he knew the envelope was sent by Sands. One of the tickets was for a pair of diamond studs that Mabel had given Taylor for Christmas two years before. A message was enclosed with the tickets.

> *So sorry to inconvenience you even temporarily. Also observe the lesson of the forced sale of assets. A merry Christmas and a happy and prosperous New Year.*
>
> *ALIAS JIMMY V.*

"Jimmy V.," Mabel knew, referred to a 1920 movie, *Alias Jimmy Valentine*, about a reformed convict forced to expose his past as a safecracker in order to save a girl who gets locked in a safe.

Now Taylor had a new servant problem. That very morning, Taylor had had to bail Henry Peavey out of jail. He'd been arrested the night before for soliciting young boys in Westlake Park. Mabel laughed. Taylor offered dinner, and she refused but accepted a gin and juice cocktail that Peavey made. After Peavey left for the evening, at about 7:20, Mabel kidded Taylor about his butler's fancy getup of green golf stockings and yellow knickers. Then they got down to serious talk about books. They talked about "a book by that Chicago newspaper man," as Mabel remembered, Dos Passos's *Three Soldiers.* Taylor unwrapped the books he had bought her that afternoon at C. C. Parker's Bookshop. One was a newly translated critique of *Thus Spake Zarathustra,* and the other was the latest short story collection of Ethel M. Dell. The heroine Rosa Mundi of the title story might suit Mabel for a movie, he thought. They talked about the kind of dramatic heroines Mabel wanted to play in stories like *The Moral of Marcus,* the sort of thing Taylor directed and Sennett did not. Then they chatted about their separate dates for the Cameraman's Ball on Saturday night. Mabel said that she was going straight home to bed, and Taylor said he'd call her around 9:00 to see how she'd liked the books.

When Taylor walked Mabel from his apartment to her car on the street, Peavey was gone, although he had chatted with Davis for a few minutes. As Mabel stepped over the pile of peanut shells at the curb, Taylor spotted Freud coupled with the *Police Gazette* on the back seat and laughed, "Mabel, Mabel, my darling, I'm afraid you're hopeless." As her car pulled away, Mabel blew Taylor a kiss by pressing her lips to the side window. Detectives found the imprint of her lipstick there the next day. The time was 7:45. Mabel had spent no more than forty-five minutes with Taylor.

At 7:50, Faith MacLean, wife of actor Douglas MacLean, thought she heard either a car backfire or a gunshot. Backfiring was frequent on Alvarado, but the report was loud enough to cause her to go to her door directly across the court from Taylor's front door and to look out. She saw a man standing in Taylor's open doorway on his porch. "I looked at him and he stood and looked at me," she testified. He then turned around to shut the door behind him and walked casually toward her on a path that led to an alley behind their apartments. He was around 5'6", weighed 165 to 175 pounds, and wore a rough woolen jacket with a muffler and a tweed cap. He was not Edward Sands, she said.

The man had probably been hiding behind the open door when Taylor walked back in because the path of the bullet indicated that Taylor had been shot in the back, with his left arm slightly raised. The bullet had entered 6 1/2" below the left armpit of his Army fatigue jacket and woolen vest to lodge 4 1/2" from his right shoulder. Douglas MacLean confirmed the time of

7:50, and a witness in a street apartment confirmed that he had seen Mabel with Taylor at the curb at 7:45. Mabel had an airtight "alibi," but the lid was off on Hollywood, and those who had always suspected the worst of motion-picture trash were amply rewarded by the revelations to come.

Robbery was ruled out, since the murderer had ignored the gold jewelry Taylor was wearing, as well as seventy-five dollars in his pocket and objects like a costly Luger pistol in plain sight upstairs. A crime of passion was more likely and made better copy. The *Examiner* proposed a "JEALOUS MAN," a rejected suitor of "the famous actress" involved with Taylor, and they ran a photo of the missing Sands. Sheriff William I. Traeger, whose relation with the picture industry was less cozy than the other agencies', zeroed in on "the famous actress." "Somewhere in the plot, possibly as an innocent cause, but nevertheless as *the* cause, is a woman," the Sheriff reiterated. Since Mrs. MacLean had seen a man, Sheriff Traeger suggested that the man she saw might have been a woman dressed as a man.

The Sheriff's suspicions were given weight by the fact that there were not one but two famous actresses involved with Taylor. Mary Miles Minter had rushed to Taylor's apartment with her grandmother when the news broke and had become hysterical when she saw the blood spots where the body had lain. It was Mary who told reporters that "Miss Normand had been engaged to Mr. Taylor about six months," a report Mabel instantly denied. A full year later, after Mary had quarreled bitterly with her sinister mother, Charlotte Shelby, Mary confessed that she herself had been engaged to Taylor and that she had run to Mabel's apartment after Taylor's to find out what Mabel knew. They talked, she said, in Mabel's bathroom and turned the taps on full to frustrate eavesdroppers. Three years after that, in 1926, she confessed that she had visited Taylor early the same afternoon of the night he was killed.

Even without these later revelations, blonde Mary and brunette Mabel were perfect casting for a love-triangle of the Griffith sort, contrasting a voluptuous type with a spirituelle. Mabel swore that she had never been engaged to Taylor, that they were simply

"the best of pals." The headlines on February 4 implied otherwise. "MABEL NORMAND BREAKS DOWN AT IN-
QUEST," the *Examiner* reported. Mabel was said to have collapsed in sobs after Peavey described to the coroner's jury how he
discovered the body. Peavey got to the apartment at 7:30 A.M.,
after buying Taylor's milk of magnesia on the way. He picked up
the morning paper and unlocked the door. The lights were still
on.

> *The first thing I saw was his feet. I looked at his feet*
> *a few minutes and said, "Mr. Taylor." He never*
> *moved.*

Those were Peavey's words in the "Coroner's Report." The papers went in for minstrel dialect, "He looks jus' like he did when
I went to call him of a mawnin' — jus' like he was asleep."

The body was "Stone cold and very stiff and rigid," Charles
Eyton reported to the coroner. Eyton, general manager at Famous Players-Lasky, had reached Taylor's on the heels of the
police. The first person Peavey had called was Taylor's studio
assistant. The studio raced the police to the scene.

Mabel had been late to the coroner's inquest. Coroner Frank
A. Nance had been forced to telephone her at 10:00 A.M. and tell
her the jury was waiting. While her Rolls pulled up to the mob
of reporters waiting at the front of the mortuary, Mabel snuck in
the back in an unmarked car. After the inquest, Mabel went with
police Captain Adams to Taylor's apartment to reenact her last
visit. While there, she searched Taylor's desk for a packet of her
letters and telegrams that she had sent a year ago but knew he
had kept. "Why do you keep those old things?" she had asked
Taylor recently when she saw them in a drawer. "Just because,"
he had smiled. Mabel told police she wanted to keep them from
reporters for fear they would be misunderstood. Somebody had
beat her to it. Next day, February 5, new headlines blared,
"MABEL NORMAND LETTERS LOST FROM DEATH
HOUSE."

The letters became known as "the Blessed Baby letters"
because Mabel had addressed many of them to "Dearest Daddy"
from "Blessed Baby" as a private joke, she explained. Mabel felt

increasingly harassed by interviewers who didn't believe her when she told them, "I was never in love with Taylor. There was no thought or talk of marriage between us." They didn't believe her because others said different. "I know that Mr. Taylor was very much in love with Miss Normand," Peavey told interviewers. "At times I thought that she returned his love and then again it seemed to me that she was tired of him." She seldom came to Taylor's apartment, Peavey said, but Taylor wrote her notes two or three times a day and had his chauffeur deliver them to her apartment. Taylor also sent her a carload of flowers at least three times a week.

When Mabel had been in New York the year before, Taylor had sent her a telegram every evening, and she replied each morning. These were the telegrams Taylor had saved. They had also exchanged costly Christmas gifts, such as the silver cigarette case found on his body and an amber cigarette holder worth $1800. On New Year's Eve a year earlier, Taylor had taken her to a party, and Peavey said his employer wept after Mabel quarrelled with him that night because she didn't want to leave the party. As recently as a month ago, Mabel had told Peavey that she and Taylor were going to be married and would like Peavey to work for them. Peavey had often noticed however, that when he rang Mabel's house for Taylor, someone on the other end would hang up. "It was then I would believe that Miss Normand did not care for my master like he did for her."

"Shame on Henry Peavey for telling lies!" Mabel responded. "On my honor, get it straight, please," she pleaded with an *Express* reporter. "I was never in love with Taylor." Their friendship had been based on comradeship and understanding. "We loved so many of the same things — books, music, pictures." "My chief liking for him, however," Mabel confessed, "was because of his wonderful brain and the things he could teach me." After his death, Mabel discovered that she knew very little about his wonderful brain. She knew very little, in fact, about the man. She was as shocked as the rest of Hollywood to read the headlines of February 4, "DUAL LIFE OF TAYLOR REVEALED."

The man whom Hollywood knew as William Desmond Taylor, the man of whom Lasky could say, "A man of finer ideals I have never known," the man whom the Directors Association had called "A man whom every man could trust," the man to whom Mary Miles Minter had inscribed her photograph, "Artist, gentleman, man!" was not the man any of them knew. He was William Cunningham Deane Tanner, born in Carlow, Ireland, on April 26, 1872, to an Anglo-Irish family of some distinction in County Cork.

Until his murder, Hollywood knew Taylor as a first-rate director with a colorful but unexceptionable past. His wide experience was an asset. "To portray life one must have lived it!" Realart advised in a four-page spread advertising the fullness of Taylor's career in *Motion Picture World*. Taylor had lived it as an engineering student on the Continent, a rancher in Kansas, a prospector in the Klondike, an actor with Fanny Davenport's touring company, a captain in the Royal Fusiliers, a movie actor in Vitagraph's *Captain Alvarez* (1914), a director of Flying A's serial *The Diamond from the Sky* (1915), and since then a director of over three dozen films, including the prestigious *Huckleberry Finn* and *Johanna Enlists*.

Taylor was a romantic who cultivated the role of a man of mystery, not unlike the dual role of the swashbuckling Captain Alvarez who was secretly an American adventurer in disguise. He had mesmerized Mabel as Othello had Desdemona with strange tales of adventure in the Yukon, where he had shared digs with a miner named "Red" Ashford and a poet named Robert Service in a camp called "Ninety-Below Discovery." When reporters located Red after the murder, the prospector described the man he had known as "Bill Tanner" to be a smart dresser who wore tweed suits in the day and dress suits at night, who was expert at poker and tennis, and who suffered, as their poet friend said, "from a grief you can't control." In Hollywood as in the Yukon, Taylor hinted at a tragic past. He had spent time in prison, he had confessed to a friend, to protect the honor of a woman he loved. The story, however, proved to be the plot of *The Judge's Wife* that Taylor had directed for Neva Gerber.

Neva Gerber was another actress who had been involved with Taylor and had been engaged to him in 1918 – 19. Neva had known more about Taylor than most. She knew that he had been married to Ethel May Harrison, a Floradora girl of respectable family in New York, and that he still had a daughter, Ethel Daisy. When he went to London in June of 1921, Taylor told Neva that he was going to visit his daughter, who lived with his mother and his sister in London. Taylor had returned to Hollywood "unusually depressed and irritable," Neva told reporters, because he had just learned that his mother and daughter had been killed by German bombs at the end of the war.

Not even Neva knew, however, that Taylor's daughter was alive and well and living in Mamaroneck with her remarried mother. Until the year before, neither mother nor daughter had known that William "Pete" Tanner was alive and well and living in Hollywood. Neither had seen or heard of him since October 24, 1908, when he attended the Vanderbilt Cup Race on Long Island with Billy "Fudge" Thaw. On that day Pete Tanner left behind the New York Athletic Club and the Larchmont Yacht Club and his Fifth Avenue English antiques shop and Ethel May and Ethel Daisy and lit out for the territory.

Nobody knew that Taylor had visited his daughter in New York in June on his way to London. His ex-wife had recognized a photo of Taylor the previous year, and his daughter had begun to write to him. About the same time, Taylor's sister-in-law, Mrs. Ada Brennan, living in Monrovia, California, also recognized a photo of Taylor. In January, she had asked him for money to help support the two young daughters his brother had abandoned. Denis Deane Tanner had followed his older brother from Ireland to New York in 1903, had married Ada in 1907, and had taken over the antiques business when his brother disappeared. Denis himself disappeared in 1912. Taylor had agreed to pay Ada sixty dollars a month, for Denis never resurfaced. I was startled to learn from Taylor's art director Hopkins that Denis in 1921 was living in my hometown of Riverside. Hopkins's mother, working at Realart as an art designer, had an office above Taylor's, and Taylor had introduced as his brother a man she had often seen visit Taylor by the back stairs. Nobody else saw him. Taylor usually claimed he was dead.

I discovered another odd connection of Taylor's past with my own in his ranching interlude in Kansas. William's father, a captain in the British army, had destined his eldest son for an army career. But after William failed to enter the military academy of Sandhurst and ran off instead to a stock company in Manchester, his father sent him to America. A fellow Anglo-Irishman, Frances "Ned" Turnley had bought land at Runnymede, Kansas, in Harper County, where he promised to turn black-sheep sons into gentlemen farmers. He advertised "a Western paradise where golden birds sang in the trees and silver rivers ran tinkling to the sea and the climate was so healthy it put to shame any reference to the Elysian Fields." In such a paradise, farming was dull work, so the boys set up a race track and raided the Presbyterian settlements of Harper County for ducats and daughters. While William returned to his family at Belleville Estates, in Cappoquin, in disgrace, many of the Harpers of Harper County pushed on to a paradise further West, to Riverside, California. Mabel's mystery was closing in on me.

The mystery of Taylor's past was complicated by the disappearing acts of his present. Who and where was Edward F. Sands? By February 7, the District Attorney had ordered his arrest and sent out a nationwide alarm. The *Examiner* stimulated interest in information leading to Sands's arrest by offering a $500 reward. Sands was described as twenty-six, 5'7", 185 pounds, round face, light complexion, brown hair, heavy eyebrows. The description fit the man Mrs. MacLean had seen at Taylor's door, even though she was certain the man was not Sands. Before Sands cleaned out his employer, Taylor thought him "the most marvelous servant in the world," Hopkins told me. Hopkins remembered him as a "plump, pink-cheeked Dickens character," very clever but odd. Hopkins had seen the strange parchment Sands had one day written to Taylor in his fine penmanship, saying, "I am your slave for life." Hopkins had not heard him say what others had, "He has to employ me — I have the goods on him."

Sands was a natural suspect because he was blackmailing Taylor or threatening to. More than one person had seen Sands in Los Angeles the day before the murder. The wife of Taylor's former chauffeur, Earl Tiffany, another ne'er-do-well whom Taylor had fired for threatened blackmail, claimed to have talked to Sands at length on January 31. The day after the murder, two of

Taylor's gold-tipped cigarettes were found in a garage at Temple and Hill Streets. Spurred by the *Examiner,* informants spotted Sands from coast to coast, and several men claiming to be Sands confessed to the murder in lurid prose. But nobody even knew who Sands really was.

He may have been Edward Fitz-Strathmore Sands, a navy deserter distinguished chiefly by a double nipple on his left breast. But I thought it more likely that he was the plain Edward Sands I discovered in the Los Angeles Superior Court files. This Sands had been arrested for grand larceny in 1920, a year before Taylor hired him. This Sands was young, clever, and persuasive. He had stolen tires from his employers in the Shepherd and Campbell Tire Sales Company and then persuaded them to drop charges and let him pay them back. But he neglected to pay. Next, he persuaded the judge to suspend sentence and let him off on probation. The letters attesting to his character matched Hopkins's description of an engaging young man, likeable, happy-go-lucky, roly-poly. "I'm sure he had nothing to do with the murder," Hopkins said.

By the time of Taylor's funeral on February 7, the thousands who massed at Pershing Square to catch a glimpse of the mourners entering St. Paul's Cathedral at 11:00 that morning did not care about Sands's or Taylor's past. They were there to witness the drama of the present. They were not disappointed. "MABEL NORMAND COLLAPSES AT FUNERAL! THOUSANDS ATTEND." The funeral was a nightmare, Hopkins remembered, because of the mob outside the church howling to get in. "It was like the French Revolution, horrifying, really," he told me. "Mabel was sitting next to me, sobbing and sobbing."

Thousands came to watch the drama unfolding between Mary Miles Minter and Mabel Normand, rivals for the affection of the slain man. Mounted police had to clear a path for Mabel as she struggled, borne up by a companion on each side, to enter the church. Muffled beneath her furs, her black hood and veil, "her face," reporters wrote, "was almost as lifeless as that under the Union Jack in the aisle." Taylor's flag-draped casket was flanked by two magnificent wreaths, the American Beauty roses sent by Mabel and the Black Prince roses sent by Mary. An honor guard stood at attention at the four corners of the casket that had been engraved in gold, "Our Big Brother." At its foot stood his empty director's chair. After the Episcopalian mass for the dead was over, Mabel was the last to view the body, now uncovered. "She looked long at that set, thin, aristocratic head," reporters wrote, before she collapsed "and her companions dragged her away."

What lent spice to the funeral drama were headlines two days previous, "PINK 'NIGHTIE' IN TAYLOR HOME OWNED BY ACTRESS." The actress was never named in the papers, and the nightie vanished into thin air, but the scene was now set for a myth like the Arbuckle rape, a myth of seduction and revenge, starring a monster murderess. Both Peavey and ex-chauffeur Tiffany testified that Taylor kept a woman's nightgown in a green box in his bureau drawer. Sands, they said, used to fold the gown in a particular way to keep track of when it was used. Sands was a born blackmailer. Had it not been for the later discovery of a set of love letters, Mabel would have been condemned in the public eye as the owner of the nightie and therefore a sex fiend and probable murderess.

Adela Rogers was certain that Mabel was the owner and told me that it was her husband "Ike" St. Johns who saw the nightie when he arrived at Taylor's apartment, for the mayor's office, and stole the nightie to protect Mabel. Only Adela now spoke of the garment as "little pink chiffon step-ins." At the time of the murder, Adela herself had been in New York reporting for Hearst. By the process of myth, the nightie became "step-ins," then "teddies," and finally "hundreds of pairs of panties" lining Taylor's drawers. Like other characters in this mystery, the nightie never reappeared.

The furnishings of the dead man's apartment were as subject to vanishing tricks as his life. Mabel's letters reappeared as if by magic, drawn by a wand from the toe of one of Taylor's riding boots in an upstairs closet. They were as anticlimactic as the following exchange:

Dear Mabel.
I know you're an awfully busy woman and haven't much time to grant to a poor duffer like me, but. . . .

*How about dinner together next Wednesday, and
then the Orpheum?*
> *Yours always,*
> *Bill.*

Dear Desperate Desmond:
  *Sorry I cannot dine with you tomorrow. But I have
a previous engagement with a Hindoo Prince. Some
other time.*
> *Blessed Baby.*

Two other letters, however, discovered the same day in the
same magical way as they fell from a book in Taylor's library, were
not anticlimactic. A piece of notepaper discovered with them was
anything but, despite the simplicity of the message,

Dearest —
  I love you — I love you — I love you.
> *Yours always,*
> *Mary*

The notepaper was embossed with the monogram of Mary
Miles Minter, familiar to reporters who had just discovered
among Taylor's effects a handkerchief embroidered with the same
monogram.

Confronted with the letters, Mary said that she had written
them at seventeen to her director, then forty-seven, and yes, she
had loved him but only with "the admiration and respect a young
girl gives to a man with the poise and culture of Mr. Taylor." The
public knew Mary only by the image that her mother and Zukor
had meticulously invented to clone Mary Pickford's image as
Little Eva. Adela had described her then as "a rosy round doll
with real golden curls and big blue eyes . . . and dimples, oh,
definitely dimples." One critic remembered her in a rosy glow as
"the image of girlhood itself." Minter's mother, Charlotte
Shelby, knew the exact price of that image when she negotiated
a contract with Zukor the year before: $1,300,000 for three and
a half years, during which Mary "must be seen very little in public
. . . be a real 'homebody.' . . . *And she must not marry.*"

On the screen Mary fulfilled the image of girlhood itself in back-lit romances like *Anne of Green Gables* and *Jenny Be Good*, directed by Taylor in 1918 – 19. Off the screen, Mary was headstrong, passionate, and increasingly rebellious against her archetypical stage mother. Mary celebrated her eighteenth birthday by getting arrested four times in one day for speeding in the red roadster that her mother gave her as a bribe to slow down in other ways. She once threatened her mother with suicide and had shot off a gun that some thought "the Taylor murder weapon." More than once she threatened her mother with the ultimate weapon of marriage. Immediately after the murder, Mary broke with her mother and her sister, Margaret Fillmore, the woman who was eventually to accuse Mother Shelby of the killing after two decades of battles the trio waged in the press. Mary celebrated her twenty-first birthday, a year after the murder, by suing her mother for the millions she had earned since her stage debut at age four in *The Little Rebel*. Mary told the press then that she had been secretly engaged to Taylor when she wrote her love letters and had planned to marry him as soon as she was eighteen.

The letters, written in a simple schoolgirl code, revealed the dual life of Mary Miles Minter as soon as newspapers published them in full, except for a paragraph or two "withheld out of modesty." Like girlhood itself, Mary had written Taylor that she longed to keep house for him in a little cottage where she would sweep and dust, tie ribbons on the snowy curtains, feed the birds, darn his socks, and help *him* wash the dishes. But girlhood had other dreams as well:

> I'd go to my room and put on something soft and
> flowing, then I'd lie on the couch and wait for you. I
> might fall asleep for a fire always makes me drowsy
> — then I'd wake to find two strong arms around me
> and two dear lips pressed on mine in a long sweet
> kiss.

Mabel knew little or nothing of Mary's infatuation, since Taylor had been openly engaged to Eva Gerber until they broke up amicably in the fall of 1919. Ex-chauffeur Tiffany told reporters that Taylor had seen a lot of Mary around 1919 until a change came about and "Mabel Normand became his favorite." Until Mary's letters exposed the gap between the fact and fiction of Mary as Little Eva, Topsy Mabel furnished the public with its current alibi of innocence lost. But in Mary the public found an even more theatrical image of betrayal than the Arbuckle rape. Mary was girlhood itself betrayed not by brute force but by a far more insidious evil, seduction, and not by a vulgar American fat boy but by a far more potent symbol of decadence, an upper-class English gentleman.

The stolen pink nightie was arrogated by myth faster even than the Coke bottle and was promptly embroidered with the monogram of "MMM." When Adela told me in Desert Hot Springs that "Everybody knew who shot William Desmond Taylor," she went on to explain that there were still unwritten laws in the West, and one of them was the right of a mother or father to kill the man who seduced their daughter. Adela included Mabel in her myth-making memory. "Let's lynch the son of a bitch and be done with it," Adela recalled Mabel's saying to her once, before Mother Shelby did the job herself. "We were going to lynch Taylor," Adela said, "and we thought Mrs. Shelby had a perfect right to do anything she wanted to him."

However baffled and hurt Mabel may have been by the exposure of Taylor's secret life, she remained loyal to Taylor and to her memory of him; but she did succumb to the myth of the transvestite murderer. "I am one with the rest of Los Angeles," she told Sutherland in 1927, "when I say that I think it will be found that the guilty person was a woman dressed as a man." The image was too cinematic to resist and Hollywood embraced it. To conform to Mrs. MacLean's description, Mother Shelby would have had to strap on elevator shoes six to eight inches high and strap sixty to seventy pounds of padding to her body. And as Shelby herself asked once, "Why should I make myself conspicuous by dressing up like a man?" But what was common sense pitted against the power of a double-barreled image — the seduced virgin and the vengeful virago?

The war of the Shelbys, however, waged publicly and litigiously, gave substance to a myth of corrupted innocence that had been lacking in the Arbuckle myth because the Shelbys incorporated the motive of greed. Behind the myth of sex was the dirty fact of money. Mary's threat to marry Taylor, or anyone else, threatened to void her $1,300,000 contract. It was Mary's chief weapon against the full arsenal of Mother Shelby and her jealous sister Margaret. Mary took on the pair of them in suits and countersuits until Margaret turned on her mother at last, in the climactic suit of *Fillmore* v. *Shelby* on September 13, 1938. On that day, Margaret accused her mother of being "a man-hater who worshipped a golden god." Headlines were less Biblical, "MOTHER SLEW TAYLOR, THINKS MRS. FILLMORE." She had seen her mother throw "the murder weapon" into a Louisiana bayou before the pair fled to Europe when "the murder trail" got too close. Her mother had tried to commit her to the Los Angeles County Insane Asylum, Margaret accused, to shut her up. To "protect" Mary, Margaret said, she had stolen her sister's diaries from her safe-deposit vault, because the diaries were "so diabolical and so pathetic that they made Mary Astor's diaries look like a post script." Margaret, the dark sister, was taking her revenge on both the starmaker and the star. The grand jury, however, found no evidence to support Margaret's charges and found considerable ground to distrust the testimony of a woman who had just been released from the county asylum and who would die of alcoholism within the year. Was Margaret talking fact or fiction? The war of the Shelbys did not solve the Taylor mystery because a larger war had preempted its alibis. The Taylor murder shared headlines on September 13 with another event:

HITLER DEMANDS LIBERATION OF SUDETENS.

BESMIRCHED

Mabel too felt betrayed, betrayed by her friends, by the industry, and above all by the press. She was embittered, Julia told Stephen: "The terrible unfairness of the publicity — a star so famous, so beloved — and the ones MN expected help from didn't come forth." Mack said that his first thought when Mabel called him at 4:00 A.M. on February 3 was of *Molly O'*: "There goes half a million dollars. . . . And nothing to do but sit and take it." He sent Mabel a publicity man to ward off the press. But the industry sequestered Mabel as they had sequestered Arbuckle. "Few dared to come too near the besmirched Normand," Mabel told Sutherland. Norma Talmadge dared, and Mabel was forever grateful for the way Norma drove up to her front door bold as brass. Mabel felt the industry had sacrificed her to a star in whom the investment was greater. My only bitter thought, she said to Sutherland, was that "I was tossed to the lions to save another actress, even if she was as guiltless of the murder as I was."

Mabel had got it wrong. Mabel was saved, for the moment, by the Little Eva sainthood of that other actress, which made her martyrdom apt. Even so, Mabel did not understand that she was herself implicated in "the conspiracy" charged by the press against officials of the law in collusion with industry officials. District Attorney Thomas Lee Woolwine — a personal friend of Taylor, the Shelbys, and other industry members, the official after-dinner speaker at a banquet for Arbuckle two years before — was under fire for erecting "a barricade of silence between the searchers for the truth and the truth itself," as the truth-seeking *Examiner* complained. Nine days after the murder, Woolwine was forced to step in personally "to clean up the mess." The first person he called was Mabel: "NORMAND GIRL READY FOR DEATH QUIZ GRILL." Once again Mabel was asked,

"Name?" "Mabel Normand." "Occupation?" "Motion Pictures."

On February 10 Mabel appeared at 7:30 P.M. at the Hall of Records with her nurse and publicity agent. She emerged three hours later, "very tired." Reporters noted her grey coat with plush collar and cuffs while Woolwine and a deputy posed on either side of her for a battery of photographers. "Hurry up and get it over with," she was heard to say. "I hate this stuff." When a flashbulb banged in her face, Mabel muttered, "Oh gawd" and made a dash for her car. Woolwine told the press, "I believe that little girl has told me everything she knows about this case and she's giving us every bit of aid she can." That little girl, however, was now thirty, and Woolwine had quizzed her for three hours not about her Taylor romance but about the drug trade.

Rumors of Hollywood "dope parties" had surfaced with descriptions of Arbuckle's "orgies." Mabel now found herself in the anamolous position of denying that *Taylor* had ever taken drugs. "Never in God's world, on my word of honor," Mabel told an interviewer. "Billy was one of the cleanest and most temperate of men in all his habits." Mabel could hardly reveal Taylor's fatherly role without ruining herself. "We used to think Taylor was queer for young girls because we didn't know that he was a reformer trying to save them, sort of a father figure," Allan Dwan told me.

Even before Woolwine took charge, the sheriff's office, still searching for the causal woman, had named a dope peddler said to have it in for Taylor. Taylor had caught him handing "the bindles" to "a well-known motion-picture actress" and had kicked him downstairs. Now newspapers uncovered a federal narcotics agent whom Taylor had consulted two years earlier in the East. Taylor had wanted help in breaking a drug ring that supplied an unnamed actress with heroin. The agent testified that the actress had taken a cure in the East and had returned to Los Angeles a year ago. The actress didn't need to be named. Mabel's name was in the news every single day.

City officials were as anxious as industry ones to keep Hollywood's image clean of drugs. There were already too many in-jokes about Hollywood "stardust," "snowbirds," and "sleigh-ride parties" in the "snow." Woolwine promised a "BIG FILM CLEANUP TO FOLLOW TAYLOR MURDER." Once the lid on drugs was off, hundreds of witnesses across the country offered information on drug rings, opium dens, and coke parties, one more bizarre than the next. Of the 300 people who confessed to the murder of Taylor, at least half of them were also self-confessed "hop-heads," in the idiom of the day. One of the more inventive was Harry Fields, a Detroit jailbird, who fingered "Sammy" Lee, a "well-known tong man, dope peddler and gun fighter" in Los Angeles's Chinatown. Fields had driven Lee and two others to Taylor's apartment the night of the murder, Fields confessed, and their accomplice was "a well-known motion-picture actress" who signalled to them by waving a bag of candy.

As the confessions poured in, Mabel was saved by overkill. But interrogation had been relentless, and Mabel broke under the strain. Sennett's publicity man had asked reporters earlier to lay off, "She's worn out, poor little thing. . . . She needs rest desperately." Finally a cold settled in her lungs, and she was confined to bed. "MABEL SERIOUSLY ILL OF GRIEF," the *Examiner* reported. Within the week, while federal agencies had stepped in to investigate rumors of a national dope ring, Mabel went into seclusion in a guarded house in Altadena. She was reported to be critically ill — from influenza, a nervous breakdown, and "partial paralysis."

By March 6, the Taylor case had at last moved off the front page, and Mabel had recovered her health sufficiently to attend the Beverly Speedway Races with friends. That same month, Arbuckle went on trial for the third time, Mary Miles Minter escaped to Hawaii for a vacation, and Mabel returned to the set of *Suzanna*. Her absence, Sennett moaned, had cost the studio thousands of dollars. The moment she could, Mabel too escaped. When she finished *Suzanna* at the end of May, she boarded the *Aquitania* on June 14 for her first trip to Europe. On her return in September, she told Sutherland, she was "completely cured of the things that had broken me physically and were threatening to wreck my mind." She did not know that her ordeal had only begun.

As the Reverend Mr. Stratton had predicted that syrup would not cure the organic disease of film corruption, so the film industry had predicted that "the public will not tolerate a be-smirched figure on the screen." Both predictions came true. Local censorship boards in the Midwest, in towns like Topeka and Des Moines, were the first to ban Mabel's and Mary Miles Minter's films at once, because their names were associated with a murder case. If Mabel were banned permanently, Sennett stood to lose his investment in *Suzanna* as well as *Molly O'*. In June, he hurried East to make personal appearance tours in theaters show-ing *Molly O'*. Mack was a hit at the Chestnut Street Opera House in Philadelphia, where fifteen years before he had been a chorus boy in *A Chinese Honeymoon*. Other exhibitors and other cen-sors, however, were not so easily placated. They had already warned Hollywood stars that they would "wipe them from their screens in the event they were proved guilty of any immorality or if they became involved in any indecent affair."

In the general rush to wipe screens CLEAN, Hollywood turned on its nearest ally and blamed the press for inventing guilt by association, forgetting its own dependence on associative guilt. Publicity was turning out to be a Frankenstein with monstrous power of its own. When Maude Delmont was released from prison, after conviction on a bigamy charge, she became a vaude-ville headliner, "THE WOMAN WHO SIGNED THE MUR-DER CHARGE AGAINST ARBUCKLE." Her act was to "rip wide the screen which hides Hollywood and the movie colony." The screen Maude would rip wide referred not to a wardrobe or stage screen, but to a film screen that in itself was now viewed as an object of deception, concealing within or behind its inno-cent blank face a horde of nasty images.

In the postwar climate of fear and distrust, like the climate after the Second World War, enemies were everywhere. The duplicity innate to the medium of film was associated with other agents of duplicity and subversion. A mystery-writer hired by the *Examiner* found a clue to the Taylor murder in the fact that Mabel Normand had with her in the back seat of her Rolls her own copy of Freud.

It may have nothing to do with this mystery, but that this Curse of Freud had so much to do with sex criminality is puzzling. Young people are running wild; older people are undermined by the so-called psychoanalysis.

Freud was a foreigner, a "Hun" and a Jew, whose works began to be disseminated in America during the war. Freud conspired with Hollywood to undermine American morality, honesty, and integrity with the poison of sex. No one was safe, not even the elderly, because Freud was undermining the sense of a man's personal identity by making every man an actor and a spectator of his own dirty nickelodeon peepshow. Freud's so-called psychoanalysis, like the hokum projected on a screen, made the integrity of self a lie and a delusion.

Mabel was guilty of associating not only with Freud but also with Nietzsche, that infamous Hun subverter of God as well as country. Nietzsche advocated deception, disguise, hypocrisy, lies. He undermined sincerity with irony and truth with masks. Freud and Nietzsche were secret agents undermining the image of the honest Yank.

In the climate of conspiracy, even native American romancers like Ethel M. Dell might be suspect. Dell's heroine Rosa Mundi had a dual identity as Rosemary, the lady, and Rosa, the snake dancer. She was like Mary Pickford's heroine in her 1935 novel, *The Demi-Widow*, who was both Coralee, the devoted mother, and Coco, the actress, no better than a courtesan in the eyes of the world. The vamp who pays the bills for the woman of virtue was a fictive solution for the American girl who wanted nice things but wanted in fact to earn them respectably. The fact of virtue, however, cost far more than its appearance, and Pickford knew to the decimal the cash value of both.

Mabel's wickedness, like Rosa the snake dancer's, was supposed to be fake. Everybody knew that Topsy was played in blackface. Beneath, she was lily white. Like Shakespeare's fools, Topsy disguised mother wit and virtue in the mask of vice. But what if the vice was real? What if the naughty girls who made public spectacles of themselves by dancing on tabletops, like Zelda Fitzgerald, or begging "horsebackie rides" from all the men in ritzy cafes, like Mabel, were not really innocent but really bad?

If they were really nutty or really naughty, the game was up. They were cheating on the rules which required them to not be what they seemed.

"Taylor's murder changed all our lives," Adela told me, "things before that and things after that." His murder exposed the fictions of all their lives by baring the facts of Hollywood hokum. Ben Hecht used to joke that everybody in Hollywood killed Bill Taylor until some district attorney asked him to name "everybody." Hollywood would always be a place for naming names since everybody was in the business of deception, and all identities were assumed. Taylor's double life had dramatized to Puritan America the unpalatable fact that Hollywood, like Homer, was the father of lies and that what mattered was not truth but style.

Taylor's hokum was out of style. Born in another century, he had been born to another style. He had been born the English gentleman that others longed to be, but perversely, Taylor wanted to be an American buccaneer. Dreams of gold and glory took him to the Klondike when his womenfolk closed in and, when he ran out of land and lies, to California to reinvent himself in the lies of a new art. Taylor had wanted to live by his wits, by the nerve and gall of the King and the Duke in his own filmed version of *Huckleberry Finn*. But Taylor was half a century old at his death, and his line in faking was dated, was too grandiose, too heroic. Hollywood was already turning toward a new line of kings and dukes and other royal nonesuch in a more plebian style, one that would eventuate in the Clark Gable who said, "You know, this King stuff is pure bullshit. . . . I'm just a lucky slob from Ohio."

If Mabel was not guilty of murder, she was still guilty of losing her good name. She lost a little bit more every time Taylor's name came into the news, and it came as regularly as elections every two or three years, as each new district attorney exploited the unsolved mystery to further his own career. Successive attorneys exploited the case to embarrass their predecessor just as successive Shelbys exploited the case to embarrass each other. Just a month and a half before Mabel's death, a new district attorney demanded a new interrogation of Mabel to embarrass his predecessor, who was already accused of bribery in an oil fraud and would soon be convicted and sent to San Quentin. The new district attorney was so skillful in manipulating Hollywood's hokum that he remained in office long enough to exploit a later smear campaign in the thirties into a new witch-hunt: "RED MENACE IN THE MOVIE COLONY."

Hollywood, I found, was still full of plots and counterplots in the Taylor mystery. One veteran scriptwriter told me that she had in her possession "the gun that killed Taylor." With the aid of a metal detector, she had found it buried in the yard of a bungalow Mabel had rented at Marathon and Melrose. Mabel had killed Taylor because he was going to take away her dope, the writer whispered, "Mabel got her stuff from a peanut man, but it was what was IN the peanuts that Mabel wanted."

After ten years' research, King Vidor assured me, he could verify that the murder weapon was the gun Mary shot at her mother one night, if only he could locate the bullet in the wall of the Shelby's New Hampshire Street house. Another director, Andrew Stone, assured me that Mrs. Shelby's chauffeur had seen her take the gun from her car and conceal it, but the police had never charged her because they had been paid $25,000 not to. He knew the Hollywood rates for murder because he knew how much the murderer who had killed his son in the sixties had paid off the police.

By the time I reached Mary Miles Minter in my first Holly-wood trip, I was drowning in clues. I talked many times to Mary Miles Minter over the telephone, but she would never see me in person. The image of girlhood itself had been betrayed by diabetes and arthritis, and she lived in pain. She lived in a respectable thirties house overlooking the cantilevered houses built into the Santa Monica canyon below — "basket cases," she called them — by late arrivals like Christopher Isherwood. The first time we spoke, some pipes had burst and water was oozing from the walls, sloshing under the hospital bed where she lay imprisoned and staining some photographs of William Desmond Taylor that had slipped behind a bookcase and lain hidden there for years.

Born Juliet Reilly in 1902, she had been rechristened by her mother with the name and birthdate of a dead cousin, when the

176

Gerry Society complained that Juliet was underage for the stage. Mary had always hated acting, she said, and she hated "the doll-faced automaton" in which Mother Shelby (born Lily Pearl Miles) had caged her. As soon as Mary was of age, she escaped the film industry to spend the next half century in litigation, trying to square her dreams of romance with the realities of money. When her mother died in 1957, she married her Santa Monica realtor and became Mrs. Brandon O'Hildebrandt, adding an Irish O' to his proud Danish lineage. She scorned my baptismal name, "Betty," and rechristened me "Elizabeth." "Elizabeth the Queen," she commanded, "wear your cognomen proudly and I wager you will drop that Betty business like a hot brick."

"The world does not know me, I've been too proud and too poor," she said, "but I'll carry on, believe me, I'll carry on." She had sued CBS in 1970 over Rod Serling's "Wonderful World of Crime" series, in which her image had appeared with Mabel's in the unsolved Taylor mystery. She wanted me to search the police archives for the reputed pink nightie, which she had never seen, although she had seen in their files in the sixties Taylor's jacket and vest. "Did somebody in the world embroider something on a nightgown because he hated me?" she asked.

"I don't know any human being who had enmity toward Mr. Taylor," she told me, recalling the moment in the mortuary when she placed on his silken pall a single Black Prince rose. "He called me 'a little white rose'," she remembered as if today, "and one day he knelt and told me, 'I think you bear the Holy Grail'." "I worshipped him in life," she spoke it like a queen. "I worship him today."

The Taylor mystery was a mystery that could not be solved, I discovered, any more than Mabel's could. Their linked mysteries compelled because they gave form to the central mystery of identity that was Hollywood's nature and its art. Their occupation murdered their names and made ghosts of their flesh. I remembered a story Jesse Lasky told in his memoirs of a battered typewriter he brought home from the studio for his young son who wanted to write. The boy found a name scratched in a corner of the typewriter, "William Desmond Taylor." "He wouldn't touch the thing for months," Lasky said. "He thought it was haunted."

GLOBE-TROTTER

OCTOBER 5, 1978, PACOIMA
[Lee telephoned at midnight]
*Well just to show you what kind of guy Steve is,
we had a room for him in the Ambassador Hotel —
you know that's quite a swanky place. And I let Julia
stay with him there overnight. I mean, she's 100 years
old so what difference could it make? Well the first
thing he complained about was there weren't any
drapes. And that wasn't so bad but we were in the
midst of moving out here, packing our stuff, our
house was a mess. But we had a room upstairs all
nice and clean for him and some nice pictures of
Mabel on the dresser, a nice clean dresser. Just out of
a clear sky he packed up all his stuff and said he
couldn't stay in this pigpen, that's what he called our
place. Now only a crazy guy would say that. We were
moving, like I say, and even when we weren't we
never kept our house fixed up like, you know, for
some expensive guests or something.*

JUNE 14, 1922, ABOARD THE 'AQUITANIA'
Mabel counted her steamer trunks in her first-class cabin and
left her secretary-companion, not Julia but a woman who spoke
good French, to help the steward unpack them. Mabel wanted to
explore the Carolingian smoking room, Elizabethan grill, Louis
XIV dining salon, Palladian lounge and Egyptian swimming pool.
At last she was going "abroad," to see in reality the places she had
studied in the Rand McNally Atlas and the globe of the world
that her mother had given her as a child. Geography was a passion, and she took her globe with her to California. In showing

Sutherland around the defunct Mabel Normand Studio, Mabel stumbled onto the globe under a heap of costumes. "I used to run in here from the set and twirl it around while I hurried away to the Klondike, to Madagascar and Paris and Peru," she recalled. "While Nappy was dashing wildly around looking for me, I'd be strolling through the bazaars of Bombay."

Now Mabel was hurrying away to the bazaars of Europe in order to escape Taylor's ghost. Bearded by reporters on the dock, Mabel had refused to answer any more questions about the murder. "I've been running away from it for months," she told them. Mabel was taking not only her first trip abroad but also her first long vacation in years. Mabel was the last of her peers to go. Arbuckle had made a triumphant tour in 1921 just before the scandal. Pickford and Fairbanks had taken Europe by storm in 1920 in one of the most publicized honeymoons in history. Chaplin, after his 1921 divorce from little Mildred Harris, had made a royal progress any king might have envied and hundreds of emigrés did. "He Came to America Travelling Second Class," *Photoplay* entitled Chaplin's return, "He Went Back as the Most Distinguished Passenger."

So many stars were making the Grand Tour in 1922 that *Photoplay* commented, "Paris has become a suburb of Hollywood." Mabel's Grand Tour was to begin in London and move on to Paris and Berlin. While Mabel stayed at the Ritz, her press agent made certain that London and her fans back home knew where she was. Reading Thomas Burke's *Limehouse Nights*, Mabel set out to see Limehouse for herself, the agent reported, decked out in her diamonds and furs. At Pennyfields, the Cockneys quickly recognized her and cried "Mybel! Mybel!" until a London bobby rescued her from the mobs and returned her to the Ritz. If the Fairbanks had their mobs, so did Mabel.

After Mabel toured the Continent, she returned mid-September on the *Majestic.* Pola Negri was aboard, making her first trip from Warsaw to become the first of Hollywood's imported sirens in a film aptly named *Bella Donna.* When Pola confessed that the first movie she had seen was a two-reel comedy of Mabel's, the pair became immediate friends. Pola, who had survived tuberculosis as a child, believed that Mabel even then showed the exhaustion of a tubercular. Mabel, however, felt rested and full of fun, and she coached Pola on how to become a greater star than Gloria Swanson. "Always say 'No'," she counseled. Swanson herself was about to say "Yes," to the Marquis de la Falaise de la Coudraye and to raise the standards considerably of other Loreleis abroad.

Sennett's publicists had been playing up Mabel's extravagance to compete with the new glamor queens like Gloria, who glittered with conspicuous consumption. In December, *Photoplay* ran four pages of fashion photos entitled, "Youth and Moonlight and Paris, An Impression of Mabel Normand's New Clothes." Mabel posed in silver lamé turbans and mauve capes, in ostrich collars dyed purple, in afternoon coats embroidered with steel nail-heads, and in evening wraps of tiered silk fringe collared in monkey fur. In her suite at the Hotel Crillon, Mabel was reported to sit on the floor while she pointed at parading mannequins, "I'll take it, just like that — dress, hat, shoes and all." When she returned, Violet Unholtz told me, her clothes were all a size and a half too big and had to be cut down to fit.

She did not return to Hollywood, however, until spring. When she landed, her publicity agent sued her for $2500 he thought owing and attached her trunks at the dock. He lost his case, but he augured trouble of other kinds. Mabel's longtime pursuer Norbert Lusk caught up with her at the Hotel Ambassador. He had not seen her since the Goldwyn days when, a young man in love, he had "waited for word from her that didn't come." Now she seemed "changed, yet unchanged." She was more bookish and wrote poems, but only for herself, she said, for she "couldn't bear to be laughed at in *that* way." In London, she told him, she had met H. G. Wells and G. B. Shaw, whom she found "quizzical and very clever." She would have met Sir J. M. Barrie at the Ritz, but she dawdled so long in her bath that he fixed the fire in her grate to warm her and left.

Now that her vacation was over, her doctor had ordered complete rest. Lusk indicated why.

Scampering over to a desk, she cried: "Isn't it outrageous? I have to autograph five hundred of these Suzanna books before I can get away! It's slavery.

*Tell me what to write on the flyleaf for my French
teacher. I've been studying three years and don't know
a thing, but he's a darling old peach."*

*She needed no prompting. "Don't you dare like
this book better than you like me. Votre gamine
terrible — Mabel! I bet I know more French than
Mary Pickford at that," she crowed, inked to the
wrists as she went on scribbling.*

Mabel was soon to play *votre gamine terrible* to Mack when
she got wind of the fact that Sennett had been offering the lead
of his next film to another girl. *Six* other girls, Mabel told Sutherland and named them. They were all Sennett bathing beauties,
all "adorably young" as advertised, and Mabel was enraged. In
November, she told Lusk to take charge of her mail while she took
off again for Europe. Lusk was to cable her if he came across any
loose jewelry. "I don't expect any," she told him, "but somebody
might have a weak moment." He was also to send Goldwyn's
memoirs as they appeared in *Pictorial Review.* "I want to see what
he says about me." This time Mabel met Barrie in London, and
she wrote Lusk, "He made me think of Peter Pan grown old. He
wears a shawl." The mail brought no jewels, Lusk said, but a
quantity of lover's laments from suitors who imagined Mabel had
promised to marry them. "I felt sorry," Lusk said, "for the delusion of anyone who believed he could pin her down."

Mack thought he knew how to handle Mabel's elusiveness.
When she extended her first post-European vacation too long in
New York, he threatened to give *The Extra Girl* to somebody
else. Mabel was not in a mood for threats, and she called his bluff
to show Nappy he was suffering delusions of grandeur. Mack
delayed his revenge until his memoirs in a curious mixture of
complaint and brag. "She ordered the smartest clothes Parisienne
couturieres could overcharge her for, danced with princes, and
flitted about the cafes." While it was true that she gave high-
diving exhibitions on swanky English estates, rumors that she
dove naked into the ship's swimming pool were unfounded, Mack
said, "in all personal things she never violated good taste."

To get at Mack, Mabel made the most of a brief flirtation
with Prince Ibrahim, "nephew of the khedive of Egypt," whom

she had met at the races at Deauville. He had given her "many a laugh," she told Lusk, and had followed her to Paris with four turbaned genii bearing rare perfumes, Kashmiri shawls, and talismans of gold. The genii would stand, arms crossed, in the corners of her hotel suite while she and the prince conversed on a divan. "They didn't seem to cramp his style much," she said, "but the ship reporters back in New York read into our acquaintance a romance that never existed."

Mack was free to think what he liked when she flashed a big square-cut diamond on her engagement finger and denied that it meant a thing. Mabel returned, finally, to Los Angeles on March 4 and was met by a mob of reporters and friends at a reception at Santa Fe station. Mabel denied any rumors of marriage. "When I get married, well, it's not going to be a middle-aged man in Europe and it is going to be an American," Mabel told them. "No titles for me." Mack's publicists, however, made the most of the rumors since titles were as necessary as diamonds to a well-dressed star.

Mabel's little red-morocco address book confirmed that the prince was largely a diversion for the press. Mabel had trouble even getting his name right. She had crossed out "Prince Braham" in her book and had rewritten "Momahed Ali Ibrahim." Other names and addresses put the prince in perspective, encased as he was between the Hispano-Suiza garage and Van Cleef et Arpels in Paris, and followed by Marie Dressler and Sophie Tucker in London, along with F. Hall, "K" Division, Limehouse Police Station, who "showed us around docks."

Mack delayed release of *Suzanna* until he finally copyrighted the film on January 4, 1923. He wanted to wipe the screen clean of the Arbuckle and Taylor scandals and project "the Mabel of the early Sennett days, the carefree Mabel with the red cheeks and the laughing brown eyes." In *Suzanna* Mabel was to be "the same carefree devil-may-take ragged little angel of *Mickey* and *Molly O'.*" Sennett labored hard to make her so. He also labored hard to make Mabel the dramatic star she yearned to be. He invested more money in *Suzanna* than ever before. He labored over his plot: "Girl peon in love with one of noble birth is eventu-

ally happy with him after it is learned she is also of the nobility."
He labored over his dialogue: "If she is a lady, I'm glad I'm a
peon." He labored over the music cue sheet: "Don't use Toreador
Song except for a few bars. . . ."

Still critics complained that the story was "very weak and
very silly," the action "spotty and trite," and Mabel's talents
wasted. The public demanded "Pollyantics" from Mabel, and he
gave it to them, Sennett thought, letting the cross-eyed Ben
Turpin get the laughs from the Hee-Haws. But Mabel knew
something was out of whack when she read a critic who advised
audiences to sit through *Suzanna* in order to see the Hal Roach
short at the end. It was an Our Gang film in which "the dusky
Farina does some of the best work of her career." Mabel was
being replaced by a real Topsy, eight years old.

I found a clue to Mack's and Mabel's failure to bring off
dramatic comedy when I found Mabel's couturière, Violet Unholtz, in her nineties, living with her daughter in the cherry
orchards of Yucaipa. Mrs. Unholtz, a tiny dignified woman in a
lace collar as straight as the row of curls on her head, did not want
to see me. "The past is past," she said. "I want nothing to do with
it." Her daughter Lois, who was a child actress with her brother
Bobby on the Sennett lot, was equally firm. "I was there, so I
know there wasn't nothing to it," she said. When Mrs. Unholtz
relented and plumbed her memories, she remembered how Bobby
used to play with the rubber fruit on the hem of one of Mabel's
gowns and how scared he was of the big chow "Ojai" that Mary
Pickford had given Mabel as a pup. When Ojai died, Mabel
buried him in her backyard and put his framed portrait on an easel
above the grave. It was during *Suzanna,* Mrs. Unholtz remembered, that Sennett's mother moved to California for good with
the little girl she had adopted for the grandchild she had not got
from Mack and Mabel. What Mrs. Unholtz remembered best
was how Sennett tried to change the way he made films when he
made *Suzanna.* "They put Comedy to sleep and tried Drama,"
she told me, "but Drama was not Sennett's line. Drama is slow
plodding and Comedy is Bing, Bang, Bing."

Despite this change of rhythm, two critics at the time sin-
gled out *Suzanna* for special praise. Robert Sherwood included

Mabel's performance in his 1922 – 23 list of Best Individual Performances, calling her "a bright star the sparkle of whose wit
cannot be dimmed by the stodginess of the story in which she
appears." The discerning critic C. A. LeJeune called *Suzanna*,
more surprisingly, Sennett's finest film: "A fairy-tale bit of pantomime, beautifully massed, fantastically lighted, and richly played
by Mabel Normand but indeterminate in its goal." Divorced from
the goal of slapstick, Mack and Mabel floundered. Mrs. LeJeune,
writing in 1931, blamed American women for killing slapstick
because "they wanted romance and pathos, heroism and gallantry
in their entertainments, and slapstick denies all these things." All
these things were things that Mabel wanted and that Mabel
thought she had found in a role like Suzanna and in a man like
William Desmond Taylor. "You see," Mrs. Unholtz said, "in the
old days we picture people believed in *never ending time.*"

I-DON'T-CARE GIRL

Mack and Mabel's timing was notably bad. Ten days after Mack released *Suzanna*, Hollywood was hit by its third, and in some ways worst, scandal. On January 14, matinee-idol Wallace Reid, who had the looks of a Gary Cooper, the ease of a Clark Gable, and the charm of a Jimmy Stewart, died of drug addiction. Hollywood mourned as never before. In Hollywood, if Arbuckle was liked and Taylor was admired, Wally Reid was loved. Lasky called him "the easiest actor to cast and work with in the whole of my experience." *Photoplay* had recently said that if President Harding got $75,000 a year, Reid should get a million because he might not do much good but he couldn't do nearly as much harm. As it happened, Reid did a great deal of harm because his death once again shattered public faith in the sanctity of the images they worshipped.

Everybody had wanted to believe that Wally was exhausted from overwork and that he was improving as fast as his wife Dorothy assured friends and fans that he was. His wife put out daily bulletins about his quick recovery until his death put period to the farce. Dorothy was forced to confess that a doctor had put Reid on narcotics after a severe head injury and that he had become addicted before anyone understood. By the time the studio caught on, Reid was so fully hooked that he spent his energies outwitting the doctors set to watch him. Since he was a sporting type, Reid concealed his hypodermic needle in a hollow golf club, or so the rumors went after his death. After his death, his wife announced that she was going to produce, as "a memorial to my Wally's great fight," an antidope propaganda film called *Human Wreckage*.

It was the first of many such films during the twenties as the wreckage mounted. Sennett had once bragged of Mabel, "Wherever she was, there was action!" Now, it seemed, wherever she was, there was scandal. The process was cumulative. Mabel was not directly tarred by the Reid scandal any more than she had been directly tarred by the Arbuckle scandal. But the Taylor scandal had left a nasty taste on rumor's many tongues that made Mabel vulnerable from then on to any Hollywood scandal involving drugs. No matter how fiercely Mabel and Mack willed the past away, the past could not be reinvented, the slate could not be wiped clean.

Increasingly, Mabel became two Mabels, a public Mabel and a private Mabel. Both identities were real and both fake. Mabel's split personality was different from Pickford's since Pickford controlled her public image of purity as coldly as a sanitary engineer. The power of the mythic Little Eva to evoke nostalgic sentiment increased the more she was distanced from her public and from her impersonator. The less Little Mary was Eva in fact, the more powerfully her public willed the fiction that innocence was forever. Mabel, on the other hand, was never in control of herself because she was controlled by her images. The power of the mythic Topsy was immediate, personal, now. Topsy confirmed the lie that even the wicked were good. But the lie was perilous because Topsy, to be Topsy, had to go too far. Mabel tried to keep her balance by splitting the public clown from the private lady, but in fact they were both masks of a self she couldn't find.

Meeting Mabel for the first time in June of 1922, columnist Herbert Howe of *Photoplay,* noted the two Mabels and confessed that the public one, "the roguish mischievous child" of the screen, had always been too hoydenish for his tastes. To his surprise, he discovered that the private one was "a brilliant charming intellectual of lightning wit." As a dedicated convert, Howe now worried about Mabel's career. He worried that she was performing too much at parties and not enough on film. In New York, Mabel was a regular at Texas Guinan's infamous parties at the King Cole Club. In Hollywood, she was a regular at the Talmadges's Friday night "cat parties." Howe warned her that a star should be seen on the screen instead of in café society. "We have taken great delight in watching her at first nights and smart shops and in her limousine," he wrote in *Photoplay*, "but how about her public?"

But Mabel was a personality girl whose screen image was inseparable from her life and whose public demanded antics wherever she went. The public demanded more of its sinners than of its saints because it wanted its sinners both ways — real and fake. Like Fatty, Mabel had always been a comic scapegoat whose role was to purge the common flesh of its excesses by embodying them — sexually, whimsically, blasphemously. The I-Don't-Care Girls of comedy were all personality girls who were at the same time mythic girls meant to violate taboos, and their worshippers demanded that the girls invest the myth with the reality of their persons. They would not be satisfied until the girls went all the way to anarchy and oblivion. That's what scapegoats were for.

In contrast to the spirituelle, the voluptuous were meant to be queen for a day — only. The Mabel Normands, the Clara Bows, the Marilyn Monroes had to burn out and wither like roses, for they were Time's Fools. They were the seize-the-day girls, the rosebuds to be gathered while ye may. They imaged the mortality of youth and beauty and merriment, not their endurance, and the scandal that overtook them all was as inevitable as "the doom of Mabel Normand." Their adorers wanted the fiction of innocent naughtiness, and if the hard facts of sex, alcohol, drugs, and age took over as innocence fell into knowledge, there was always a fresh rose to be plucked. The I-Don't-Care Girls were captive to those they captivated in a very special way. As a drug-blasted Judy Garland said once of her fans who mobbed the Palladium, no matter what she gave them, "They wanted more and more."

In April, Mabel began work on *The Extra Girl*. "Seventh-choice Mabel," she reminded Mack and made him pay for his perfidy with a new contract for two (or never more than three) films a year at $3000 a week. But Mabel's bad luck was running true to form. In August, a horseback-riding accident put her in Good Samaritan Hospital with a broken collarbone. During a party weekend, she'd been riding on Coronado Beach alone, when her horse stopped suddenly and pitched her over his head. She landed on her shoulder and passed out. A couple found a riderless horse far up the beach and traced his prints in the sand back to Mabel. Mabel was scratched and bruised, the papers reported, but in no danger of permanent scars. Mabel, I discovered later, had been drunk at the time.

Mabel's bad luck did not improve in the hospital. Another patient was Mother Shelby, who gave press interviews at her bedside in response to the accusations of her ungrateful daughter. Mary was suing her for every penny she had. Mary had kept a diary, and the *Examiner* now quoted a few of its "tear-stained" pages addressed to Taylor after his death: "You were to have been mine. Had I known you were to be taken from me no power on earth could have kept us apart." Asked to comment, Mabel told reporters, "It is too bad that my name should be dragged into this on account of the family squabbles between Miss Minter and her mother." Mabel did not know that a year later her name would be dragged into another scandal because of the family squabbles of another patient, millionaire Norman W. Church. After his wife visited him in the hospital, she sued for divorce and named Mabel corespondent.

Mabel soon returned to work, but she was not in good health. She was thin and gaunt and tired easily. Sennett's publicists tried to turn this to advantage by calling her "a slapstick Mona Lisa" in her new role. But critics of *The Extra Girl*, after its premiere on October 28, observed in its star "a certain forlorn pathos that is distinctly real." One acute reviewer noticed that Mabel revealed a dual personality. "The Normand everyone knows so well, lively, gay and mischievous is there, but almost at the snapping of a finger her buoyancy gives way to an expression of utter despair." Mabel couldn't hide the truth of her despair from the searching eye of the camera, although she smiled bravely. But critics were no longer pulling their punches and the *New York Times* said openly what many felt: "In the beginning one or two scenes are mildly amusing, but for quite a long spell one sits and thinks that Mabel Normand is a little too old to play the part of a screen-struck daughter." This time Mabel was upstaged not by dusky Farina but by one of Colonel Selig's lions. "The lion is the whole show, far more amusing than Miss Normand."

The Extra Girl was Mabel's swan song without her knowing it. "I think you will be proud of your old moody Maberu San," she had written Lusk, using his joke-Japanese name for her. "She did not guess that her days as an actress were numbered," Lusk commented. *The Extra Girl* is the only one of her three Sennett features to survive, and I could see for myself the sadness of her face in repose. Yet many of her comic scenes are as funny as ever, particularly when she battles with her father over a forced marriage and when she muffs a screen test wearing an unmanageable hoop skirt and pantalettes. The story is lost somewhere in the usual hokum (and the surviving film is so fragmented that it suggests lost footage or botched re-editing), but the chase scene is surely the most exciting Mabel ever made. The chase was too exciting, Mabel told Sutherland, since it involved a real lion supposed to run amok in the studio and to corner Mabel in a closet, where she wards him off with a feather duster.

The behind-the-scenes stuff was even more exciting. Mabel was supposed to lead the lion on a rope behind her, pretending to mistake him for Teddy the Great Dane. Off camera, director Dick Jones kept a pitchfork in hand in case of trouble. But unfortunately Jones stumbled and frightened the lion. The lion sprung, Mabel fell flat, and Jones stabbed Mabel in the rear with the pitchfork intended for the lion.

The Extra Girl was at the far end of the curve of Mabel's career. At the near end was an early 1913 short called *Mabel's Dramatic Career,* which traced the story of a kitchen scrub who becomes a star at Keystone Studios. "Time Passes," the subtitle says. Mack, the rube that Mabel left behind, enters a nickelodeon and sees the star threatened by a villain on the screen. "It's Mabel," he cries, and rips up the screen with his six-shooter, mistaking the fake for the real. A decade later, it was still Mabel, but the plot and the mood and the fakery had changed.

What is visible in the *The Extra Girl* is an unexpected overlay of sadness and loss. The old folks are left behind in River Bend, USA, to mourn an empty place at the table while their little girl has run off to Hollywood to seek her fortune in the movies. This time, however, Cinderella doesn't make it. Mack claimed that he wanted the film to be a "realistic" portrayal of the fate of hundreds of thousands of girls who flocked from small towns all over America to Hollywood in search of stardom. In the final scene, the small-town girl who failed to become a star has returned to River Bend and married her old beau. They sit with their little boy watching home movies. Mabel's line ends the film, "Dear, to hear him call me 'Mama' is better than the greatest career I might have had." Sennett has changed the line for the worse from his written scenario, in which the boy asks his mother who the pretty lady is on the screen. "Why that is mama," Mabel replies, "acting in the movies when she was young and foolish."

BAD-LUCK MABEL

SEPTEMBER 16, 1977, BEVERLY HILLS
[Looking through the publicity releases in the Mabel Normand file in the Library of the Academy of Motion Picture Arts and Sciences, I found one dated August 28, 1924, from the *Daily Express* that began, *"Miss Mabel Normand — you cannot keep that name out of the news — returns to the screen in* The Extra Girl." In the margin a contemporary hand has scribbled in red pencil, *"Ha, Ha!"*]

JANUARY 1, 1924, HOLLYWOOD
Meditating in his eight-foot marble bathtub in the tower on the Sennett lot, Mack was pleased with himself and with Mabel. Despite mixed reviews of *The Extra Girl*, box-office receipts were good in the States and sensational in Japan. At the Mission Theater, Mabel had recently appeared at a benefit showing for the Japanese Earthquake Relief Fund, for which admission was a can of food. "A can if you can" advertised the film and the star's good works. The film was going so well that Mack had negotiated a new contract with Arthur S. Kane of Associated Exhibitors for a series of features starring Mabel.

Personally, too, things were going well with Mabel and Mack. Mabel had come to his New Year's Eve party the night previous, had behaved herself, and had thanked him for "a beautiful dinner." It was almost like old times, before Taylor, before Goldwyn. . . . Mack would send her a magnificent bouquet tomorrow to the Good Samaritan Hospital where she was scheduled for an appendectomy early in the morning. He hoped to god she was getting a good night's sleep. Maybe her luck had turned. What

191

else could happen? The phone rang and Abdul, his Turkish masseur, answered. After a few moments, he handed the receiver to Mack. It was Mabel, calling from the Wilshire Boulevard Police Station, completely hysterical and saying someone had been shot.

On January 2, Mabel was back in the headlines. The *Examiner* ran a photo of Mabel in a demure straw boater under the heading, "MABEL NORMAND'S HOST SHOT BY CHAUFFEUR!" The subhead was worse: "Edna Purviance at Party; Driver States He Used Mabel's Gun." At 8:30 the night before, Mabel had been quizzed by the same police detectives she had come to know intimately after the Taylor shooting. As Detective Cline made out his report, he asked Mabel once again. "Name?" "Mabel Normand." "Occupation?" "Motion Pictures." Edna Purviance was with Mabel at the station, and she denied that anybody was intoxicated, although "it would be foolish to deny that there had been nothing to drink during the afternoon." Police told newsmen that the actresses were in "a high state of exhilaration from New Year's celebrating" and that Miss Normand was so anxious to set right her chauffeur's story that she was incapable of coherent statement. Reporters noted that Mabel was "lavishly dressed" in black velvet and diamonds. They also reported that when the police had arrived at the apartment of Courtland Dines, Mabel's host, Dines was propped up in bed, smoking, and refused to move. Police had had to strap him to a hospital stretcher to remove him violently "in a cloud of cigarette smoke and profanity." Mabel's denial that she had had anything to do with the shooting became a stock Hollywood joke for stonewalling, "I was not in the room when the shot was fired."

Headlines the next day compounded confusion, "GREER REVEALED AS FORMER CONVICT! MISS NORMAND SUFFERS BREAKDOWN." Mabel's chauffeur, Joe Kelly, who confessed that he had shot playboy Courtland Dines, was not Kelly at all but an ex-convict named Horace Greer. Greer had escaped in 1914 from the chain gang of the Oakland City Jail where he had been sentenced for petty larceny and had come to Hollywood for a new life under a new name. Dines was reported to be fighting for his life in great agony at the same Good Samaritan Hospital where Mabel was also a patient. Actually, Dines was not badly wounded, and Mabel was simply going ahead with her appendectomy, but rumors and headlines multiplied as the principals contradicted each other's stories.

Mabel's story was that Edna had called her mid-afternoon on New Year's Day and told her to drop over to Dines's apartment at 325-B North Vermont. Dines, at thirty the twice-divorced son of a Denver oil tycoon, had been dating Edna for several weeks and said of Edna and Mabel, "We three were just the best pals in the world." Mabel arrived around four o'clock, she said, and started to clean up the mess from the night before with a broom and mop "and otherwise did a great maid act." She had not meant to stay, but Dines began to tease her about his Christmas present that he had forgotten to take from her house. So Mabel called her housekeeper and told her to send Joe Kelly over with it. The housekeeper reminded her of her operation the next day, but Mabel told her not to worry. Around seven o'clock, Dines insisted that they all dress for dinner. Mabel followed Edna into the bedroom to help hook up her evening gown. "Say, you dirty dog, where's your powderpuff?" Mabel remembered asking. Then she heard firecrackers explode. "I used to throw firecrackers . . . at Ben Turpin," Mabel explained to the police, "until he threatened to quit his job." Firecrackers seemed to be popping all over the house, when Dines appeared in the bedroom doorway, smiling funny. "Well," he said, "I got plugged." Blood began to seep through his shirt front. Mabel and Edna laid him on the bed, tore off his clothing and put a dressing gown on him. The next thing they knew, the police burst in and an ambulance arrived.

Chauffeur Horace Greer, alias Joe Kelly, told a different story. He had shot Dines in self-defense, he said, when he saw Dines reach for a bottle to slug him with. Then he had driven to the Wilshire Police Station, thirteen blocks away, to give himself up. When Mabel had telephoned home for the package, Mrs. Burns had told Greer that Mabel would be better off without such friends. "Then in a fit I sort of ran upstairs and grabbed the gun," Greer explained and added, "I have lung trouble and heart trouble and can't stand up and fight." Greer knew that Mabel kept a .25 caliber pistol in her bedroom dresser drawer. Greer had once asked Mabel's maid to get it away from her because they were all afraid that Mabel might use it on herself. Mabel was given to fits of depression, and when she drank she was impossible to control. The maid couldn't give Greer the gun, she said, because Mabel checked it every night.

When Greer reached Dines's apartment, Dines kept him waiting outside. "It was cold out there and I got quite peeved," he admitted. When he entered, Mabel was lying on a divan and "in no condition to stay any longer." Greer insisted that she come home, when Dines sneered and reached for a bottle. "That was where the trouble came in." Inspector Cline asked what he meant by trouble. "I just shot him, that's all," Greer replied. "I was so nervous that the darn gun kept on shooting. It fired three shots, I think, and jammed." Mabel told the police that her director Dick Jones had given her the gun as a joke when they were filming *Mickey.* The boys had tricked her into believing she was a crack shot by letting her shoot at a row of bottles that a cowboy, standing just behind her, would hit. Dines kept Mabel "all hopped up," Greer complained. When Cline asked him whether he meant dope or liquor, Greer replied, "Liquor, I guess." "Is Miss Normand using dope now?" Inspector Cline persisted. "Not that I know of," Greer answered.

Dope had surfaced again. "He was just full of hop," Dines said of Greer, "that's the only way I can figure it out." Dines's story was that he and the girls had been "sort of arguing" about Mabel's going to the train to meet some friends. "I told her she was in no condition to go out in public," he said, but Mabel wouldn't listen and called Greer to take her. "You know how Mabel is," Dines continued. "No one can do much with her." Dines instanced a party at the Coronado Hotel a few months before where Mabel had gone horseback riding and had broken her collarbone "because she wouldn't listen to reason." Dines said that when he refused to let Mabel leave the apartment, her chauffeur took out a gun and started shooting.

Newspapers had a field day with snapshots of the three best pals in the world clowning aboard playboy Freeman Ford's yacht on a weekend cruise to Catalina. They had struck "all sorts of silly poses in exuberant moods," Edna explained to reporters, but others might have said they were roaring drunk. Edna and Dines "had an understanding" that they were engaged, she said, but Mr. and Mrs. Tyson Dines promptly disputed her claim. "We would not have approved of such a marriage," they announced in Denver. Nor did they approve "the sweet time" their son detailed in letters to his friends back home.

> Every afternoon I leave my office right after lunch
> and we go to Mabel's house, or to Edna's, or to the
> home of another actor. We drink and play around
> and you never tasted such Scotch highballs. It
> certainly is a lot of fun. Then we have a new club
> called the "Beach Club" at Santa Monica. We play
> around on the beach in our bathing clothes until we
> are tired, then we go into the clubhouse and drink
> highballs and smoke in our wet bathing clothes.

One of Dines's friends described him to a reporter: "When he was sober, he was generous, interesting, thoughtful and a delightful fellow to know. But," he added, "he wasn't sober so often of late."

Neither was Mabel. "That woman when she is sober is the sweetest little woman in the world," Greer said damningly in Mabel's defense. Mabel's housekeeper compounded the damage by explaining that even though Mabel did not drink heavily, "she always hated not to be a good sport." To defend his own actions, Greer told police that a week before the shooting he had brought Mabel home late when "she was not as she should have been." He went up the steps with her as he always did, he said, "because she wore a great many jewels and insisted that I see her safely in the house." Greer said that he told her then, "Miss Normand, if you don't stop running around with those people, I'm going to quit my job." Mabel had told him, "Don't scold me now, Joe."

Scolding did no good, as others would testify. An actress, whom Taylor was directing just before his murder, recalled in the thirties that Hollywood's reputed misbehavior in the twenties had been greatly exaggerated. At Arbuckle's last big party before his scandal, she explained, nobody misbehaved — nobody except Mabel Normand. But even then, everything was under control.

Mabel's chauffeur had "seized her firmly and carried her to her car in spite of her violent protests," she said. "He was merely carrying out his unique orders — orders from her — as we all knew."

In the Dines shooting, the *Examiner* tried to play up a sex angle between the chauffeur and the famous actress, like a *Lady Chatterley's Lover*. "Was Greer secretly in love with Miss Normand?" they asked. But the angle lacked credibility, and reporters settled for a class angle between the chauffeur and the rich playboy. "Greer's insistence and Dines' disdain, the aristocrat looking down at the chauffeur, the Russian wolfhound lifting his lip at the sturdy airdale," one journalist wrote. "The consciousness of class . . . almost cost Dines his life." Some reporters opted for psychology and attributed Greer's dementia to media overdose. "To the world he was just a chauffeur, but in his own imagination Greer was a mighty champion of his particular goddess, who happened to be Mabel Normand." Greer was proof of the subversive power of movies to corrupt imaginations and to split identities. Greer told the police that when he got off the train in Los Angeles he took a new name because he was determined to become a success and to make "Joe Greer" the emblem of that success. He too might be a star.

He did star in the *People* v. *Horace A. Greer* before the grand jury on January 16, 1924. After a week's testimony, during which rumors of Greer's cocaine addiction increased, the judge reprimanded witnesses for conspiring "to keep from the court many things that the court should know about this case." Five months later, when the case went to court, the jury found the defendant *not* guilty of assault with intent to do great bodily harm, wilfully and maliciously, and Greer returned to anonymity. No jury, however, could clear the name of "the besmirched Normand."

BANNED

"This film star has been entirely too closely connected with disgraceful shooting affairs," the State Attorney General of Ohio announced in banning Mabel's films. In the aftermath of the Dines shooting, Will Hays was reported to be speeding from Chicago to Los Angeles "with his chin out." While Mabel was recovering from her appendectomy in the hospital, she hired a lawyer to answer telegrams from censorship boards across the country demanding explanations. After Kansas announced that all Normand films would be "eliminated" from the screen, Mabel was said to have wept through the night "in hysteria." Arbuckle's former attorney made matters worse by defending Mabel in the press. An artist should be distinguished from her work, he said, and exampled George Eliot. "Just imagine the world's being forbidden to read *Adam Bede,*" he said, just because the artist was a woman living in sin with a married man.

When Sutherland interviewed her in 1927, Mabel still wanted to set the record straight: "No ban ever was placed on any of my pictures because of the Taylor murder and the Dines shooting, in both of which affairs I was promptly held guiltless and nowise responsible." Mabel meant that Hays had never placed an official ban on any of her pictures. He didn't need to. The public did it for him. In a last-ditch effort, Sennett sent Mabel in the spring on a personal appearance tour in the East and mid-West. Lusk advised her against it. "She was no campaigner, no spellbinder," he said, "but a spontaneous comedienne." The trip began ominously with the Illinois Federation of Women's Clubs joined with the Women's Association of Commerce in Chicago. They summoned Mabel there to present her side of the story. But when she arrived on March 20, at the LaSalle Street

Station, Mrs. George Palmer, President of the Women's Clubs, publicly withdrew the invitation. "The majority of Illinois Club women wish to see neither the actress in person nor on the screen." Mabel was humiliated but managed to wisecrack, "Gee, if anyone ever shoots off a firecracker when I'm around. . . ."

Mabel's wisecrack was a pitiful squib to throw against her massive notoriety. Mabel went on with the tour and received mayoral keys to cities stretching from Kansas City, Kansas, to Philadelphia, but the tour was a disaster, and she knew it. When she wasn't intimidated by the people she was supposed to woo, she mimicked them behind their backs, Lusk reported, and "sometimes not far enough behind." Mabel told Lusk that she felt betrayed and exploited:

> *They tried to get money from me for their charities.*
> *They'd take me to orphanages and institutions to see*
> *the dear little kiddies. . . . Then they'd show me the*
> *toilets and say it was sad they were in such bad*
> *condition, and would I contribute for the children's*
> *sake? Darling, if I have to repair water closets to keep*
> *on the screen, I'll stay off, thank you.*

For years the public had been fed publicity stories of Mabel's generosity, her love of children, her benefits for orphanages and similar charities. For years the public had spent their money at the box office to make Mabel rich. They must have felt she owed them something. Mabel must have felt that no matter what she gave them, they wanted more. Because Mabel was intensely loyal, she took the public's fickleness as personally as she had once taken Mack's. "Mabel used to think the whole world was her friend," Lusk wrote, but she discovered at last that "there is an awful lot of hypocrisy in this world."

Mabel's response to trouble was to head for Europe, and she spent the summer there, from June to August. Sennett denied that he had canceled Mabel's contract and announced that she would soon begin *Mary Anne.* "As long as the public continues to demand Mabel Normand," Mack said, "my company will continue to employ her services." But his remark was disingenuous for the public had stopped demanding Mabel Normand, and he knew she would never make *Mary Anne*. Columnists championed Mabel in the pages of *Photoplay* against the "smug hypocrites and bigots" who had become "dictators of personal liberty." "Mabel is jinxed," Cal York wrote, "but she's also charmed." Many readers disagreed. "If Mr. York thinks he can stuff the public on Mabel Normand's virtues, he is very much mistaken," a letter writer complained. The quarrels between Mabel's defenders and detractors filled the letters column, but Mabel's fans were not helped by the star herself.

Mabel's old champion Herbert Howe defended Mabel against the complaint of an American matron he had met abroad who had been disgusted by Mabel's unseemly behavior on a night train from Rome to Venice. "It seems Mabel created hysteria among the passengers by sticking her head out of the compartment every five minutes to yell, 'Cuckoo!' and to hurl a silver dollar at the porter." Howe's defense was increasingly lame: "Mabel was above all mortal law, being in reality an angel who simply will play jazz on the harp instead of the standard anthems." In reality, Mabel was getting too old for such pranks, and other jazzing angels were flexing their wings. In 1924, Clara Bow was only nineteen, but Paramount had learned from Mabel the need to legislate restraint. Her contract with Zukor stipulated an amazing $500,000 bonus if Clara did not "run wild" too publicly. Meanwhile, the only begetter of the "It" Girl, Elinor Glynn, predicted that Mabel would rise again like an angelic host. "She will even rise above her own inner enemies, those enemies of the spirit which we all have to destroy."

Those enemies of body and spirit had a head start. A 1924 feature entitled suggestively, "The Inside Dope on Movie Stars," exposed at last the fiction that had buoyed Mabel's return to Sennett and had recreated, endlessly, the same little raggedy angel of *Mickey*.

> Her eyes are bulging and they have lost their old
> luster. Her voice is dull and, at times, wandering. She
> is still pretty. Her clothes are in beautiful taste.
> Recently she bobbed her hair in a spirit of mischief
> when a friend dared her to have it cut. . . . She

expects to work again, but the old Mabel Normand,
of the serio-comic smile and quick wit, is gone.

Carefree Mickey was gone even before Mrs. Georgia W. Church dealt Mabel a final blow in September by naming Mabel corespondent in Mrs. Church's suit for divorce against her husband. It didn't matter that Mabel was only one of three women named and that the other two supplied substantial evidence of Mrs. Church's loss of sanity. What mattered was that Mabel, after Arbuckle, Taylor, and Dines, was now in the news for a sex scandal with a man named "Church."

In charging her husband with cruelty and infidelity, Mrs. Church accused Mabel of consorting with her husband in the Good Samaritan Hospital the summer before:

> . . . *the said Mabel Normand was then accustomed*
> *to run in and out of his room attired, as to her outer*
> *garments, only in her nightgown and to have drinks*
> *with him there; and the defendant showed to the*
> *plaintiff flowers in his room which he said were*
> *brought or sent to him by Mabel Normand and*
> *afterward . . . Mabel had told him that if he did not*
> *keep still she would tell him naughty stories and she*
> *kissed him goodbye on his departure from the*
> *hospital.*

Mabel was outraged. She told reporters that during her two weeks' stay, she was never out of her own bed, that she had once seen a nurse wheel past her door a patient whose hands and arms were drawn in front of him in a painful position (from some accident to his hands, she was told), and that she had waved the patient a cheery goodbye when he went home. But as for any other contact, Mrs. Church's charges were absurd. "Why, boys, cross my heart," Mabel said, "I would not know that man if he were sitting here in this room listening to me." As for sending him flowers, "Good grief," she exclaimed, "don't he have enough money to buy himself all the flowers in California if he wants to?"

Against the advice of Mack and all her friends, Mabel decided to sue. "There is a limit to all human endurance and I have reached mine," she said, in filing on October 10 a libel complaint against Mrs. Church for $500,000. Mabel's lawyers stated that the divorce complaint "named Miss Normand in an unsavory manner and thereby damaged the film star's earning capacity in motion pictures." Mabel had determined to become "a pioneer," she said, on behalf of other maligned motion-picture people. "I've made up my mind to quit being good natured about all this dirt being dished out about me," she said. She had remained silent through all sorts of lies, but now she was going to protect herself. "They've just got to quit kickin' my name around," Mabel complained, offering them further opportunity. Mabel couldn't understand that lies were her business, even if some were truer than others. Mabel's name had ceased to be her own the moment she chose her occupation. On November 20, the State Superior Court ruled against Mabel on technical grounds. Mrs. Church had made no direct charges against Miss Normand herself, but rather against Mr. Church.

Sennett had had enough of name dropping. Mack dropped Mabel's contract by telling her a lie. He told her that Hays had banned her films. Mabel was angry and sceptical. She asked her friend Judge William P. James, who was visiting New York, to drop by the Hays Office there and find out what was happening. The judge wrote her in late October from the Hotel Commodore:

I think I wrote in my last letter that the Hays office here gave me to understand that they had issued no sort of ban against your pictures. Anything that was reported to you must have been upon the responsibility of your producer alone.

Mack wanted to appear loyal, and he remembered himself that way in his memoirs, "I offered to start her in a new picture immediately, but she wouldn't consider the idea." In fact, Mack had had enough of Mabel, and he now washed his hands of her.

For the next few months, Mabel killed time. She considered an offer from British National Pictures to move to England. She considered an offer to make films with comedian Larry Semon. She took a course in Advanced French at UCLA. And she picked up a new beau, director Paul Bern, who'd been hanging around, waiting, ever since he met her at Goldwyn's. Known as "the priest of Hollywood" for his wonderful brain, Bern wooed Mabel as Taylor had, with learning and fine jewels. Gossip columnists noted that they made a handsome couple at the premier of Fairbanks's *The Thief of Bagdad* at Grauman's Chinese. Mabel was wearing the sort of ermine and white satin that a later girl friend of Bern's would make her trademark. Jean Harlow would be the first to turn the voluptuous type blonde.

While her career fell apart, Mabel bought her first house, a "Beverly Hills Italian bungalow" which still stands at 526 Camden Drive, due south of Sunset Boulevard and the Beverly Hills Hotel. The area was just developing then as other stars followed Gloria Swanson's move from rented court apartments to bungalows to Mediterranean palaces. Mabel's house was neither bungalow nor palace but a solid, two-story, rough-stuccoed, flat-roofed building that, from a contemporary snapshot, rose stark naked from a lawn bare of shade or shrubbery. Age has improved it, and today palm trees and a tile roof have softened its outlines as it stands in a neighborhood of quiet affluence. But it was on the interior that Mabel lavished her attention. Other photos show Mabel's living room grandly got up with an immense antique Sarouk, plush settees, a Della Robbia reproduction covering one wall, tapestries covering another, a framed photo of Norma Talmadge on a fringed velvet cloth, and flowers everywhere, at least a dozen room-size bouquets.

When Mabel moved in, Blanche Sweet lived on one corner, actor Tom Moore on another, and young Basil Rathbone on a third. Mabel was at loose ends and drinking too much, Blanche remembered. Blanche remembers that Mabel invited her over one afternoon and boozily tried to entertain her with funny stories about herself, like the time a friend had advised her to cure a sore muscle with Sloan's Liniment. Mabel poured a bottle of it in her bathwater and "nighed burned her insides." But Mabel wasn't funny anymore. She was a drunk.

In June, Mabel announced that she was leaving Hollywood for good and returning to her real home in the East. She was going to start a new career on the stage and had just signed a five-year contract with producer Al H. Woods to star in a musical comedy called *A Kiss in the Taxi*. Mabel threw a large farewell party at her new house for all her old friends. "It's her great chance and Mabel knows it," a reporter wrote. It was also her only chance, and she took it, despite her terror of the stage, because Woods had persuaded her that a stage appearance would get her back on the screen.

When Mabel left for New York on August 3, friends and photographers crowded the station to see her off. She posed with the gang on the caboose of the Santa Fe Limited and smiled. But in her low cloche hat and short silk coat she looked like a wrinkled flapper and like a stranger to herself. To prove that she was through with Hollywood, she announced that she was writing "The True Story of Hollywood" based on her diaries, a real Hollywood autobiography — "with all the dirt in it." She also kept her house, in case.

A Hollywood elegist in the thirties, contemplating the number of deaths in the twenties by murder or suicide, concluded that Hollywood's speed was inhuman, since it sent so many bright stars into eclipse. "It sent Mabel Normand away and she never came back." Mabel had come back too often, and although she would return to Hollywood within the year, she never came back as a star. Later, Mabel blamed a fickle public and press for hounding her out of pictures as they had hounded Arbuckle. But who was to blame? The entrapments of image-making were too new and immediate to be understood by its victims. At one moment, the media made them gods. "Hey Fatty! Are you *human?*" asked a Paramount ad in 1919. "Are you a *wizard?* Or just a *genius?*" At the next moment, the media reduced them to subhuman simulacrums. "You are mere photographic types," *Motion Picture News* warned actors after Arbuckle's arrest. "You think you have been touched by divine fire, whereas you have only been touched by Celluloid."

Celluloid was new and the movies were magic, but the message was old as time. "Don't get too big," Allan Dwan had warned Hollywood friends. "You can last forever at the bottom or in the middle, but you get to the top and you're doomed."

RAGGEDY ROSE

OCTOBER 10, 1978, PACOIMA
[Lee telephoned at 8:30 A.M.]

I'm supposed to be fixing some breakfast for Julia, just some roast beef, mashed potatoes and tomatoes cut up in little squares to eat with a toothpick. But she can't hear me.

Well, the first Friday in every month a Father comes over. He's practically as blind as Julia so a girl in the Church comes with him. Julia gives him $10 for the Church and when the Father's in the other room I give the girl a hug and a kiss. But I musn't talk sex to you all the time. I'm supposed to talk about Mabel.

AUGUST 28, 1925, STAMFORD, CONNECTICUT

Mabel stood in the wings of the Stamford Theatre in a long curled wig and a ruffled organdy gown. She was waiting for her cue to enter as the wife of a philandering husband in the opening performance of *The Little Mouse*. She tried to remember her friend Nazimova's instructions when she had gone for her daily voice lesson beside the pool that would become the central attraction of Hollywood's Garden of Allah Hotel. Mabel had called Nazimova by her writing name, "Peter Winter," and "Peter" had told her over and over that even if her voice was soft and throaty she could learn to project it. Others had called her voice "hoarse and adenoidal," and when Mabel got to New York, she sought help from such stage notables as Laurette Taylor. Mabel had confessed to Lusk that she was "scared stiff not only at the thought of facing an audience but of being kidded behind my back by Broadway actors in the cast." From the wings, she had just spotted her old rival of Goldwyn days, Geraldine Farrar, sitting in the front row of the theater. Mabel's throat clamped tight with fear. She knew was going to bomb.

In New York, Mabel rented a lush apartment at 100 West Fifty-ninth Street on the Park and went straight into rehearsal. But her producer pulled a fast one. Instead of the musical she'd been promised, he pulled out an old chestnut roasted by the critics under seven earlier titles: *Oh Diana, Diana of the Movies, The Five O'Clock Man, The Blue Mouse, Lonely Wives, Oh Madeleine,* and *Naughty Diana.* Now it was *The Little Mouse,* and the producer had not even given her the fun role of the vamp in this old farce, but had cast her as the dull virtuous wife. He had given her a good contract, however, beginning at $1500 a week plus 10 percent of the gross. After the play, she was to make films for him on a sliding pay scale that would reach $8000 a week in the fifth year. Now she wondered if she'd even make it through opening night. She had never acted on a stage in her life.

Mabel's worst fears were confirmed by the critics. Mabel "spoke hardly above a whisper at times," the Stamford reviewer wrote. "She appeared to be under an unusually [sic] nervous strain." The show moved on to Long Branch, New Jersey, and then to Brooklyn before it closed September 16. "We owe her thanks for added proof of what has so often been asserted," said an unkind New Jersey critic, "that there is a vast gulf between motion-picture work and acting."

Mabel knew that she had failed in everything but courage, and she was desolate. Fans congregated at stage doors wherever she appeared, Julia told Stephen, but Mabel refused to continue the show. A Broadway playwright promised to write a comedy for her but couldn't get beyond the second act. Mabel busily wasted the entire winter in New York. She called in her entourage, Lusk said, "and settled down for a winter of reading, church-going and supervising the mending, pressing and inventorying of her stockings, handkerchiefs and lingerie that was always going on." If she couldn't be an actress, at least she could be a lady. Besides, Mabel rationalized to Lusk, "I have to stay here, I'm still under contract." Lusk understood that despite her forays down Eighth Avenue, flashing her furs and diamonds, "she was giving up without herself knowing it."

What Lusk and others knew was that she was drinking herself into oblivion. Julia preferred not to remember. What Julia remembered was only what was beautiful. Mabel liked "always to surround herself with high-class friends," Julia said to Stephen. She liked to give quiet parties for very conservative and literary people like "Carl Van Vechten, Miguel Covarrubias, Heywood Broun and Edna St. Vincent Millay." Julia remembered meeting the sweetheart of millionaire W. K. Vanderbilt, who took them to her "swanky apartment" to meet other gentlemen of culture. Julia did not remember what another memoirist of the period recalled. Edmund Wilson in his diary of the twenties remembered that Mabel was a regular at Julius's Bar in Greenwich Village, "a more or less horrible bar," open all night and always crowded, "with its extraordinary pictures, Mabel Normand, etc." Wilson's "etc." was eloquent of what Julia forgot.

OCTOBER 20, 1978, PACOIMA
[Lee telephoned at 8:00 A.M.]
Yeah, Cody's really a mean dog — to other people. He never bit family. I got to watch the gate every minute. He'll kill people — part pit-bull and part some little black dog. He's bit me a couple of times but he's gettin' old now, slowin' down. Bit the County Assessor once and the Insurance man said I'd have to get rid of him so I got rid of the Insurance man.

Did you get the nudist magazine I sent in that suitcase full of trash?

MARCH 24, 1926, BEVERLY HILLS
Mabel had just come back to Hollywood, to her Camden Drive house, and opened *Motion Picture World* to find an open letter filling an entire page.

WELCOME BACK TO THE SCREEN, MABEL NORMAND
Your return makes us all happy for you have the gifts, the training, the personality and the technique which is the supreme technique — the one which is

so sure that it does not show. You have that rare
thing, that possession above price, Mabel Normand,
the charm of spontaneity!
The best o' luck, Mabel Normand, and again
welcome back to the screen.

MARY PICKFORD

Pickford's letter cheered me mightily, Mabel told Sutherland, after the humiliation of her stage debut. Mary understood the source of Mabel's greatest pain, that all the training and experience of a decade's work in film counted for nothing on the stage. Mabel could no more transfer to the stage the art of pantomime that she learned for the camera than those vaudeville veterans Weber and Fields had been able to transfer to the camera the art they had learned for the stage. In praising Mabel's spontaneity, Pickford now tactfully suggested to Mabel how foreign to her own talent and craft was the stage's demand for repeated performance.

Mabel had come back to Hollywood after many had missed her on the screen. The influential critic Iris Barry in her 1926 volume *Let's Go to the Pictures* compared Mabel favorably to the new crop of comediennes — Constance Talmadge, Dorothy Gish, Louise Fazenda — and lamented that "Mabel Normand, with more talent than ten of her sisters, is almost forgotten." Barry, like LeJeune, discriminated between farce and dramatic comedy and understood the unique values of slapstick. "Mabel comes in between the clowns and heavies," Barry wrote. "Mabel is the one and only true female comic."

Hal Roach brought Mabel back to Hollywood in March with a three-year contract for eight short comedies and eight features. Her old friend Dick Jones had left Sennett to become production supervisor for Roach Studios, and it was Jones who asked Roach to hire her. "The bringing back to the screen of Mabel Normand was a master stroke," Roach Studio ads said at the time, but Roach told me that he hired Mabel because "Jones thought she needed the dough." Roach was more interested in his own comic stable: Will Rogers, Harold Lloyd, Laurel and Hardy, and Our Gang. Our Gang had just made a comic burlesque of *Uncle Tom's Cabin,* and Mabel must have winced to see her mug in the Roach advertising lineup squeezed between Will Rogers and dusky Farina in her Topsy role.

No sooner had Mabel returned than the Taylor ghost reappeared in headlines, "MYSTERY OF WILLIAM DESMOND TAYLOR'S MURDER IS SOLVED, KILLER KNOWN DECLARES KEYES." District Attorney Asa Keyes and his deputy (who both landed in San Quentin in 1930) had just completed a four-week investigation in Chicago and on the East Coast, following "new information" supplied by Mary Miles Minter in New York. While Mabel had been living at Central Park South, Minter had been living in Central Park West. She engaged in charity work now that she had retired permanently from the screen, after a settlement of $300,000 with Zukor. Four years after the murder, reporters were again hammering at Mabel's door. "Persecution!" "I am being harassed," Mabel complained. "I have answered a million questions regarding the Taylor murder case. . . . I tell you my nerves are frayed."

What new information Minter supplied was never made clear, but she had implicated somebody. Headlines like "HOLLYWOOD WOMAN TAYLOR SUSPECT" did Mabel no good no matter how often Attorney Keyes stated, "Miss Normand at no time had any connection with the Taylor murder." Nor was she in the room when the shot was fired, Hollywood joked. Keyes announced the startling news that Minter had been in Taylor's apartment the day of the murder and that an arrest was imminent because he had enough evidence in his suitcase to convict two men "now in Chicago." While Mabel had nothing to do with the murder, Keyes said, "she had valuable evidence that will help to clear it up." Valuable evidence instantly vanished. Deputy Davis complained that his briefcase had been stolen, along with newly recovered evidence (two long blonde hairs) from the police department safe. The Taylor mystery continued to thicken with killers unnamed and unknown.

For Roach, Mabel was scheduled to make six shorts before January, but she made only five before her contract was dumped: *Raggedy Rose, The Nickel Hopper, Anything Once, Should Men Walk Home?, One Hour Married.*

"I know of no reason why I should not have gone ahead and fulfilled my contract with Roach, save for a couple of facts," Mabel told Sutherland. "I got married and I got pneumonia." Roach also had money troubles and had to cut back. Mabel was expendable even though she was doing good work. To return to two-and three-reel shorts after full-length features was a humiliating comedown for Mabel, but Roach knew how to use her to her best advantage in the new contexts of comedy.

Roach understood story structure in a way that Sennett never had. Roach recently explained that "Mack knew how to do slapstick, but he never knew why he did it." Mabel's talent, like Mack's, was for a comic situation or scene rather than for sustained narrative. Mabel filled and elaborated "the moment" the way Chaplin did, but she needed help in putting the moments together.

Four of her five shorts for Roach have survived and make one wish that she had teamed with Roach earlier. She is still doing Cinderella turns, but Roach exploits them for sight gags of a kind that would soon make Laurel and Hardy famous. Mabel in *Raggedy Rose*, for instance, is a junkman's apprentice whose job is to collect the junk thrown at a pair of fake cats she winds up to yowl. Love enters the picture when the hero tosses his boot at the cats and knocks Mabel cold. Mabel in *The Nickel Hopper* is a nickel-a-dance girl whose feet are mangled first by the young but fat Oliver Hardy and then by the young but tall Boris Karloff. When Mabel spurns the hero's Rolls for her own Model-T, the car collapses around her in a heap of tin, anticipating a dozen Laurel and Hardy scenes of a clown left with nothing but a steering wheel and a subtitle, "The engine must have been cold."

Mabel's best short, *Should Men Walk Home?*, was her last, released January 14, 1927, under the direction of Leo McCarey. McCarey, who became an important comedy director for Laurel and Hardy and the Marx Brothers, dropped the Cinderella plot and made a crook comedy that shows what Mabel might have done had she been born later or understood her talent better. Paired with a handsome second-story man, Mabel plays a jewel thief distinguished by incompetence. At a party where fat Oliver hovers over the punch bowl, Mabel drops the stolen diamond in the bowl, a fountain, even a baby's diaper before house-dick Eugene Pallette can catch her. Promising to reform, Mabel drops silverware from her sleeve as she exits. McCarey's farce is more sophisticated than Sennett's because the tempo is different. McCarey explained once that he deliberately altered the rhythm of Sennett's slapstick, slowing down what Mack had speeded up and underplaying what Mack had overplayed. If speed was the key to the Old Comedy, slow and deliberate motion was the key to the New. Mabel's flexibility could have made her the catalyst for McCarey that she had been for Sennett.

Oddly enough, it was Mabel, McCarey said, who sparked Laurel and Hardy's famous traffic-jam scene in *Two Tars* by a real-life scene of cumulative destruction. As McCarey tells it, Mabel, Roach, Charley Chase, and a few other comics were in New York in McCarey's hotel room, where he was dressing for dinner but unable, as always, to tie his bow tie. "Let's nobody tie his tie," Mabel said, and they all walked out on him. An hour or so later, after McCarey had called Hollywood to locate a tie-er in New York, he caught up with the gang in a restaurant, and the first thing Mabel did was to pull out his tie. "You little son of a bitch," McCarey yelled and in revenge pulled out Roach's tie. Roach pulled out Chase's, and the idea spread across the restaurant. First it was ties, then collars, then tuxedoes, which they ripped up the seams with their dinner knives. The scene makes one wonder what would have happened had it been Mabel rather than Mae Busch who went on to play with Laurel and Hardy.

But Mabel had peaked too early. "How many stars pull like the one and only Mabel?" Roach had advertised *Raggedy Rose.* "Her first picture in a long time — and the public is hungry to see her." The public was hungrier to see the new wave of far-ceurs like the Marx Brothers, who announced that at the close of their stage-hit *Cocoanuts,* their first film would be *The Marx Brothers at Yale.* Comedy was changing fast, and while Mabel began to adopt the look of baby-faced Harry Langdon, unless it was the other way round, the old-time human caricatures were being phased out by the newspaper cartoons that would eventu-

Top   The bungalow court on South Alvarado Street where William Desmond Taylor was shot February 1, 1922. Arrow points to 404-B.

Middle (*l. to r.*)   Edward Sands, Taylor's valet; William Desmond Taylor; Mary Miles Minter, starlet; Charlotte Shelby, Mary's mother.
Bottom   Diagram of bungalow court as it appeared in Mabel's biography in *Liberty* magazine, September 27, 1930.

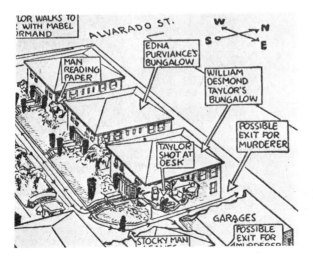

Top William Desmond Taylor in an official studio portrait for Famous Players-Lasky in 1921.
Bottom Mabel's photo was found on Taylor's body in a gold locket attached to his watch chain. The inscription reads, "To My Dearest."

Top   Mabel with her tutor George "Frenchy" Jaumier at a charity rodeo in Hollywood, where Mabel sports a diamond ring after her second trip to Europe, in 1922.
Bottom   Mabel with Duke the lion in *The Extra Girl*, released October 1923, just before Mabel's films were banned.

Top   Mabel with the Mayor of Omaha, Nebraska, on her unsuccessful tour in 1924 to salvage her reputation and her films.
Bottom   Mabel cutting up with Edna Purviance and Courtland Dines on a weekend cruise to Catalina Island before Mabel's chauffeur shot Dines on New Year's Day, 1924.

Top   Mabel on the side porch of her new house at 526 Camden Drive in Beverly Hills.

Bottom   Mabel quits Hollywood "for good" to start a new career on the New York stage in August 1925. Here to see her off are (*l. to r.*) Paul Bern, Ben Turpin, Marie Prevost, (unidentified), Jack White, Mabel, "Frenchy" George, Rena Borzage, (two unidentified women), Frank Borzage.

OPPOSITE PAGE
Top   Mabel with Dick Jones at Hal Roach Studios to shoot *Raggedy Rose*, November 1926, when Mabel returned to Hollywood after bombing in New York.
Bottom   Mabel relaxing on the set of her last film, *One Hour Married*, February 1927, five months after she'd married Lew Cody.

Top   Mabel poses with Lew for publicity shots after they ended a drunken party by eloping on September 15, 1926.
Bottom   Mabel with Lew, left, Raymond "Hitchy-Coo" Hitchcock, right, at the premier of *Bardelys the Magnificent* at the Cathay Circle Theatre in 1926.

Top Mabel's funeral, February 29, 1930. Honorary pallbearers at the right are Sam Goldwyn, Mack Sennett,
D. W. Griffith.
Middle Mabel's last portrait, in 1928, after tuberculosis
had been diagnosed.
Bottom Mabel's star as it appears today in the Avenue of
the Stars on Hollywood Boulevard.

ate in the replacement of Mabel Normand by Minnie Mouse. When Mabel broke her contract in January "by mutual consent," she was immediately replaced by a human comedienne who took the I-Don't-Care Girl to a new plateau of the voluptuous. She was replaced by the platinum blonde gold-digger Jean Harlow.

MRS. LEW CODY

NOVEMBER 1, 1978, PACOIMA

Dear Betty —

So first here is the recipe for Cody's Stinky Dinners. #1) Take a big washboiler, a six gal. size, and put in about 17 lbs. of corn beef with a couple head of cabbage and about 5 lbs. each of carrots, onions, parsnips and potatoes. Put the meat in with water in the morning and add vegetables about an hour before dinner.

#2) Now here's the name's-sake salad. Take one slice of Bermuda onion about 1/2" thick, put one slice of orange about 1/2" thick on top of that and drown in French dressing full of garlic chopped up fine.

#3) For dessert we bought pastry we called "truffles," shaped like a snail and filled with whipped cream. We bought 'em from our bootlegger. They were to take the nasty dinner taste out of your mouth. By each plate we put a little box of bicarbonate of soda.

XXX,
Lxx

SEPTEMBER 18, 1926, HOLLYWOOD

Lew Cody, who was to be master-of-ceremonies that morning at The Breakfast Club broadcast in Hollywood Bowl, arrived disheveled and a little late, still dressed in his dinner clothes. When he reached the radio microphone, he explained to his audience, "Fellows, I went to a party last night. It was my wedding party. I married Mabel Normand."

While his audience registered surprise, nobody was more surprised than either Lew Cody or Mabel Normand. Sennett refused to believe it. "I have never understood it, I cannot explain it, I do not even believe it. But it happened," he said in *King of Comedy.* "After Mabel Normand became Mrs. Lew Cody I never saw her or spoke to her again." Until then, through all that had happened between them personally and professionally, Mack still thought of Mabel as his girl. Now he could not forgive her any more than she could forgive him.

Mabel had made headlines once again: "ELOPEMENT OF MABEL NORMAND AND LEW CODY ON SPUR OF MOMENT SURPASSES THRILLS IN FILM DRAMA." Mabel and Lew posed for the press that afternoon in front of Cody's Beverly Hills house, and Lew explained their decision with a laugh: "Well, it's been on both our minds for a long time, only we didn't know it." Julia, who imitated her employer and married briefly a man named Benson, was horrified at Mabel's marriage. At first she refused to believe it. Then she refused to accept it. "They never lived together as man and wife," she assured Stephen.

The wedding surprised Mabel's suitor Paul Bern as much as it did Lew or Mabel. Bern had continued to pursue Mabel, despite a heavy dose of the Mabel treatment. "Mabel wouldn't give him the time of day," actress Leatrice Joy told me, remembering a scene when she was married to the romantic John Gilbert. Bern had dropped by to show the Gilberts a diamond and emerald bracelet he intended to give Mabel that night. Just then the phone rang for Bern. Mabel was calling to cancel the date. In a rage, Bern tore the bracelet apart and threw the jewels into the canyon below. Like Mabel's other lovers, however, Bern remained devoted to Mabel, and unlike other lovers he remained loyal throughout her long decline.

Mabel had trouble explaining her marriage to herself. Mabel had known Lew for a good fifteen years, and Mack had known him since they trouped together in an operetta called *The Dairy Maids.* Paramount advertised Cody as "the famous Beau Brummel of the screen, man about town, handsome lover of the movies, and modern Don Juan in general." He had been born Louis Coté, a French-Canadian, in Berlin, New Hampshire, on February 22,

1887. Since Cody had helped to create the type of villainous dandy, Mabel had cast him in that role in *Mickey*. Since then, Cody had become known as the Butterfly Man, after the title of one of his many films in which he played a "he-vamper," films like *Broken Butterfly, For Husbands Only,* and *Exchange of Wives.* Cody, in fact, had been instrumental in turning the dandy from a villain to a rogue-hero by making seduction comic. A 1920 *Photoplay* caught his tongue-in-cheek manner by describing Cody in *Broken Butterly,* "plying his wiles, his moustache, his tight cuffs, his fancy shoes, his curious waistcoat, his naughty eyes, his well-creased trousers, his multitudinous jewelry, and other devices, not forgetting his nonchalance — never must we forget his nonchalance! — upon a child of the Canadian woods."

Lew was entirely a creature of his tailor-made role. The I-Don't-Care Girl had married the actor known as "the devil-may-care man." He lived near Mabel at 609 North Maple Drive, in "a Spanish-Moorish palace," famous for the front door in which guests carved their names before eating his epic corned beef and cabbage dinners or gazing at his living-room tapestry of a nude with a tiger creeping up her flank. He was as famous as Mabel for elaborate private jokes. He liked to dress in the full uniform of a vice-admiral when he cruised in Keaton's "yacht," a car Keaton had outfitted with bedroom, kitchen, and bar. He was as famous as Mabel for not showing up on the set. Robert Florey remembered one afternoon when Cody kept a cast of 200 waiting while he passed out smuggled bottles of Pommery-Grenot to friends in his dressing room until Cody passed out himself. He was even more famous than Mabel for getting drunk. His gang of the Four Musketeers — Jack Pickford, Norman Kerry, and Marshall Neilan — symbolized, Florey said, *"toute la gaîté d'Hollywood,"* as they stormed Vernon's, the Hotel Alexandria, the Sunset Inn, and every bar in Tijuana.

Unlike Mabel, Cody had been married twice before — to the same woman, Dorothy Dalton. He would have married her a third time had he not slept through their scheduled wedding with a hangover and woken up twenty-four hours too late. Mabel told Sutherland that she married Lew the night a guest canceled out on a dinner party she was giving at her house and Mabel asked

Lew to fill in. Around midnight, when the party was going good, Lew got on his knees in a burlesque marriage proposal, and Mabel, in the same spirit, accepted. Guests demanded they elope. Lew called up the Beverly Hills Police chief for a motorcycle escort, borrowed twenty dollars from him to pay for the license, and the wedding party piled into Mabel's car to speed at eighty miles an hour with police sirens screaming to Ventura. Just like a film drama, they roused a justice of the peace, who pulled his pants over his pyjamas, wed them, and sent them back to Beverly Hills. While Lew went straight to his Breakfast Club, Mabel went straight home. Julia told Stephen that Mabel was "just heart-broken when she realized she'd married him," and she roamed the house upstairs and down when she got back. "And to think his name is on her tomb," Julia lamented. Lee said simply, "When they did it, Cody and Mabel were both dead drunk."

Adela Rogers paid tribute to their marriage in a 1929 feature she titled "The Butterfly Man and The Little Clown." When I asked her if she could explain Mabel's motives, Adela said that Mabel was very lonely and liked to go dancing with Lew at Vernon's, where Harold Lloyd and Bebe Daniels were winning all the cups. "All the gals were anxious to get dates with Lew," Adela explained, but Lew and Mabel were more like pals. "Mabel was like two fellows," Cody said. Because of Lew's Don Juan reputation, when the publicity organization WAMPAS gave the newly-weds a party, they presented Mabel with "Lew's little black address book," an out-sized baby crib, and an epigram: "Marriage is like prohibition — you'll have a helluva time enforcing it in Hollywood." In fact, however, Lew was much less interested in pursuing women than in pursuing a good time with his pals. After his nearly fatal heart attack in 1929, when his doctor forbade all visitors, Cody replied, "If I must die, I'll die as I've lived — laughing," and he sent for his pals.

Mabel's and Lew's elopement confirmed the public's view of "The Real Hollywood" pictured by a 1927 *Variety* as "a Land of Cockaigne and Cocaine, Champagne and Extra Girls." Even when Scotch cost eighty dollars a case and champagne a hundred, *Variety* noted, bootleggers were thick at every studio, where they handed out brass tags engraved with the bootlegger's phone number and the patron's personal order number. This was the Hollywood where extra girls were on twenty-four hour call at Henry's Deli, where director Mickey Neilan served 500 pounds of caviar at a time in washtubs at the Garden of Allah, where Norma Talmadge filed her jewels by color in her shoes — diamonds in white shoes, sapphire in blue — and where Mabel got drunk with Connie Talmadge in the ladies' lounge of the Hotel Alexandria.

But there was another Hollywood that Mabel had never been asked to join, the respectable Hollywood of married domesticity modeled on Pickfair's model couple. This Hollywood had complicated rules that allowed the mistress of San Simeon equal but separate rights with Mrs. William Randolph Hearst (herself a former show girl). It allowed Joseph P. Kennedy, a well-known family man from proper Boston, to provide separate but equal accommodation on the same Atlantic liner for his wife Rose and his mistress Gloria Swanson. However adaptive its rules, this Hollywood appeared on the society page instead of in scandalous headlines, and this Hollywood Mabel joined at last by joining the institution of marriage. When an old married friend gave Mabel a wedding shower, Mabel was overcome by the occasion and burst into tears. When the eminently respectable Mayfair Club invited Mabel to join them, she joined. The truth was that Mabel liked being married. She had simply married the wrong man.

MABEL DYING

NOVEMBER 5, 1978, PACOIMA

Dear Betty —

*About Cody and alcohol. He used to get 3 or 4
gals. of alcohol from a Hollywood drug store and his
chauffeur James Glen would make it into gin by
adding 4 gals. water to 1 of alkie. About the only
exercise Cody ever done was to lift up the glass or
bottle. He never used to go to bed until he was so
drunk he couldn't stay up any longer. His manager
had to give him an ice cold bath before he went to
the studio to get him sober enough to work, but this
was before my time.*

*I never heard of him taking any cure. His doctor
said it would be his end if he didn't stop drinking.
So he didn't stop and so it was his end.*

Lxx

FEBRUARY 15, 1927, SANTA MONICA

When Lew and Mabel got married, Roach offered them his
yacht *Gypsy* for their honeymoon, but Mabel returned to the
studio the day after the wedding to finish shooting *Anything
Once.* In January, as Mabel remembered to Sutherland, "I didn't
feel like working, and when one isn't happy one cannot work
— at least I can't." Despite the circumstances, Mabel took her
marriage seriously and at first liked playing the role of nest-maker.
The couple planned to take a trip to Europe together during the
summer, and Cody was making two pictures at once for MGM
in order to get enough time off. Meanwhile, they were looking at
Beverly Hills real estate for a house big enough to hold their

combined wardrobes, they joked. Until then, they kept both their houses and trouped back and forth for parties.

A month after Mabel left Roach, she became seriously ill with pneumonia and was removed to Santa Monica Hospital under the care of Dr. H. Clifford Loos, Anita's brother. The first reports were of "an abcess on the right lung," but they were quickly corrected to "a congested condition." Mabel was in a high fever and delirium but passed the crisis two days later at 8:00 P.M. Cody, who had remained with her at the hospital, went home. The doctors had finally diagnosed tuberculosis. Although Mabel's condition was kept both from her and from the public, her friends knew and knew there was no help for it. She had probably been tubercular for at least a decade, since 1916, when she would work harder to make up for the long bouts of illness and would drink harder to make up for the energy she lacked.

When he first came to Hollywood in the early twenties as a journalist, Robert Florey told his French readers that he naively believed headlines like "MABEL NORMAND A LA MORT" until "Frenchy" George assured him that "MABEL NOR-MAND DYING" was Hollywoodese for a head cold. At the end of the twenties, "MABEL NORMAND DYING" was a frequent headline, and it was fact, not fiction. Over the next three years, despite frequent spells of recovery, Mabel was dying by inches. Because she had so long been a symbol of Holly-wood's gaiety and vitality, "Mabel Normand Dying" became now a memento mori, a symbol of the mortality of Hollywood itself.

Mabel spent the next two months in the hospital, recovering, while Julia answered the flood of telephone calls and letters and flowers from friends and well-wishers. While Julia kept few mementoes of Mabel's living, she preserved every minute of her dying. She kept amusing notes that mother Peg Talmadge wrote from New York. Peg had just been buying presents for her "little girls" — "one or two little things from Woolworths (and damn nice for 10 cts.)" Or she had just been to a party with one of the boys who "wants to play 'Hide the Slippers' and little games where you get lost 'n everything, do you get me?" Julia kept a telegram from Norbie Lusk, from "My Heart Which Will Always

Be Mostly Yours." Julia kept Mabel's thank-you telegram to one of her "real" artists, James Montgomery Flagg, who sent her books. She kept fan letters. One fan from Australia sent Mabel a "charming book of Australian views." Another wrote from Stamford, Connecticut, to tell Mabel that she had known her brother Claude and to "ask Mr. Cody does he remember the bartender at Beslers on Main Street near the Alhambra Theatre." A friend who, with her husband, had been part of Mabel's wedding party wrote to say they were "broke for fair" and could she borrow the thousand or so "you offered that night?"

Mabel's brush with death impelled her toward Hollywood's large pool of psychics. Mabel got a fortune-teller to come to the hospital to read tea leaves. Julia saved the notes Mabel had scrawled from the reading:

> . . . *man comes to my house . . . feels badly about*
> *something, ashamed. I'm going to get a present,*
> *something to wear. Man who is feeling badly is going*
> *to bring it. Someone around my house very nosey,*
> *part of my wish here, not a good wish . . . an old*
> *lady sitting in a chair, waiting and waiting to hear*
> *from me. . . .*

The fortune-teller seemed to be describing Lew, Julia, and Mabel's mother, but you couldn't be sure. Mabel also consulted a numerologist who expounded Mabel's numbers. Her destiny was number four, her heart's desire was number four. These were good numbers, but her birth number was bad. "All the troubles and discord in your life have come thru your birth number," the reader advised. "You brot in a large Karma." He advised her to develop her Spiritual Body, "For you are God's perfect child. You are victorious, a bringer of good, like Calvin Coolidge, Warren Harding and Henry Ford."

Hollywood had always believed in numbers, and I picked up on Mabel's birth number, number six, when I came across a former silent-film star, Mary MacLaren, whose interest in numerology was keen. I found Mary in a soiled raincoat and cloth sandals, wearing an unraveled sweater for a scarf and feeding twelve cats and an aged toy poodle that was blind, stiff, and entirely denuded of hair. Mary, who had married a British Army Colonel in 1924 and had gone to live in India, who had danced once with the Prince of Wales and dined often with the Duchess of Sutherland, now lived on the porch of her bungalow, dispossessed by a hypnotist who claimed her house. Mary lived among moldy boxes of junk, garbage cans, opened tins of dog and cat food, and the combined excreta of her numerous pets. The number six, she told me, was fatal. By numeric equation, six was the number of my Christian name. "Betty, my dear, I would make this the last day of my *life* to wear that name," she commanded. "Change it today!" Like Mabel, Mary wrote poetry, and she took a magnifying glass from the Friskies box she carried for a purse to read me her last poem.

> *Every plant*
> *Every tree*
> *Every bird*
> *Every bee*
> *Every creature that I see*
> *Is a blessing to me*
> *From God.*
> *I feed as many as I can afford*
> *Praise the Lord.*

At Julia's instigation, Mabel had turned to the Lord even before her illness. She had met Father Vincent Chiappa, S.J., of Loyola College, and through him was helping to support an orphanage. Julia saved a letter from Father Vincent to Mabel, dated April 18, 1925, that suggested in Christian terms the way in which Mabel was split between good and bad "numbers."

> *Dear Child in the Sacred Heart:*
> *Your 150 orphan girls and your adopted children*
> *are crying and praying for their adopted Mamma.*
> *God wishes the complete surrender of yourself to*
> *Him by purity of mind, heart and body. . . . You*
> *have a noble and generous friend in Mr. Howe and a*
> *real guardian Angel in Miss B. You know her. But a*

deadly enemy in the person of anyone who defiles
your mind or body by ought contrary to God or
virtue.

The date suggests that Julia sought out Father Vincent when Mabel returned to Hollywood from New York, once again determined to make a clean start. But Julia suffered from a split that was rather like Mabel's and that surfaced in her letters to Stephen. Lee told me once that Julia had almost stayed in the St. Clara Convent in Wisconsin where she had been raised because she thought she had a vocation as a nun but found out she loved the world too much.

Father Vincent called Mabel "a chosen soul" and bombarded her with holy cards and holy medals until he died in 1929 at age fifty-eight. Father Vincent was but one of many Jesuits whose relation to the movie colony was close physically as well as spiritually. Sunset Boulevard was bounded by Loyola on the West and the Church of the Blessed Sacrament on the East. Father Vincent, however, tended to be too close in the pursuit of his duties and was reprimanded by his bishop for "his too apparent eagerness in the direction of nuns in convents."

Julia saw in Lew Cody that deadly enemy who threatened to defile Mabel's mind and body. But Mabel was genuinely fond of Lew and wanted to make him a good wife. I discovered this in a brief note, written in Mabel's hand, that Lee came across when he was sorting through his "stuff and stuff and stuff." It was a "Blessed Baby" letter and revealed a side of Mabel that she seldom let show beneath the mask of the regular fellow.

> *My Boy —*
> *What a naughty baby and how neglected you have been. Is going to make the house adorable for his return — will fix all those broken "funny old chain things" on the electric lights, will buy 2 doz. kitchen glasses, 2 doz. colored tall high ball glasses. Now young man to proceed further in our domestic lyric — also 1 doz. bath towels, 1 doz. sheets and 1 doz. pillow slips, 2 blankets — that very naughty Toby's*

outside sport is to tear them to pieces — also my
unmentionables. Will send Toby to his devoted
friend Rockie to play a harmless game of Running or
Solataire.

I'm in my bed my Big Boy but I'm not lonesome
with everyone here, only I'm happy I'm home waiting
for you.

— Baby

The note was undated, but Mabel had come home from the hospital sometime in April. The first thing she did was to celebrate by throwing a big party that must have put her in bed for another month. By this time Lew had quarreled with MGM and had quit to make an extended vaudeville tour on the Orpheum circuit. He was away when Mabel had a relapse and returned to the hospital in July. On July 28, 1927, the day I was born in a hospital in Riverside, Mabel was sixty miles away in a hospital in Santa Monica, deathly ill with 'flu and pleurisy.

By November, Mabel was well enough to take a trip East to join Lew for his performances in Washington, D.C. According to a news clipping, Mabel lost a $2000 diamond pendant "somewhere between the Willard Hotel and Le Paradise" after his show. Before Mabel returned to Hollywood, there were public quarrels and rumors of divorce, which both hotly denied.

Sometime in the fall of 1927, Sutherland interviewed Mabel and fell for her like all the rest. Sutherland's pet name for her was "Tibby," and he autographed a photo of himself with a message and Mabel's pet name for him: "Well no matter who gets the air, it was worth everything on earth that has any value, Tibby — 'Rio Rita.' " Mabel told her "Rio Rita" that she still hoped to recover fully and, when she returned to pictures, she intended "to do some lovely things in the modern vogue in comedies." But she sensed that 1927 was a turning point and that her moment was past.

In 1927, Al Jolson's *The Jazz Singer* ended silence. Only the year before, a Requiem High Mass at the Church of the Good Shepherd, Mabel's parish church in Beverly Hills, had ended the career of the screen's most eloquent silent lover, Rudolph Valentino. Only a year later, a letter from the William Morris Agency would ask Mabel to make a personal appearance tour for the new "talkies," together with Harry Langdon, Our Gang, and Al Jolson. Everything had happened so fast. Only fifteen years before, Mabel had made her first trip West on a crack modern streamliner, speeding at sixty miles an hour. Only a year later, an airplane pilot friend would write Mabel from New York to say that he had made a wonderful trip East, averaging 113 1/2 miles an hour from Los Angeles to New York.

NOVEMBER 10, 1978, PACOIMA
[Lee telephoned at 9:00 A.M.]
I just didn't want to go through the day without hearing your little voice. Are you ever constipated? I've got a little book here of Gaylord Hauser's, Eat and Grow Beautiful, *that's got your picture just inside the cover. At least I think it's you but it's a rear view and it don't have any clothes on. I wanted to ask — did you think I wanted to sleep with you? I coulda slept with Mabel's sister Gladys but she was kinda greedy. I just passed up the opportunity.*

JANUARY 5, 1929, SANTA MONICA
For Mabel, the year 1928 was a blank. For the first time since 1921, Mabel's name was entirely out of the news except for two small bits that framed the year. In January, a wisdom tooth upset Mabel's plans for a vacation trip to Denver where Lew was performing. In December, she made a little home movie as a Christmas present for Lew, "her first picture since retirement." She made it with the help of an MGM cameraman and director Frank Borzage in the vestibule of her Camden Street house, but "the story was a secret." She wanted Lew to have it before he left New York to extend his vaudeville tour to England and France.

Lew did not make the tour, and Mabel never made another picture. On the evening of January 5, Mabel suffered intense pains in her chest, her lungs hemorrhaged, and she was immedi-

223

ately taken to Santa Monica Hospital. That very evening, Lew Cody and Robert Florey were in New York, watching Max Schmeling beat Joe Sekyra in Madison Square Garden, when Lew clutched his chest in intense pain and collapsed with a heart attack. Florey's call to Mabel and Julia's call to Lew went unanswered, as their doctors West and East conspired to keep any news of their patients out of the papers in order to keep Lew and Mabel innocent of each other's crisis. Their tragedy had the timing of farce. For the next six weeks, each separately struggled to survive. Not until March 20 did the news break, "SCREEN PAIR FIGHT SERIOUS ILLNESS."

Only then did Mabel's doctor advise reporters that both of Mabel's lungs were infected with tuberculosis revealed by recent X-rays. He planned to remove her to strict seclusion in Pottenger's Sanatorium in Altadena to aid in her fight against t.b. Cody, meanwhile, had improved sufficiently to make the trip West but was still in seclusion at a health resort at Lake Arrowhead. He would soon be allowed to return to his beach home north of Malibu at Playa Del Rey to complete his recovery. "Neither are aware of the serious condition of the other," papers reported.

Under the headlines "MABEL NORMAND SINKING," reporters had a field day making up dialogue for a movie scenario.

> *"How is Mabel?" Lew Cody inquired.*
> *"She's fine," he was told, "and awfully anxious to see you."*
> *"Well, I'll be all right in a few days," Lew said, "but in the meantime don't tell her I'm ill. Let her think I'm still in New York."*
> *Almost at the same time in his Beverly Hills home, his wife, Mabel Normand was saying:*
> *"What word did we get from Lew this morning?"*
> *"He's fine," they told her, "and expects to start home in a few days."*
> *"Tell him I'm coming along fine," smiled back Mabel, despite the fact that life is slowly slipping away from her.*

Mabel — "once popular as a screen star," a reporter had to explain — had not passed the crisis of her fever until the end of February. While her doctor knew she would not get well, he felt she could now be told that her husband was out of danger.

Because Julia hated Cody, she was convinced that he neglected Mabel callously after he learned she was ill. When Mabel was still at home, Julia was the nurse in charge, and she kept a daily memo calendar from February to the following August. It told a different story from the synopsis in her memory. Lee came across the calendar after Julia went to a sanatorium in the Valley. On the calendar, Julia noted Mabel's pulse and temperature twice a day. After March, almost every other day she noted: "Dr. Cook visited, gave iron. Mr. Cody called."

Before Cody knew Mabel was ill, he called from "the Warwick Hotel in New York," then from Arrowhead, where he "sent flowers and Easter hat." Finally he called from his beach house, "The Light House." On April 11, Julia wrote, "Mr. Cody here today with nurse." After that, Cody visited Mabel regularly until August 28, when Mabel was finally removed to Pottenger's "very sick with neuritis." It would be Mabel's last trip.

I had decided that Julia was simply jealous of Cody until Lee sent me two bits of paper, torn from a spiral notebook, enclosed in an envelope of snapshots. The paper was covered with Mabel's penciled jottings, and I had to guess at the date. It had to be before Lew went off on his vaudeville tour.

> *Friday: Lew did not come for dinner — at Snows*
> *since Thursday night — drunk when he telephoned.*
> *Afraid to see him — hid upstairs. Came over,*
> *smashed in back window of door — raised hell —*
> *servant leaving, said he would break his neck.*
> *Telephoned him later — was then terribly drunk —*
> *said he would not take me on trip to Chicago to see*
> *fights.*
> *Saturday: J. [Judge] James here, called Lew to come*
> *for dinner — women over there — refused — left his*
> *house with her.*
> *Sunday: Nurse here — J. James, Lew here for dinner.*
> *Nurse told all our fortunes. J. left.*

They were sad notes from the hand of the girl who had written "our domestic lyric" and who had not married Mack because she found him with another woman on the eve of their marriage. Had Nurse told her fortune then, would she have seen a Lew Cody in her heart line, in her life line? I was sorry that Mabel had burned her diaries — or had had Julia burn them for her — but I understood.

GOOD NIGHT MABEL

NOVEMBER 15, 1978, PACOIMA

Dear Betty —

Well one Mabel story I remember. I used to carry Mabel around the house when she was too weak to walk. And one night I was sitting downstairs in the living room when Mabel comes wandering down the stairs. She said, "Lee, I just dreamt about you. I dreamt that you took me waaaay, waaaay out in the ocean on a ship and we never came back and I didn't give a damn." I carried her back upstairs and put her to bed.

Lxx

AUGUST 28, 1929, ALTADENA

When they took Mabel to Pottenger's in August, Julia slept in an adjoining room and handled all the letters and calls. Lusk said that he received a note from Mabel written in Julia's hand: "I'm doing all the doctors tell me to do, because I want to get well and go to New York again." Lusk found it strange to read her words in somebody else's handwriting, "like an impostor." As an actress, however, Mabel had been an impostor all her life, miming silently somebody else's words. Even the disease that attacked her seemed to belong to that simulated life, separating substance from shadow and wasting the one while illuminating the other. As Mabel's flesh grew weaker, her image grew stronger, her image of wild-child innocence. "She couldn't have lived longer," Lusk wrote. "It wouldn't have been right for her to grow old."

Mabel was actually thirty-eight the year she lay dying, but

nobody saw her that way. They saw a wasted child who could die but could not grow old. Her fans and friends deluged that child with fruit and flowers in such abundance that she sent the stuff on by truckload to a veteran's hospital in Albuquerque. Friends wrote notes to cheer her, and Julia saved them. Gloria Swanson scolded Mabel for not keeping her promise to play tennis. Mary Pickford thanked Mabel for "the dear little jacket" at Christmas, for the flowers at Easter, and hoped to see her soon "because it has been such a long time since we laughed together." Paul Bern, signing himself "Pinkus ben rabbi Jauno," joked that he wanted to visit her, "but somewhere in the offing is a doctor who will raise hell and kick me right out on-the-place-where-I-usually-sit."

Everybody saw Mabel the way they had always seen her, as a mirror of their own desires. Since she had reflected on celluloid an excess of life, she reflected now an excess of spirit. After her actual death, Hollywood conveyed what Mabel meant to them by inventing scenes of a little girl dying bravely, in several takes. Gene Fowler invented a scene of tough-sweet comedy for a pair of worldly clowns. "Lew, I want you to buy me an ambulance," Mabel says. "It's the only way to travel. You can lie down, smoke, and if you get in an accident, you're all undressed for the morgue." Since Mabel was a child with a child's passion for opening presents, Fowler wrote, Lew promised to bring her a double bag of trinkets the next day. "Don't let anyone open them please," Mabel whispers to her nurse just before she dies.

James Quirk of *Photoplay* wanted a scene of comic farce, so he staged a dialogue between Mabel and a friend just returned from a Mexican revolution. The friend had met an aviator there, he told Mabel, who used to tighten his steel leg with a screw driver. "Liar," Quirk has Mabel shout, laughing and wheezing her last. Anita Loos wanted a moral tragedy and narrated a scene of Mabel dying of drugs, attended by her doctor brother: "She was too far gone to be moved, so Clifford had a screen brought from her house and placed about her bed, where, thinking she was in her own room, Mabel died in peace." Adela wanted soap opera, "the girl who loved laughter" abandoned to her fate, a dying clown, dying alone. And Mack Sennett? Mack wanted a lover's farewell. "Those flowers over there," Mabel says with her last breath, "they're from Mack aren't they? He did not forget me."

Nobody forgot Mabel. They just kept on reinventing her. Julia, outraged at all these "barefaced untruths," reminded Stephen that she had been the sole guardian and faithful servant of Mabel's long passing. "I was so tired, worried and concerned," she told Stephen. "I got so thin, I fasted, gave up meat, candy, mortified myself, offering up to God to please spare Mabel's life." Julia sent for Mrs. Normand and hoped she would stay on to help care for Mabel, but after a couple of days, Mabel sent her mother home.

On December 22, 1929, the Taylor mystery troubled Mabel for the last time, "TAYLOR MURDER SENSATION. KEYES DENIES HE BLOCKED DEATH INQUIRY." The new district attorney, Buron Fitts, in cahoots with the governor of California, had found a new witness who would "prove" Taylor had been shot by "a motion picture actress." The new witness, however, was a druggie convict who traded fake testimony for a parole and who then skipped to Mexico. An old witness, Henry Peavey, resurfaced in San Francisco to say that he had heard a movie actress quarrel with Taylor on the day of the murder but he had been silenced by the then deputy attorney Keyes. Mabel's doctors refused to allow Mabel to be interrogated. Her last murder headline was "MISS NORMAND TOO ILL FOR TAYLOR QUIZ." Five days after Mabel's death, Keyes was sentenced to San Quentin for conspiracy and bribery, and twenty-two months after Mabel's death, Peavey died of alcoholism in a Napa hospital for the insane. The Taylor mystery remained a mystery.

By February 2, Mabel was too ill to be told that her father had died that day. Mabel's sister sent Julia a black-edged card announcing Claude G. Normand's death at age fifty-nine of pneumonia. "Julie darling," Gladys wrote, "whatever happens please don't allow Baby to see this — at least we can spare her this." I found the card in one of Stephen's files, and a visiting card was stuck to the back of it. It was dated January, 1930, and signed "To Mabel Norman: Hope you recover soon, Samuel Goldwyn." There was no word of any kind, Julia said, from Mack.

By February, Mabel was no longer allowed to see her chow puppy that she had named "It Girl" after Clara Bow. But the doctors could not stop Mabel from seeing, or pretending to see, things that amused her. She loved to tease her nurse Emma Johnson, Julia remembered, because Emma was so prim. "Out of a clear sky Mabel said one day, 'Emma, I can see the lace on your panties when you stoop over.' "

On the evening of February 22, Julia sent for the nearest priest, from Montabella. "He anointed MN, also the nuns from Mount St. Mary's came and brought Holy Water, the Blessed Candle, etc.," Julia wrote Stephen. Early in the morning of February 23, at 2:25 A.M., Mabel died. "I was at Mabel's side holding the Candle," a reporter quoted Julia at the time. "As the end neared, she folded her hands across her bosom and endeavored to repeat a little prayer Mrs. Benson whispered in her ear. But her lips could not form the words. Only her eyes spoke." It was an appropriate ending for a star of silent film.

Her death certificate listed pulmonary tuberculosis as the cause of death. They took her body to Renaker's Mortuary in Monrovia and then to Cunningham and O'Connor Funeral Directors in Los Angeles. While Cody picked out a "beautiful bronze casket" and a crypt in the new mausoleum of Calvary Cemetery, Julia clipped a lock of Mabel's hair and saved it in an envelope on which she wrote, "Cut off at undertakers when we put up hair for last time."

Across the country, headlines read, "MABEL NORMAND AT PEACE," but the question, Who *was* Mabel Normand? still plagued reporters trying to distinguish fact from fiction in their newspaper morgues. The *New York Times* obituary spoke of her early poverty as an art student, "forced to support herself by any means available while the art studies waited." The *Los Angeles Examiner* spoke of the wild extravagance of the star who booked return passage for a dozen friends on the Atlantic liner that had just docked in order to buy all the girls a new wardrobe in Paris on the trip back. The *Los Angeles Times* spoke of an elfin tomboy who was "literally devoured" by the life she had longed for. An editorialist in the *New York Times* tried to sum up the paradox of a star who had lived "foolishly generous and gloriously oblivious of self."

"Not since Valentino's funeral has there been such a throng," the *Examiner* reported under headlines for February 29, "THOUSANDS MOURN AT NORMAND RITES." At 11:00 A.M., Father Michael J. Mullins read the Requiem Mass at the same Church of the Good Shepherd where Valentino's had been celebrated. Mabel's casket was half-covered with a blanket of orchids and lilies-of-the-valley. Within the satin lining, Mabel seemed a mere girl, in curls and pink chiffon, dressed "as though she were going to a party."

The mourners were a living history of the silent film they had created. Her honorary pallbearers included Griffith, Sennett, Goldwyn, Chaplin, Arbuckle, Sterling, Bern, Sid Grauman, and Eugene Pallette. A Polish photographer, Albert Kopec, who had filled Sennett's studio books with stills of Mabel, brought a 16-mm camera and shot a few feet of film outside the church as the pallbearers placed Mabel's casket in the hearse. I found Kopec in Hollywood, and he told me how Mabel had liked to go to Polish dances with him, "You should have seen the boys when I walked in with Mabel Normand." Among his files, Kopec discovered that he still had a print of Mabel's funeral. In a series of frames, I could see three short men standing in a row in the sunshine to the right of the hearse, at least they seemed short until I realized that they were Griffith, Sennett, and Goldwyn.

King Vidor attended the funeral with Irving Thalberg and Edgar Mannix, and his memory of the event memorialized the end of an era. Vidor had been waiting in Thalberg's office that morning to hash over a murder script when Thalberg emerged in his usual rush, pushed Vidor and Mannix into a car, and sped off to a church. Lew Cody ushered them into a pew. "Who is it?" Thalberg wrote on a note to Mannix, who replied, "Mabel Normand." Vidor recalled with a shock the girl of his boyhood dreams, the "beautiful, lithe-figured" diving girl who had drawn him to Hollywood in the teens. Thalberg, however, was a man of the future. "Too many murders," he wrote Mannix again on the note. He didn't mean Mabel. He meant the mystery plot of his new talkie, *Billy the Kid.*

"Too many murders" was not a bad epitaph for Mabel, but it had a hard-edged thirties sound. Other tributes, as usual, reflected the speaker more than the girl. A bizarre tract called "The Blue Flame" remembered Mabel as "a red poppy among the lilies," fighting bravely against the white plague and the newspapers that murdered her when "they wrote of the fertilizer instead of the flower." Cody's tribute had the casual cool of a pal: "She was just a little girl who neglected to look before crossing the street." Sennett's tribute had the virtue of brevity: "I never married. There was only one girl."

Mabel furnished her own best epitaph in a poem she titled "Short, Short Story," that began "I'm bad, bad, bad!"

> *If there was one sprig of poison-ivy*
> *In a field of four-leaf clovers*
> *I'd pick it up.*
> *If it was raining carbolic acid,*
> *I'd be the dumbbell sponge.*

The stories of bad, bad girls were usually short, but still they had to pretend not to care. I found out how much Mabel cared in a few more penciled pages of Mabel's diary that fell from a book Lee sent me that had belonged to Mabel. It was titled *The Answering Voice: One Hundred Love Lyrics by Women*, edited by Elinor Wylie. The diary pages were dated February, 1927, when Mabel suffered her first tubercular attack.

> *Feb. 4: Began to get sick opening night of Greta Garbo and John Gilbert,* Flesh and the Devil.
> *Feb. 15: Went to hospital.*
> *Feb. 19: Peg Talmadge here in afternoon, long talk. love Peg. Gastly to be in bed, loved her visit — liked today, only I read Nietzsche, depressed me somehow. J [Julia] has the room full of flowers, great friends. How long will they last?*
> *I dislike people sending me flowers and then consider their duty done. Loved L. Carter's flowers best, broke, could have spent that money on herself — Hope the dog misses me and I could go home —*
> *THIS THING IS APPALLING (WHO CARES?)*
> *Feb. 20: Flowers. Dr. Loas visited. Also Dr. Dazey. Dazey sensible odd person. Like him best. C. [Cody]*

had people at beach house for sandwiches, also play
pool. Lonesome, will hate tonight. J. Phoned. Paul
Bern, La Varnie, Mrs. Manait — wish they were sick.
(Later) Strange what sickness does to one. Dr.
came in. He has wonderful hands, not beautiful yet
full of a strange singular expressiveness. Probably
Leonardo da Vinci had hands like that. With such
hands one can do anything. Sometimes when he's
talking, he will gradually close his fingers into a fist,
then suddenly open with a gesture of silent good. Has
control of his destiny. I don't believe he believes in
God.

I never felt closer to Mabel's mystery than at that moment.
For one thing, February 4 had rung a bell. Mabel used to write
out telegrams in pencil on Western Union forms, which Julia
would copy over and send. I had seen one addressed to Greta
Garbo, at the Miramar Hotel, dated February 4, the night Mabel
took sick.

Altho' you have only appeared in this country in
three pictures I saw you tonight for the twelfth time.
You were more gorgeous than ever, a great picture, a
great performance from a great artist.

Mabel's generosity was as spontaneous as her talent, but I wondered whether Garbo's radiant image had made Mabel feel like
an impostor from a forgotten era and a lost art. Garbo's spiritual-
ized sex and fleshly wisdom made nonsense of the old divisions
between Griffith's fleshless girls and Sennett's bathing beauties.
Worse, Garbo's ageless sorrow made the American innocence of
all of them — Mabel and Pickford and the Talmadge sisters and
even the Gish girls — look old.

"THIS THING IS APPALLING," Mabel had written of
her own mortality, and the next moment, "WHO CARES?" Her
words were an epitaph for an era. Mabel's carefree youth imaged
Hollywood's in the teens of the century. Her growing wildness in
the twenties touched in some way on every major scandal that
made Hollywood giddy after the war. Her long day's dying at the
end of the twenties matched the dying of that silent world of

gesture which she read in her doctor's expressive hands and which Hollywood would call a dead language in 1930. Hollywood let itself go in mourning Mabel, for in grieving for its first little I-Don't-Care Girl, Hollywood was grieving for itself. Throughout the fall and winter of 1929, Hollywood broadcast a nightly tribute in the new language of sound. Radio stations ended their evening programs every night with a personal message, "And to you, Mabel Normand, out there in the hospital, good night."

MABEL LIVES

NOVEMBER 25, 1978, PACOIMA

Dear Betty —

Before I forget, I saw Mabel's trunk in the garage yesterday. It's got 3 or 4 shelves spaced for shoes — her shoe trunk is what it was — about the size of a steamer trunk. Must have cost about $200 at one time, worth a lot more now. There wasn't nothing in it though. It was empty.

Lxx

FEBRUARY 12, 1927, BEVERLY HILLS

Three days before Mabel went to the hospital, she made out her will, which contained the proviso: "To my husband, Lew Cody, I give the sum of one dollar, only, for the reason that he is well provided for in his own separate property and is capable of earning his own support." "That is the way I wanted it," Cody told reporters, after the probate lawyer had estimated Mabel's estate to be worth $300,000. Mabel left everything to her mother but one dollar. This was not the dollar Minta Durfee meant when she said, "If there is anything better in the next life than this, then Mabel Normand is in the dollar seat." Even in the next life, bad-luck Mabel had left behind her, good intentions not withstanding, a legacy that brought little but grief.

Since Mabel had named no executor in her will, Cody was named by the courts. Mabel's mother immediately sued Lew over a $50,000 trust fund Mabel had set up in 1922. While the Normand family's expectations of Mabel's fortune were high, by Hollywood standards Mabel had been so "foolishly generous" that she was poor. In 1930, Sennett estimated his worth at

$15,000,000. Mabel's lawyer had overestimated the total value of Mabel's house, jewelry, furniture and investments. Mabel left exactly $73,835. Her "fabulous jewelry," said to be worth $100,000, was now estimated at $20,000 and brought less than that when sister Gladys sold it at auction in 1931.

Julia was bitter, for Mabel left her nothing in her will, and Gladys let Julia pick but a single jewel for herself before Gladys "pitched things out right and left." When Mabel's mother died two years later, what was left of Mabel's estate — now reduced to $37,000 — was split between Gladys and Claude, along with the house in Staten Island. Gladys immediately sued Claude for the house and lost. Gladys, too, was bitter. She covered a ledger-sized address book, front to back, with strange slanted handwriting, interlarding addresses of the famous with meditations on fame and mortality. Next to Sennett's name she wrote, "Trying to recapture the past can only lead to futility." Next to Julia's she wrote, "Gone with the wind." But Gladys found Julia on February 11, 1959, and wrote to her then: "Today, dear God, Ash Wednesday. Much water has gone over the dam since 1930." I thought of Goldwyn's reflection, "We have passed a lot of water since then." Gladys, who lived obscurely in Greenwich Village until her death in 1970, appointed herself the keeper of Mabel's memory. After Mack in the sixties signed a release for Mabel's life story, Gladys warned Julia, "Well just one thing, Julie, if there happens to be one thing detrimental it had better be removed while it is in the can or it will be just too bad."

Mabel's brother Claude was bitter and so were the children who survived his hanging. His son Livingston, who found his father's body when he was a 19-year-old sailor home on furlough, would answer none of my letters. Claude's daughter Mabel would talk to me only on the phone and with the greatest reluctance. "Talking about Mabel Normand is taboo," she explained. Everyone used her, lived off her, fought over her, and yet everyone ended up broke, she said. "Mabel caused nothing but tragedy — I can't explain it." Mabel Normand Rycowitch, who looked very like Mabel in her photos, had done some modeling, like Mabel, until an auto accident ruined her face. "There's always been somebody in me that's never been able to come out," she confessed to me. "I think I made a lot of wrong decisions because I tried to get away from Mabel Normand — I tried to run away from her ghost."

JULY 11, 1981, PACOIMA

Betty darling — Julia continues about the same. Lately she has slipped a little. I'm about as healthy as ever and go to the Sanatorium every day. A few of my girl friends had a grand party for me for my March 1 birthday. I was 81. They are all born-again Christians and my # 1 is a Jewish girl. They are all about 26 years old.

Like you said, I run into very few people that remember M.N. they are too young and the older ones are God Bless dead.

Much love,
LXX

Lee often signed his letters, "God bless you honey always and remember He died for you and me." Julia felt that Mabel had died for you and me and that her cement star in the Avenue of the Stars was but an earthly reflection of her star above. Wherever I looked for Mabel in Hollywood, I felt the conjunction of earthly and heavenly stars. When I visited Pickfair and saw for myself the famous leopard rug, the urn given by the King and Queen of Siam, the portrait of Mary in blue in the beige-silk drawing room where music softly piped, my guide to this shrine was a large woman named Valerie Sorelle. Valerie had fallen in love with the actor Buddy Rogers when she was eight and her loyalty to the man Mary married had never wavered. She kept the faith equally at Pickfair and at her Long Beach church where she preached and did psychic consulting. "It just puts something in God's banking account for us," Valerie said, looking through me with her turquoise eyes framed by jet black hair. "I never mind drawing from it because I try to keep my balance pretty good."

I had trouble finding God's banking account for Mabel. I looked for Mabel at Pickfair, but I didn't find her there. Nor did I find her at the Knickerbocker Hotel, now an old folks home crowded with wheelchairs where Mabel and dozens of other silent stars had run through the lobby and where the husband of Geraldine Farrar shot himself. I did find in an upstairs room at the Knickerbocker a retired naval commander who had lived next to Sennett at the Garden Court Apartments for many years. "Sennett had made a lot of girls," the commander remembered, "but the only girl he ever talked about was Mabel Normand."

I looked but didn't find Mabel at Republic Studios in the Valley, where a bronze plaque fixed to the sound stage of the "Mary Tyler Moore Show" had been dedicated to her memory on December 27, 1940. A court jester and a celluloid ribbon in bas-relief framed the message on the wall: "May we never forget her — a great soul who pioneered and gave purpose to the early motion picture." But Mabel wasn't there. Instead, there was a guard who had written a TV murder mystery and who wondered if I could get it published for him.

Nor had I found Mabel in the wardrobe trunk of the Hollywood Museum in Lincoln Heights Jail. I found her in nothing as factual as cement or bronze or leather and silk. I found her rather in the images of memories that were as fake and real as the images of movies. They were fictions that made flesh dissolve and time stand still. They were lies that denied time and mortality. "We picture people believed in never ending time," Violet Unholtz said and so could not believe in death. Griffith worshipped the health guru Bernarr MacFadden and so "believed that he could live 140 years if he watched himself." Mary Pickford, fortified by whiskey and her Runner's Bible, believed that she conversed nightly with her mother long after Charlotte Pickford had gone to her grave. Minta Durfee believed that her grandfather could not quite raise the dead but he could stop the dying, for he had the gift of healing, Minta said. "He could stop bleeding and he could take the warts right off of people."

The picture people and their pictures engaged in an act of faith. "First I think it's true, then I believe it's true, then I *know* it's true," said the keeper of Pickfair. I thought of all those people who had said, "I know. I was *there.*" And I thought of Minta who had said to her memoirist, "Don't bother with all that history stuff, I'm telling you the *truth!*" Was the true Mabel Normand to be found?

"Where in the end do we search," St. Augustine asked, searching for truth many centuries ago, "but in the memory itself?" Stephen searched his memory for tragedy and I searched mine for comedy, and we found both in the name of Mabel. But Mabel's occupation undid us all. Mabel's occupation was like death itself in its dispossessions. As a changeling, Mabel embodied the mystery of memory, of identity, of truth even to herself. Because she invested her image with so much life and because she gave so much of herself away, she laid claim to our memories. She claimed the lot of us who tried to track her down, piece her together, reform her, run away from her, or possess her. To the most possessive, she was the most elusive. To Mack Sennett, Sam Goldwyn, Bill Taylor, Paul Bern — it was she who possessed them. She possessed, possesses still, her guardian angel Julia, who most wanted to purify her. She possesses still her namesake, Stephen's mother, who most wanted to run away. She possesses still her grandnephew Stephen, in whom even now "MABEL LIVES." She possesses now even her searcher, who most wanted to solve her mystery. I found myself recently filling out a library card with the name "Mabel Fussell."

To search for Mabel was to search for something that was not meant to be found but could only be felt in the searching. "Here however we are always seeking," St. Augustine had written, "and the joyous possession of that which is found is not the end of the search." Who was Mabel Normand? Mabel, I found, would remain as mysterious as the murder of William Desmond Taylor. Nor would there be an end to my search, for what I had found instead of Mabel was the power of her image to possess the living. If I could not exorcise for Stephen the doom of Mabel Normand, at least I could share his haunting.